Shining

Like

STARS

AN EVANGELISM HANDBOOK

Shining

Like

STARS

DOUGLAS JACOBY

Illumination Publishers International
www.ipibooks.com

ipi

Shining Like Stars

An Evangelism Handbook
Fourth Edition

Book Design: Toney Mulhollan
Printed in the United States

Published by
Illumination Publishers International
1190 Boylston Street
Newton Upper Falls, Massachusetts 02464
www.ipibooks.com

ipi

Contents

PART IV

EVER BRIGHTER

Grounding new believers in the Word and the mission

PART V

BURNING HEARTS

Conclusion

Preface to the Fourth Edition

The first edition (blue) of *Shining Like Stars* was published in 1987. Substantial revisions were made for the 1990 (yellow) edition. In the same way, massive editing preceded the release of the millennial (spiral bound) edition in 2000. Once again it is clear that extensive revision is in order. It is not clear what form the final version of the book will take, and so the present volume can be described as no more than a "fourth edition." Please consider it a work in progress.

If you have read any of the earlier versions, you will notice a host of changes. Some are significant corrections of a theological nature. As my understanding of God's grace has deepened, I have seen many deficiencies in the earlier editions, especially in their overly mechanical approach to evangelism and reliance on human wisdom. Other changes are simply the cutting away of the superfluous or the polishing and sharpening of the dull. A good amount of new material has also been added, in part to set forth the rationale for personal Bible studies with non-believers, and in part to clarify a number of unfortunate impressions from certain sections of the earlier versions. In short, a new edition was sorely needed.

How this book can help

This is a book on personal evangelism. It is challenging. It is practical, with dozens of in-depth studies to be shared with non-Christians and even young Christians. Through the past twenty years it has helped many people, And yet the book cannot change your heart – that's between you and God. You'll have to make a personal decision to face reality head-on and let your light shine. But if your heart is right, the book can help you in several ways:

- It will challenge you to overcome shyness and live boldly for the Lord.
- It will draw your attention to opportunities God is giving you every day to reach out to those around you.
- It is brimming with effective study materials you can use to help your non-Christian friends come to faith, and new believers grow in their faith.

Three Books

This book is admittedly the "word of man" (1 Thessalonians 2:13). It can only point us to the master evangelist, Jesus Christ, suggesting a number of possible approaches as we share the life-giving news with outsiders. The only book with *real* authority is the Bible itself. And yet as has been said, for many people, we who are Christians may be the only "Bible" they will ever read, and the only "Jesus" they will ever see (2 Corinthians 2:14-16). Therefore my hope is that *this* book will ground us more deeply in *the* book so that our lives will truly be a book known and read by all.

As Christians who are "shining like stars" (Daniel 12:3, Philippians 2:15), may we drink deep of the Holy Spirit, who always insists on making Christ known!

Douglas Jacoby
Marietta, Georgia
January 2006

PART I

LIGHT OF THE WORLD

"You are the light of the world. A city on a hill cannot be hidden. Neither do people light a lamp and put it under a bowl. Instead they put it on its stand, and it gives light to everyone in the house. In the same way, let your light shine before men, that they may see your good deeds and praise your Father in heaven" (Matthew 5:14-16).

Jesus taught that his followers were destined to exert an illuminating influence on this world. The light that burns in a heart touched by the Spirit of God ought never to be extinguished or hidden; rather, it must be fanned into hotter flame and more visible incandescence.

First things first. Chapters 1 to 3 of *Shining Like Stars* deal with our life decision to let that light shine.

1
Where Are You Hiding?

I believe that you, the reader, want to serve God and make an impact on the world. People don't usually buy books on evangelism unless, deep down in their heart, they want to be evangelistic. Yet all of us can, at times, slip into neglecting the very things which mean the most to us. A husband neglects the wife of his youth, a daughter forgets to write to the one who brought her into the world, a disciple slips in showing gratitude to the God who saved him.

Hide and Seek?

When it comes to evangelism, many of us do more than merely neglect it: we actively *hide* from it. Are you hiding? Adam and Eve hid among the trees in the Garden. Moses tried to hide behind his brother Aaron, while Saul hid among the baggage. Even Peter, in a moment of weakness, denied Jesus and hid himself among the guards around the fire. People hide not only because they are confused about the facts or unsure of what to do, but also because they are unwilling to face reality head-on.

This book is written for those who are serious about evangelism. Now I know that all Christians are serious about evangelism, in one sense. We strongly believe in it. We all heard the call to discipleship as we were making our decision for Christ. At baptism we said "Jesus is Lord"—a lifelong promise to obey his word, follow in his steps and be fishers of men. But how are we really doing in our own evangelism? Are we hiding? The serious Christian always wants to take it higher.

Jesus said, "You are the light of the world. A city on a hill cannot be hidden." At times don't all of us hide our light? He continued, "Neither do people light a lamp and hide it under a bowl. Instead they put it on its stand, and it gives light to everyone in the house. In the same way, let your light shine before men, that they may see your good deeds and glorify your father in heaven" (Matthew 5:14-16). This passage is simply the Great Commission in another form.

Have you been hiding? And if so, where? What are your excuses, who are you trying to hide behind, or what trivial thing is distracting you from your mission? (Or is your conscience clear?) Let's agree to come out into the open. We have nothing to hide and we certainly do not want to hide from our mission. If this is our attitude, we'll all "shine like stars" (Daniel 12:3, Philippians 2:15).

Is God Calling Me to the Mission Field?

"Okay," you think, "No more hiding. I'll come out into the open. But I know what this means. I'll have to throw in the towel on my degree, my job plans—everything!—and move overseas. Maybe preach to the pygmies..." This form of self-delusion does at least sound somewhat glorious. But such thinking is flawed, for the mission field is not just "over there"; it is right here! If we aren't ready to strike up conversations with those around us, invite them to share in our lives, our faith, our Lord—how is it suddenly going to become easier if we move to a foreign country, with all the extra challenges such a move would entail?

No, if we're not shining like stars here, we are simply not ready to go to a foreign field. The truth is, we are always surrounded by fields "white/ripe unto harvest" (John 4:35). God is in fact calling every one of us to the "mission field." It may well be a mission field in Africa, Asia, or somewhere behind the "bamboo curtain." More likely it is in our own country. The point is to be ready, all the time. Ready to "go anywhere, do anything, give up everything" for the cause.

I remember a time in my life when I thought missions meant only *foreign* missions, and the more foreign the better! The enormous continent of South America, with its hundreds of millions of denizens dying in darkness, captured my imagination. I began reading the Bible in Spanish, even trying to pray in Spanish. So when I was initially invited to join a mission team to London – you know, English-speaking England — I didn't react well. "London? That's not glorious enough," I was thinking. "They speak the same language as we do (almost). Would I really be laying it all on the line if I went there? I'm destined for a higher calling," I mused.

And yet London was awesome! I was proud to be on the mission team – and wish more of us were excited about being on "mission teams"! I rapidly became an Anglophile. I have watched the inspiring film *Chariots of Fire* ten times! Everything British was better, and in a funny way I secretly became ashamed of being so "American." I even tried to change my accent. (As easily as the leopard changes his spots, to use the idiom of Jeremiah.) "Hank the Yank," they called me, and many others of us too. We meant well—but how we stuck out! As things turned out, I ended up living abroad for 12 years—in England, Sweden, and Australia.

The point is, you can do it either way. Preach in your own country, or move somewhere else. That is, if you are convicted that the Lord has a plan for your life, that he has sent you on a mission. And the alternative?

Hide. Is that what you're doing?

2
The Mission

In the last chapter we were asked a question: "Where are you hiding?" In this chapter another vital issue receives our attention: the mission. Often in the Word we read of people *sent* on missions: Jonah to Nineveh (Jonah 1:2), Isaiah to the Israelites (Isaiah 6:8-9), Saul to the Amalekites (1 Samuel 15: 18-24), Jesus to the earth (John 1:11-13). Are you clear on your mission? This means commitment to God, living your life for him (2 Corinthians 5:15).[1] This means doing great things for God, praying grand, global thoughts, not puny, parochial prayers! And this means thinking, believing, dreaming, living and dying heroically. As Horace Mann remarked, "Be ashamed to die until you have won some victory for mankind." And as the apostle remarked, "Grace to all who love our Lord Jesus Christ with an undying love" (Ephesians 6:24). Undying love—you're in it for the long haul, disciple. True zeal is more than skin deep. It is not some ephemeral, Sunday costume you don every week. God's claim on our life is total, not partial. Have you compromised your mission?

Slain by a Fierce, Wild Beast!

Deep in our hearts many of us have always suspected this is the way it must be—if there is a God, his Word is true, and we are to follow him. Ever since I was a little boy I knew (from Sunday school) that we were supposed to live for God. I heard about people who sold everything and lived in poverty—and something in my soul responded, "I should live that way, too." There was a certain attractiveness to the grand old hymns, waxen candles, walks through cemeteries, thinking about God. Even confirmation classes intrigued me! And I still remember the words of a song I heard when I was six or seven years old:

> I sing a song of the saints of God,
>> patient and brave and true:
> They toiled and they fought and they lived and they died
>> for their own good Lord they knew.

And one was a doctor and one was a priest
and one was slain by a fierce, wild beast:
And there's no, not a reason, no not the least
Why I shouldn't be one too![2]

My conscience was mildly haunted by the words of that song for another twelve years—especially by the thought of being slain by a beast! Could there be something so worth living for that it was also worth dying for? The words remained in my heart, until I began to consider the Bible more seriously. Looking back now, I believe I was just waiting for a chance to become committed. (Maybe you were, too!) When I met men and women who lived as committed a life as the one they taught (and sang) about, the old chords were set vibrating, and I knew my quest, in one sense, was at an end.

The world is looking for a cause, something to live for. Usually people rally behind one cause or another, but seldom the right one. It is up to us to show them that Jesus Christ is worth living for. And dying, if that is what we are called to do. It's all part of the mission.

Holiness an Option?

Is holiness an option? Is the mission only for those who feel comfortable with it, or are we all called to "fish" (Luke 5:14), to "gather" (Luke 11:23)? In these days of "church of your choice" and "non-judgmentalism," is this level of commitment just one more jaded theme we could just as well do without? Or is this not the narrow path that Jesus walked, and which he bade us come and walk as well? The Hebrew writer was lucid: "Make every effort to live in peace with all men and to be holy; without holiness no one will see the Lord" (Hebrews 12:14). The Scriptures are clear: Holiness is no option. Let the world mock, and let the religious world defend its shallow religiosity with theology Felix would have applauded (Acts 24:25). Lukewarmness is not an option because God, the holy God, is not an "option." God commands us to be holy because he is holy (1 Peter 1:15-16; Leviticus 11: 44-45, 19:2, 20:7).

It should be no surprise that the Holy Spirit makes us holy. It flows through our veins, a transfusion of life and determination coursing through every artery and capillary. The person who claims to have the Spirit must live a holy life, or the game is up! By their fruits you will know them (Matthew 7:20). Without holiness no one will see the Lord.

Although in time the emphasis on holiness declined, especially after the legalization of Christianity in the 300s, God never lowered his standard or the requirements for discipleship. The concern for holiness continued unabated for nearly three centuries before the early church had finally cooled off. Consider the second-century sermon called 2 Clement. Clearly, at this time, there was still a concern for holiness. "What assurance do we have of entering the kingdom of God if we fail to keep our baptism pure and undefiled? Or who will be our advocate, if we are not found to have holy and righteous works?" (2 Clement 6:9b) Reading the "Church Fathers," or Patristic writers, can be enormously beneficial, affording clearer insight into how the original church evolved into the confused state of modern "churchianity," and bringing us closer to the radical spirit of our earliest brothers and sisters in the faith.

We read in Romans 12:11, "Never be lacking in zeal, but keep your spiritual fervor, serving the Lord." *Fervor* is the Latin word for "seething, heat; ardor, passion." The verb *fervere* means "to boil." This fervor, energy, or heat, is the difference between pulseless, morbid religion and vibrant, vital faith. No amount of explanation about how a corpse is really "alive" is going to convince anyone with eyes in his head. Living faith has a pulse because it is energized by the very Spirit of God (James 2:26).

'When You're Hot, You're Hot'

""When you're hot, you're hot. And when you're not, you're not," the saying goes. God's word demands that we be hot, not cold or lukewarm. The success of the mission absolutely depends on it!

> "To the angel of the church in Laodicea write: These are the words of the Amen, the faithful and true witness, the ruler of God's creation. I know your deeds, that you are neither cold nor hot. I wish you were either one or the other! So, because you are lukewarm—neither hot nor cold—I am about to spit you out of my mouth" (Revelation 3:14-16).

These words are addressed to a church that used to be hot, but had slipped into the self-satisfaction of lukewarmness. Sadly, only a few decades later this church seems not to have repented. Other churches that received letters in Revelation 2-3 were still in existence (like those in Ephesus and Philadelphia, for example), but the second-century writers sent no letters, as far as we know, to the church of Laodicea. It seems this first-century church dwindled in faith and in numbers, ultimately vanishing off the screen.

Jesus Christ looks not just at heart, faith and intent, but also at deeds. "Holy" and "hot" are nearly synonyms when it comes to commitment. Furthermore, the Scriptures affirm that cold is actually better than lukewarm (Malachi 1:10, Revelation 3:15). Religious experiences are no substitute. Truly spiritual people don't gather "miracle" stories and seek after a spiritual buzz (Colossians 2:18); they do the work of God (Matthew 7:21-23).

Can you honestly say that you are "hot" for God, his word, his will, his people, his plans? You can if his mission runs in your veins.

'Inwardly Boiling'

Hundreds of millions claim to be Christians, despite the fact that their "pulse" is next to impossible to locate. Dead faith creating dead weight in dead churches proclaiming a cause long dead. Imagine your friend asking you to go and check a pot of water on the stove.

"It should be boiling by now," he says.

You check it swiftly dipping in your finger (just to be safe), only to feel tepid water. "Still cold!" you reply.

"No, it should be boiling by now," he returns; "please go back and check again."

You check once more and feel only lukewarm water.

What would you think if he said, "I know it's hot; it must be boiling. Yes, it must be '*inwardly* boiling'"?

What if he persisted in spouting off slogans like "What counts is heart, not heat," and "Lukewarm water needs time to 'mature'," wouldn't you eventually come to question his sincerity, or his understanding of words such as "hot," "cold" and "boiling"? He then further defends his doctrine: "No water is perfect"; "All water has the right to seek its own temperature"; "Being nice is what counts, not being hot"; or perhaps "The warming up is more important than the heat." The theology of lukewarmness continues to blossom: "We truly believe in inner boiling," and "Judge not water's heat," and finally, "Hot-water-only-groups are too exclusive!" Would you not be right to accuse him not only of illogic but also of special pleading?

So it is with holiness. The commitment of discipleship is nonnegotiable. The fervor of spiritual zeal is defined by God, not by man. No one has the right to dilute holiness, then say "It's good enough."

Fake versus Real Zeal

Zeal can be faked. Showing up at church—even smiling, clapping, saying "Amen"—may fool others, but it cannot fool God (Galatians 6:7). He knows whether we are about his mission or not.

Do you have a zeal that's real, or are you the "hype type"? Still confused about what God thinks about faking dedication, feigning devotion, falsifying discipleship, fudging holiness? The tale of Ananias and Sapphira (Acts 5:1-11) reveals the heart of God on this matter. When this couple faked commitment instead of being honest about where they were, we read that they were lying to the Holy Spirit (v. 3) and testing the Spirit of the Lord (v. 9). God the Spirit is offended when, instead of allowing him to make us holy, we make a farce of faith. No more showy, shallow, sham religion!

How can we claim to be God's people when we are lacking in zeal? Many people lack the truth, and yet sometimes are just as zealous in their religion as real Christians are (Romans 10:1-2). Zeal does not mean loud "Amens" and boisterous behavior, but being filled with the Spirit of God and modeling the walk we talk about. After all, as Mark Twain said, "Few things are harder to put up with than a good example." When people see that kind of zeal, they will know it's real.

Never, ever forget who you are and whose you are. True Christians are *a holy people on a holy mission in a holy church serving a holy God.*

Notes

[1] Much of the material following in this and the following chapter has been adapted from chapter 12 ("A Zeal that's Real") of *The Spirit* (Newton, Massachusetts: IPI, 2005).

[2] Lesbia Scott, 1929.

3
The Lifeblood of the Church

Evangelism has been described as the lifeblood of the church of Christ. It is a major part of our mission on here earth and deserves our time, energy, and wholehearted labor. At this point, it should be states that mission and purpose are different things. Our *purpose* is to enjoy our relationship with God and make it to heaven; our *mission* is to change the world. When mission and purpose become confused, spiritual burnout is not far away.) As vital as evangelism is—yes, the very lifeblood of the church!—it is not everything. As with physical life, blood is vital, but so are the heart that pumps it, the organs that draw from its supply, and the brain which regulates the whole. Are you clear about your purpose? About your mission? And about the difference between the two?

The mission is two-fold. We are called to preach the Word and to help the poor. Although ultimately one's spiritual condition, not one's medical or economic situation, is what counts, still we are called as the people of God to both facets of the mission. True Christians love the poor. True Christians also love the lost and share what they have found with them. It is fundamentally unrighteous to neglect one or the other.

Let's zero in on our evangelistic responsibility. Just as Jesus sent his disciples out to preach the Word and to minister to the needy, so the Spirit sends us today on the same twin mission (Mark 3:14).

Lifeblood

World evangelism is our consuming passion as disciples. It was the will of God in the first century, the mountaintop mandate of the Lord Jesus and the lifeblood of the New Testament church. The situation is no different today! While we humbly realize it is possible, our generation is probably not the last in human history (1 Thessalonians 5:1). Thus surely our common goal must be to bring Christ to every nation—to saturate the earth with the gospel in our lifetime, by all means possible.

Our first-century brothers and sisters, moved by the Holy Spirit, caused quite a stir when they preached the radical message of the gospel. The Spirit insists that we work together to turn the world upside down.[1] How do we know that? Because the Spirit inspired the entire Bible. Europe, Asia, Africa, Australia the Americas—the entire world!—can be and must be evangelized if we, as God's children, are to be faithful to our Father's wishes. On this there can be no compromise. Nor should we ever leave our "great work" in order to negotiate with the critics (Nehemiah 6:1-14).

I am privileged, as an international traveler and Christian speaker, to have preached in over fifty nations, and keep up a correspondence with persons in over a hundred nations. (Not that I don't enjoy sharing about the Lord in my home country.) My teaching ministry is a thrill, a joy, an honor, and an all-consuming passion. You are probably not an international evangelist, but that doesn't mean you don't have a *message*, a *mission*, and a *ministry* right where you live. All Christians have the message (the gospel), a mission (to make Jesus known, through word and deed), and are in the ministry (a royal priesthood, in the words of 1 Peter 2:9).

Hopefully you don't have to be *told* to share your faith before you do so. The good news is so "good" that it is contagious, explosive, and nearly impossible to contain (Jeremiah 20:9). As someone has said, "The Spirit of Christ always insists on making Christ known" (see John 15:26).

We're Outta Here!

How determined are we to follow the Spirit and to refuse to tolerate unspirituality? Years ago (in the '70s, in fact), my brother and I were driving down the East Coast of the United States, attending various Christian conferences. The first message at one conference we had registered for was on the topic of evangelism. The speaker began by describing evangelism as a "talent" or "gift." The experts, according to this man, had calculated that only ten percent of Christians can be expected to evangelize, since for ninety percent of us, it is not our gift.

But there is a difference between gifts and commands. For example, we are all commanded to encourage others (Hebrews 3:13), yet some of us have the gift of encouragement (Romans 12:8) and will find that what may be hard for others is relatively easy for them. While it is true that some of us find some of the commands easier to obey, we must never minimize a command into an option under the claim that "It's not my gift"! Evangelism is not an option. After all, in Ephesians 4:11, the gift is not evangelism, but evangelists—the leadership position.

As the conference speaker was droning on, I thought of the ten lepers (in Luke 17) and how only one returned to thank Jesus. (Yes, only "ten percent" had the decency to show appreciation for what God had done in their lives. The "ten-percent rule" applied here, though not as meant by the speaker!) After the talk, I turned to my brother Steve and said, "I'm outta here!" We walked out, We were not interested in explaining away the Great Commission or consoling ourselves about our lack of commitment.

How about you? Are you hanging out only with those who have low expectations for world impact? Are you attracted to a fellowship that says "I'm okay; you're okay," "Judge not," and "Lukewarm is acceptable"? Putting it another way, do you count the hours that go by between times of sharing your faith, or the days? How often do you share your life with friends in your home (1 Thessalonians 2:8)? The Holy Spirit is not a spirit of timidity, but a one of power, love and self-discipline. The next time a thought of compromise starts to "lecture" you on why you do not have to obey the Great Commission, just say, "I'm outta here"!

The Acts of the Spirit

Probably the place God has most clearly shown his will that all disciples be evangelistic is the book of Acts. The title "The Acts of the Apostles" is really a misnomer, since only Peter and Paul receive significant coverage in this book. Many scholars contend that Luke's second volume should really be called "The Acts of the Spirit," since it is the Holy Spirit who essentially serves as "Director of Evangelism" and "Chief Empowerer of the Christian Movement." This is key in understanding the plan of Acts. In our lives we have no more powerful advocate in evangelism than the Holy Spirit himself. Let's examine a few of the ways the Spirit assists us.

After Pentecost, first-century Christians were not interested in concealing the gospel—only in revealing it. When the church was scattered in the Great Persecution after the martyring of Stephen, many shared their faith—not just the top leaders! (Acts 8:1, 4). Acts records the birth and growth of the church during its first three decades. Several aspects of the explosive expansion of the church are noteworthy:

- The bold proclamation of the message by all the disciples.
- The universal opposition met with by the church.
- The rapid growth of the fledgling movement.

Since the same Spirit empowers us today, is there really any reason not to expect the same working of the Spirit in our own lives? Why not study Acts with an eye on the spirit of the Christians as the Spirit impelled them to take the Word to a lost world?

Boldness Booster

Timidity has never been the way of the Spirit! The Spirit will help us to change in any area of our life necessary in order for us to become effective evangelistically. Have circumstances gotten you down? Are you not as bold lately as you have been in the past? If so, claim the power of the Spirit as the early Christians did when under great pressure: "Now, Lord, consider their threats and enable your servants to speak your word with great boldness" (Acts 4:29). Was that prayer ever answered? (Would God let any prayer like that go unanswered?)

> "After they prayed, the place where they were meeting was shaken. And they were all filled with the Holy Spirit and spoke the word of God boldly" (Acts 4:31).

A miracle? Perhaps. (The shaking is immaterial.) They sincerely desired boldness, prayed a prayer for boldness and emerged from that prayer meeting bolder than ever! Coincidence? Hardly! God is waiting and willing to fill with his Spirit any of us who need to grow in the area of boldness.

The Spirit-Directed Outreach

The book of Acts shows just how involved the Holy Spirit is in the enterprise of evangelism.[2] Let's take a quick tour through Acts and notice how often the Spirit is mentioned in connection with outreach:

- Through the Spirit Jesus briefed his apostles, explaining the kingdom of God and preparing them for the mission soon to commence (Acts 1:2).
- The Spirit would empower the Christians systematically to evangelize the world: first, the city; then, the outlying towns and villages; finally, faraway lands (Acts 1:8).
- The Spirit brought the international crowd together to hear the good news of Jesus Christ (Acts 2:5).
- The Spirit filled the praying Christians with evangelistic boldness (Acts 4:31).
- The Spirit equips obedient disciples to speak even in the face of opposition (Acts 5:27-32).
- The Spirit made it clear that racial divides are no obstacle to the kingdom of God (Acts 8:14-17).

- The Spirit advised the early missionaries where to preach and when to move on (Acts 8:29, 39).
- The Spirit encouraged the church, leading to numerical growth and spiritual sobriety (Acts 9:31).
- The Spirit made it dramatically clear that we are to focus on the central elements of the gospel, not the peripheral ones, when the Gentiles were ushered into the kingdom (Acts 10:44-48, 11:12-18).
- When the Spirit and faith fill a person, many people are brought to the Lord (Acts 11:24).
- The Spirit conceives missions plans (Acts 13:2) and sees them through (Acts 13:4).
- The Spirit sometimes blocks missionary plans (Acts 16: 6-7).
- The Spirit places leadership, particularly eldership, over those who have been led to Christ (Acts 20:28).

Surely we can be confident that the same Spirit has been working in our own generation to bring down walls of Communism and Apartheid, thus opening the door to the evangelization of our world. Jesus concluded the Great Commission by saying, "I am with you always, to the very end of the age." Is it not through the continuing work of the Spirit that his promise is being fulfilled?

The Spirit Changes Hearts

The Spirit works with us in our evangelism. We do not need to rely on our own wisdom, but we must rely on the power of the Spirit (1 Corinthians 2:1-5). According to John 16:8, the Spirit convicts the hearts of non-Christians. The Word is the sword of the Spirit (Ephesians 6:17). Here is the world evangelism plan in a nutshell:

- The Spirit changes the hearts of followers of Christ.
- Disciples of Christ preach the Word wherever they go.
- The Spirit works through the Word to change the hearts of nonbelievers.

Conclusion

The early church took the Great Commission (Matthew 28:18-20) to heart and made a concerted effort to implement Jesus' command to preach the gospel.[3] They obeyed the Great Commission because they understood the Greatest Commandment (Matthew 22:37ff). Love for God always comes before love for the lost, and when the order of the commands is reversed, skewed theology and lopsided lives result. Understanding the intent of the master evangelist, the apostles saw most of the territory around the Mediterranean evangelized within their lifetime. Inroads were made deep into Africa, Asia and Europe. In the following centuries, before the legalization of Christianity in 313 A.D., the fledgling faith continued to expand, the message being carried nearly worldwide—in some form at least—by the time of the Reformation.

Sadly, although the original nuclear church exploded into action, it later slackened. Worldliness and materialism crept in. Soon Christians failed to forge unity. Instead, they "forged" it – only in pretense, as powerful leaders used their weight to intimidate. Amazingly, within a generation of the legalization of Christianity, the persecuted church became the persecutor —torturing and killing those who would not conform to official church doctrine. The slide into the spiritual Dark Ages was rapid and drained the true church of its lifeblood.

Yet today again the Spirit of God is moving in the world so that the torch is being rekindled. The truth is being proclaimed. Are you part of this great conflagration, in your heart of hearts?

Evangelism is the lifeblood of the church. Let's preach the Word, and pray for God to saturate the earth with the message. We leave the results to him. (It is not our job to control outcomes; those we leave to the Lord.)

Notes

[1] The phrase "turned the world upside down" comes specifically from Acts 17:6 (RSV). Technically, the verb means "to upset" (disturb, as in the sense of disturbing the peace) more than to "up-end." When the Latin Vulgate translation was produced, Jerome chose the word *concitant,* which means simply "rouse, stir up." The same word is found in Acts 21:38, referring to "the Egyptian." Thus the phrase is a negative, not a positive one.

[2] Much has been made of Acts 17:26-27, "From one man he made every nation of men, that they should inhabit the whole earth; and he determined the times set for them and the exact places where they should live. God did this so that men would seek him and perhaps reach out for him and find him." Is it true that God *directly* determines where people live—125 Main Street (as opposed to 127 Main Street)—in order to place them in proximity to disciples? God's providence is awesome and evident everywhere. But when Acts 17 is preached this way we are not talking about providence, but a subtle form of predestination.

The theological problem is that if God has determined where those who will be saved live, and when they will be there, then he has *de facto* consigned others to situations in which they will not have an opportunity to respond to the gospel. Then there is the textual problem. The RSV, among many good translations, renders Acts 17:26 more accurately in this instance than does the NIV. We read, "And he made from one every nation of men to live on all the face of the earth, having determined allotted periods and the boundaries of their habitation" (RSV). There is an allusion here to Deuteronomy 32:8. Paul is not talking about local geographical predestination, but rather God's *providence.*

[3] Technically speaking, the intentional effort to evangelize the world began with the First Missionary journey (Acts 13), eighteen years after the resurrection.

PART II

STARS IN THE UNIVERSE

"Do everything without complaining or arguing, so that you may become blameless and pure, children of God without fault in a crooked and depraved generation, in which you shine like stars in the universe as you hold out the word of life—in order that I may boast on the day of Christ that I did not run or labor for nothing" (Philippians 2:14-16).

When we have the attitude of Jesus Christ, we will naturally and sincerely hold out the Word of life, above all in the major arenas of our personal witness: neighborhood, workplace, and school. These are the focus of chapters 4 to 6.

Afterward we will explore three rather more challenging arenas. All of us want to be a great example to our families. We yearn to leave our mark on the world. And we would give anything to have the confidence of Christ when in the presence of the "ultra-religious." Accordingly, chapters 7 to 9 cover evangelism at home, with foreigners, and with the extremely religious.

It is God's will that all Christians "shine like stars"—wherever they are, whatever the time or circumstances.

4
From House to House
Neighborhood Evangelism

There is a direct link between selflessness and evangelism. Selfish people, like selfish children with their toys, do not "share." But when we have the attitude of Christ, we naturally hold out the Word of life. As Paul wrote,

> "Do everything without complaining or arguing, so that you may become blameless and pure, children of God without fault in a crooked and depraved generation, in which you shine like stars in the universe as you hold out the word of life..." (Philippians 2:14-15).

And when we hold out the word of life, we will "shine like stars." What is essential is the heart of a servant, not an attitude of entitlement (Philippians 2:1-11). What a contrast this creates with the surrounding society! When we have the attitude of Jesus (Philippians 2:5), our "default mode" is to be evangelistic. Yes, I know we're *commanded* to "go." And yet I have found that most Christians, when they are at peace with God, feel loved by their leaders, and are growing spiritually, *automatically* share their faith with others. All the king's horses and all the king's men couldn't stop them!

Outside the home, the three major arenas of personal witness are neighborhood, workplace, and school. The early Christians let their light shine publicly, as well as "from house to house" (Acts 5:42). In considering the goal of world evangelizing the world, or even just a city, the importance of neighborhood evangelism cannot be overestimated. This is where the majority of the people will be reached. This is the largest evangelistic "field"—dwarfing by comparison any college campus or workplace.

Relational Evangelism

At the outset, let me say that most Christians are not *naturally* good at relationships. We struggle. We need help. There is a simple reason for this. (a) We have come out of the world, (b) in the world people are generally poor at relationships, and (c) conversion does not immediately alter this deficit. Growth in Christ is a *process* which requires our effort (Philippians 1: 25, 2 Peter 1:5-9). It takes time! In the meantime, all of us have to struggle to become more relatable, less self-conscious, more patient with our fellow humans. (I do. Don't you?)

In this chapter we will focus first on single adults, then on married adults. In reaching these two groups effectively, it is obvious that different approaches are necessary, owing to the diversity of needs and outlook.

Reaching Single Adults

Let us define the "single adult" as follows: someone who is not a teenager, not a student, and not retired. (These categories have their own special needs, which will be touched on later.) Typically, they are in their twenties to thirties, working and without family responsibilities. Nothing else about them is typical (race, income, social background), except that they are at that stage in life where they may be the most "open" to the gospel. They are young enough to accept new ideas, available enough to study the Bible frequently, and flexible enough to adjust relationships, residence and whatever else is necessary to change in order to serve God more fully.

Furthermore, older, more "stable" people are commonly reached through relationships previously established with single adults, as opposed to direct invitation from an unknown Christian. In combination, these factors obviously make the evangelization of this group of people both urgent and strategic.

So how do we effectively go about it? Single adults can be met in a number of ordinary ways. Use your time wisely and invite people while at work. How about restaurants, or recreational facilities? Trains, planes, buses—generally any mode of transport has potential. The most important key is to start conversations. In my experience, the overwhelming majority of Christians undergo a quantum leap in evangelism if they simply set their minds to start conversations. If you are looking for a formula, try these steps:

Smile; establish eye contact. People will usually warm to you as you warm to them.

Start a conversation. Any subject will do. Be friendly. Most people would rather have someone interesting to talk to than sit in silence or pretend to be busy.

Say something "spiritual." I don't mean, "Brother, art thou redeemed?" I mean, turn the conversation to spiritual matters. If you mention something about your religious activities, or your reading, or your faith, and the other does not "pick up" on it, that may well be a clue that they are not interested, at least at this point in their life. If their interest is piqued, then keep sharing. (Do let the other person talk, however! No one enjoys a chatterbox.)

Invite them in. Maybe it will be an invitation to a church service. More effectively, how about an invitation to coffee, or lunch, a party, or a sport activity.

The beauty of this method is that anybody can do it. It all starts with conversation—an effort to communicate, to reach out.

Once I conducted an experiment. I challenged myself to meet as many people in a day (and invite them to church) as possible. The only rule: I would not strike up conversations "out of the blue." I pledged to meet them "naturally." I started conversations while standing in lines, eating at restaurants, walking in the park, and so on. A few times I even managed to strike up conversations with small groups of people. All these interactions took time, and by the end of the day—in which I did most of the things I normally did, including errands—I was tired! Yet before I retired that evening, I had invited 48 men and women; nearly all were single adults. That was an eye-opener!

Evangelistic Keys

Let me offer some keys to effective evangelism of singles:

Group evangelism times. Get a small group of Christians together after work or on a weekend day to share their faith, then to have a meal together.

Have follow-up parties together. So many contacts, not followed up on, are lost. "Strike while the iron is hot." Follow-up needs to be emphasized—never forget that evangelism is not simply inviting people, but teaching people the gospel and winning "as many as possible" (1 Corinthians 9:19).

Set up personal studies. It is important to set up personal studies,[1] as many and as quickly as possible. Not only is this important for effectiveness, but it is also important for the morale of the group. The sooner the Christians are involved in studies which make progress, the more encouraging an experience it is for them. The leader should keep track of the more receptive people being studied with and the progress that is being made.

Friendship and fun. Two further ingredients that make for effective evangelism are friendship and fun. Don't underestimate the importance of having a good relationship with someone you are studying with. In fact, if a non-Christian has several good relationships in the church before becoming a Christian, it will both help him to make the right decision and also serve as a source of security and stability in the first few months as a Christian. Get your whole Group Bible Discussion reaching out to each of the visitors, especially, to those who are progressing well. Remember that you're asking people to make decisions that will radically change their lives—they need to know that you care.

Prayer. Pray for your ministry to grow. Keep a prayer list for your own personal devotional times. Pray as a small group. Pray with others over the telephone. Have the occasional early morning or late night (or all-night) prayer time. Set up prayer chains, or times of prayer and fasting. Seek other ways to rely on the Lord as you hold up one another's arms.

Activities. In line with the idea of friendship and fun, activities of all sorts really help to make a Group Bible Discussion fruitful. Some Christians may not be able to get many people to come to a Bible study, but they certainly know how to get someone to come to a party! Here are some suggestions for activities that have worked well in the past:

- Dinner/Barbecue before Bible study, or apart from the Bible study. If you can, have an international dinner or one that focuses on one particular nationality. Have food, music and clothes from that country—perhaps even a slide show.
- Show a movie after the study.
- Camping—go to the country with visitors for a night or two. This is easy for singles and is great for developing relationships with people who are moving along well in personal studies.
- House-Warming Party—when you move into a new apartment or home, have invitations printed and put them through the doors of all your neighbors, immediate and not so immediate. You'll be amazed at how many show up.
- Ordinary Party—at your parties use all available talent to the full. Many churches are blessed with a lot of musical talent. It is not uncommon at our parties for these brothers and sisters to give off-the-cuff displays of their "skills and thrills." It definitely negates the idea that church is a place for people who have nothing to offer!
- Sports and games of all kinds are useful activities.

- Use public holidays—they are great occasions to get people together.
- Wine and cheese parties. Once we even organized a *non-alcoholic* cocktail party. I was the bartender! A huge number turned out. (Yes, we were up front that there would be no C_2H_5OH!)

Hopefully these ideas will get your creative juices flowing. Singles like fun, spontaneity, and creativity. You will be effective if you can be a pace-setter as far as social life goes. No one should have a busier social life than a Christian, and in particular a single Christian.

The difference

The main difference between singles and marrieds is the amount of free time singles tend to have. Their interests are not "divided" (1 Corinthians 7:33-34). They are able to meet for meetings and studies much more often and family men and women. This is especially true of singles under forty.

A word also ought to be said about some of our older singles. Most in their forties and above, or in some larger ministries, the fifties and above, will appreciate not being included with the twenty-somethings! (If you don't understand why, ask one; he or she will not hesitate to tell you!) Friendship is based not just on common interest, but also on common position: position in life, position socially, and so forth. I would not, in general, expect an older single to keep the same pace as someone ten or twenty years younger.

Reaching Married Adults

By virtue of their age and experience in life, evangelizing among married adults often, but not always, requires a different approach from that which we have looked at so far. The biggest enemy of the married adult is a complacency of sorts. It is that feeling of having in some sense "arrived"; he has a wife, he has a job, he is raising (or has raised) a child or two—and he does not need *your* advice about how to live, thank you very much! This is especially the case if you don't have much of a job (in his eyes), no wife and no children of your own. "What do you understand about life, anyway?" he will ask.

In reaching this group you're at an obvious advantage if you yourself are a married adult—particularly if your marriage is an excellent one. (Make sure you are praying every day as a couple; hold each other accountable to some goals; find a couple to help you, with whom you can open up.) Whether you are married or not, a high premium is placed on qualities such as patience, sensitivity, tact and hospitality, as well as over-all exemplary lifestyle. You'll be evaluated at the workplace, in the home and the neighborhood. More than with singles, students or teens, you have to *earn* the right to teach this group of people the gospel. This makes sense, when you think about it, because married adults carry more responsibility than singles. A decision for Christ affects not only themselves but also their spouses, families and careers. When the future of your family is at stake, you want to be sure of what you're getting yourself into!

None of this should be taken as endorsing compromise or any form of watering down the gospel. It is, however, a call for patience, perseverance and the utmost effort to make the gospel attractive by our own lifestyles.

The rewards of perseverance are great indeed. This group carries a healthy maturity and stability into the church. It is from the ranks of married adults that elders are raised up. Because of generally higher incomes, this group may also be valuable as financial contributors to the church. And they are the ones who'll reach more married adults!

Suggestions

Here are some suggestions for effectively evangelizing married adults:

Open your home. As the apostle Paul writes, "practice hospitality" (Romans 12:13). Have marrieds over for meals; let them see you in your home—the well-run Christian family is a great drawing card and a reflection of how "together" your life is. Moreover, it shows them that you value their friendship and their openness to the gospel.

Don't overdo it. This is especially important at work. Again, you need to win their respect. Mistakes have been made all too often by overzealous young single adult Christians who have tried to preach too much too fast to too many. (Ever done that?) In Mark 4:33 we read that Jesus was more considerate in teaching people "as much as they could understand." What your married coworker needs to see in you is a reliable, cooperative employee (or employer). This will earn is respect and pave the way for later instruction in the gospel.

Respect their priorities. Their spouses, children and jobs are priorities. Don't make unreasonable demands on their schedules. Once a week may be the most you'll initially be able to study the

Bible with them. One of the challenges in reaching out to this group of people is to get into their schedules, which between jobs and family are very busy. Make appointments well in advance, even two or three weeks ahead.

Have activities for families. While some of the suggestions for singles (above) will work, family activities make allowances for a broader range of ages, and of children's ages. (Remember, those kids may need to go to school the next day. And the parents will need to get them ready in the morning.)

Childcare. At Group Bible Discussions, as well as at activities, make sure facilities are available to take care of children. If you can, do your best to take the children off the parents' hands and give them a good time. You'll have won some valuable points with them. The more children a family has, the less available time they will have for "spiritual" activities. In addition, the more often the sickness of one child will keep a parent at home. (Remember when you were sick as a child? Who did you want—a babysitter or your mother?)

Be helpful. Look for ways to help out. If you're perceived as interfering, though, hold back. Married people are accustomed to being in a world that is so hectic that very few people make the time to help others. This is a great arena in which to let our light shine.

Seek wisdom. For example, do not project false costs. Exaggerations of Biblical passages pertaining to the cost of discipleship are particularly dangerous when applied to this group, because the damage will be greater. "To become a Christian, you're going to have to give up your job and stop spending time with your family" are a false cost. Wife, children and jobs are Biblical priorities (Ephesians 5:22-6:8, 1 Timothy 5:8, Colossians 3:22-25). Much sensitivity and understanding need to be exercised in counting the cost with married adults. Obviously, this does *not* mean watering down the biblical standards. You may need to sit down with your married adult friend and help him work out a reasonable schedule that will place his/her priorities in balance. The next section, on what demands will be made on the married adult Christian, will helpful with this.

What Can Be Expected?

We have discussed at some length the limitations that can hamper married adults and the implications for effectively reaching out to this group. These limitations apply to all married people, Christians as well as non-Christians. What can be reasonably expected of married disciples? How can they get involved evangelistically? Here are some ideas that may help.

Work out a schedule. Go through the individual Christian's schedule, making sure his priorities are considered. Priorities are as follows:

- Relationship with God—ensure that regular quiet times are scheduled into their routine. Given most people's busy schedules, this probably will need to be in the morning.
- Relationship with family—the married adult's most important earthly relationships are with spouse and children, in that order.
- Relationships in the body and church attendance—schedule in church meetings, Group Bible Discussions and time spent in one-another relationships. If you add to these time spent at work, it becomes clear that time available for meeting and studying the Bible with people is limited.
- Special note: When working with seniors, the priorities are the same, but how they are expressed will be different. Health considerations may make attendance at all the church services and activities difficult, if not impossible. Never doubt that seniors may want to change. Yet the complications of life, even the magnitude of many of the routine tasks that younger persons perform without any difficulty, require us to show extra consideration and sensitivity. These same principles apply also to physically challenges Christians regardless of age.

Evangelism in the workplace and neighborhood. Encourage married adults to see the workplace and neighborhood as their personal ministry. Encourage them to be the best neighbors and best workers they can be. Emphasize reaching out to people in these places and having vision for them to become Christians. Undoubtedly, things will move more slowly than in a singles ministry, so encourage the Christians to be patient in developing their ministries.

Evangelistic lifestyle. Encourage them to develop an evangelistic lifestyle, inviting people while shopping, when traveling on public transport, etc., and making the most of every opportunity.

Group evangelism with singles. From time to time, encourage urge married adults to go out with the singles in group evangelism times. This may well be feasible on Saturday afternoons, for example.

Bible studies. Challenge them to strive to have at least one person they're studying the Bible with. If you are too busy to share your faith, you are too busy—you may be gaining the world and losing your own soul! Come to an assessment of how many people an individual can study the Bible with effectively without abandoning his other legitimate priorities. Bear in mind that effective studying involves time for relationship building as well as time for personal Bible study. If you're mentoring a married adult, love them enough to ensure that he or she is involved in following up with and studying the Bible with someone.

Conclusion

In this chapter we have looked at some of the ins and outs of community evangelism. We've seen its importance and examined the specifics of working with two major groups in the community: single adults and married adults. One last suggestion: Draw a map of your neighborhood or a diagram of your apartment building that includes at least twenty houses or apartments that are near yours. Write in the first and last names of all your neighbors living in these places. If you do not know the names, develop a plan for finding them out. Turn this map or diagram into a prayer and planning list for reaching out.[2] Then proceed, with prayer and genuine concern, "from house to house."

It is clear that community evangelism must be the major emphasis in our thrust to win the world for Christ. This is where the majority of the people are! We must devote ourselves need to evangelistic principles and practices that are effective with people in the community, in order to make this one of the strong points in our ministries. Only then will we "win as many as possible" (1 Corinthians 9:19).

Notes
[1] The rationale for personal evangelistic Bible studies will be laid out in chapter 10.
[2] Suggested in *The DPI Leader's Resource Handbook* (Woburn, Mass.: Discipleship Publications International, 1997).

5
God's Ambassador at Work
Workplace Evangelism

If we were to take to heart the lesson of the last chapter, and became proficient only in ministry to our neighborhoods, we would probably have more people to follow up with and study the Bible with than we have time. And yet there is another phenomenal arena for daily evangelism. It is the workplace. In fact, in the book of Acts (God's evangelism textbook!), we see all sorts of men and women—working class, upper class, every class—being won to the cause of Jesus Christ.[1]

The Ambassador

Imagine it: You're sitting in your den watching the nightly news. Dinner is in the oven, and you have just stopped for a few minutes to rest. Your feet are propped up on the coffee table, and, wouldn't you know it, the phone rings... On the other end of the line is a very official-sounding voice saying your name in a very official-sounding way. Then you hear the voice. The same voice you just heard on the nightly news. No mistaking it. It is the President. *The* President! "We were wondering if you would consider assuming the office of Ambassador to Bolivia?"

Even though very few of us, if any, will ever receive the offer of an ambassadorship from our country, all of us have received an even more important offer:

> "We are therefore Christ's ambassadors, as though God were making his appeal through us. We implore you on Christ's behalf: Be reconciled to God" (2 Corinthians 5:20).

This is a really big-time ambassadorship—not just between two countries, but between heaven and earth. As God's ambassadors, we have the responsibility of bringing to the world around us his message of reconciliation. Most don't even know that they are at war or that they are in need of reconciliation with God. Enter *Mission: Possible!* We get to tell them with our words, with our commitment, with our lives, with our love.

Specifically, you are God's ambassador at your workplace. Granted, you do not have a special parking place with a neatly lettered sign: Reserved for Ambassador. But you are one all the same.

Sharing your faith at work is multifaceted. It can be tricky, confusing, discouraging, exciting, terrifying and much more. But one thing it is not is optional. Before ascending to his Father in heaven, Jesus was very clear about the mission he was placing into the hands of the disciples and into the hands of those the disciples would bring to him throughout the ages: you and me, specifically. No sealed envelope with an encoded message. No cassette tape that would self-destruct in five minutes. Just the word of the Son of God and no chance of misunderstanding:

> "Then Jesus came to them and said, 'All authority in heaven and on earth has been given to me. Therefore go and make disciples of all nations, baptizing them in the name of the Father and of the Son and of the Holy Spirit, and teaching them to obey everything I have commanded you. And surely I am with you always, to the very end of the age'" (Matthew 28:18-20).

As clear as the mission was the promise: "I am with you always, to the very end of the age." Well, guess what: The age isn't yet over. Granted, it is a long age, but it will not be over until Jesus returns in the same way that he left.

As you walk into work every day, remember Jesus saying, "I am with you always." That means "I am with you now!" "You are not alone." "You are my specially chosen ambassador; together we will get the job done."

Being Real

Sharing our faith does not always mean verbally telling someone about Jesus or the church. Our daily lives—actions, reactions, interactions—share much about who we are and whom we imitate. The Word "becomes flesh" once again as we live it. The fruit of the Spirit in our lives produces the seeds for others to know God. In order for people to desire our way of life, we must come across as real people, not some plastic or stained glass religious versions of human beings. Sometimes we are so aware of needing to be a good example that we freeze up and become rigid. We are afraid of admitting when we make mistakes or when we respond unkindly in a situation.

The truth is that people who work with us day in and day out will see us sin. Accept it. Then deal with it in a righteous way that will help them to learn how they should be dealing with sin too.

We must learn to relax and to be friends to people. We cannot right every wrong they do or say. We cannot wait until someone totally cleans up his or her act and becomes a disciple before we affirm the good things we see in their lives. Friends convert friends. That is healthy, but it is not necessarily easy for most of us.

Because of the gossip, bad language, dirty jokes and complaining attitudes of those around us, we want to withdraw. What a tightrope we sometimes seem to walk! As disciples we must be discerning and learn to balance the following two scriptures:

> "I have written you in my letter not to associate with sexually immoral people—*not at all meaning the people of this world* who are immoral, or the greedy and swindlers, or idolaters. In that case you would have to leave this world" (1 Corinthians 5: 9-10, emphasis added).

> "But among you there must not be even a hint of sexual immorality, or of any kind of impurity, or of greed, because these are improper for God's holy people. Nor should there be obscenity, foolish talk or coarse joking, which are out of place, but rather thanksgiving. For of this you can be sure: No immoral, impure or greedy person—such a man is an idolater—has any inheritance in the kingdom of Christ and of God. Let no one deceive you with empty words, for because of such things God's wrath comes on those who are disobedient. *Therefore do not be partners with them*" (Ephesians 5:3-7, emphasis added).

Paul says that we obviously need to associate with people who are worldly, but we should not become partners with them. We are not to purposefully place ourselves with people who corrupt our hearts and minds. If this is happening at work and we have already spoken up, we will need to make wise choices. We may no longer be able to sit with certain people at lunch because they persist in improper talk, but we can still seek to be their friends. Learning to *engage* but not to *indulge* is the goal. To "associate with" but not to be "partners with"...

Taking Advantage of Opportunities

Paul wrote to the disciples in Colosse,

> "Devote yourselves to prayer, being watchful and thankful. And pray for us, too, that God may open a door for our message, so that we may proclaim the mystery of Christ, for which I am in chains. Pray that I may proclaim it clearly, as I should. Be wise in the way you act toward outsiders; *make the most of every opportunity.* Let your conversation be always full of grace, seasoned with salt, so that you may know how to answer everyone" (Colossians 4:2-6, emphasis added).

Since we are paid to work for our school, hospital, store, studio or company, and not paid to share our faith, we must be responsible and discerning on the job. We cannot spend long periods of time studying or talking about the Bible with others. But, God does give us opportunities here and there to share. We must have keen spiritual eyes and open, receptive hearts so the Spirit can move us, as he did Philip, to take advantage of an opportunity for the sake of the kingdom:

> "Then Philip ran up to the chariot and heard the man reading Isaiah the prophet. 'Do you understand what you are reading?' Philip asked.
> 'How can I,' he said 'unless someone explains it to me?' So he invited Philip to come up and sit with him" (Acts 8:30-31).

When people "invite" us into their lives audibly or simply by showing need, we must be ready with conversation that is "always full of grace, seasoned with salt, so that [we] may know how to answer everyone." Just as children have specific and rare moments of "teachability," so do adults. Our daily walk with God should be others-focused enough to recognize these moments.

Being Bold

Grace and patience are Christian virtues, but these should never be excuses for not being bold. Patience does not negate boldness. Patience has to do with trusting God for right timing. Boldness has to do with trusting God and saying what needs to be said or doing what needs to be done, no matter what the consequences. In our natures we tend one way or the other:

toward patience or toward boldness. Or could it be more accurately stated: toward cowardice or toward insensitivity? The cross always calls us to the center of God's will: neither to the right nor to the left.

Most of us do not want to rock the boat in our work situations. We are simply afraid that if we do, we will fall out (or be thrown overboard). I can remember sitting at the table in the teachers' lounge and wondering when or if I should say something. Although I knew all the teachers pretty well, I was actually a "substitute"—not really one of them. Was it really my place to speak up when I felt they were being unprofessional and maybe even cruel in the way they talked about a student? At that point I decided just to be a positive example. But since then I have felt that I should have said something—not to the whole group at once, but privately to the individuals I knew personally.

In another situation I was working with two teachers and a parent to put on a middle-school talent show. We had fewer students try out for the show than we had anticipated. So the kids were asking the teacher, "Is everybody who is trying out going to be in the show?" Since she thought they would not feel as special if everyone was going to be in it, she wanted to lie and say, "No. Everyone will not be in it."

I said, "But that's lying. There is a way to respond that is not lying. You can say, 'Those of us on the committee are the only ones who need to know how many are chosen.'"

She said, "Yeah. That's good."

Since it was natural for her to lie in such a situation, she simply didn't think about how she could respond in a truthful way.

Boldness in expressing our convictions about God, Jesus, the Bible or our church is imperative. How often, though, have we been like Peter? In the inspiration of the moment with Jesus he says, "Even if I have to die with you, I will never disown you" (Matthew 26:35). Then that very night he swore, "I don't know the man!" (26:74).

During our prayer times in the morning, or when we are together with our Christian sisters, we, like Peter, say to Jesus, "Even if I have to die with you, I will never disown you." Then, in the press of the day and the embarrassment of the moment, we shrink back as if to say, "I don't know the man!" Sometimes Jesus just doesn't seem to fit in our workplaces. In fact, that is why he was crucified: He just didn't seem to fit. Are we ashamed of him? Are we too cool to be associated with him? Too afraid to be thought of as strange or as a goody-two-shoes?

Lord, we believe. Help our unbelief!

How to Be More Effective Through Your Job

I will now close this chapter, having shared tried and true wisdom on workplace evangelism,[2] with some of *my own* practicals on how to become an even more effective ambassador at your workplace.

Be punctual. Come on time, or even slightly early, and leave on time. Do not "stretch" breaks or lunches without your employer's permission. This is really a matter of integrity, and how we do in this area creates powerful visible and subliminal impressions. Disciples need o be completely above reproach (Daniel 6:3).

Don't be "overrighteous" at work—to borrow that unusual expression of Solomon's (Ecclesiastes 7:16, NIV). Go easy on the crosses and religious paraphernalia. No need for showy prayers before the office lunch. (Not to say don't pray!) Avoid religious terminology, "church" jargon especially. ("I had a mega-awesome quiet time this morning.")

Control your work hours. Excessive overtime, working weekends, and evenings will, for most disciples, be detrimental. How can you share effectively if you are weak spiritually?

Be cheerful. A positive disposition is appreciated by all. Remember, we do not shine like stars when we argue and complain (Philippians 2:14). Negativity darkens our countenance and example.

Don't waste time. On the job, the Christian must make sure that he stays focused, completes his assignments in a timely manner, and in short, does what he is paid to do. Computer games—watch out! Some time I ago I erased every computer game from my hard drive. I asked myself, "Am I paid to become an expert 'minesweeper' or solitaire player, or to follow my boss's instructions?"

Be patient. Professionals cannot always drop everything and come along with you, even if you are an exemplary employee. Don't become despondent. When someone is booked this weekend, ask about next weekend; even ask about next month. High achievers will seldom have an empty schedule; they have planned ahead. So should you!

Do not be intimidated. Beware of overestimating the confidence of the professional. Underneath the tough exterior is often a hurting individual. The marriage may be unraveling, the children may be resentful, the job may bring only a hollow fulfillment. He or she needs you—not *vice versa*. Sure, anyone can learn from others, but we're talking about learning the Gospel here.

Be a listening ear. Most men, especially, have no really close friends to talk to—least of all about family, marriage, or spiritual matters. Be available, but do not be pushy.

Do not be underemployed. While the spiritual effects of being underemployed are not as significant as those of being unemployed (see 2 Thessalonians 3), still a subtle erosion of character may be taking place when we are not "stretched," or maximizing our God-given talents. Look for ways to upgrade your job situation. One caveat: never jeopardize your spiritual condition or your family relationships in doing so. It isn't worth it.

Network with Christians in similar professions. You will benefit from such a network of support relationships. Why reinvent the wheel? You can learn from their experiences.

Conclusion

Our workplace affords us many opportunities to reach the lost. To borrow a phrase from the US Army, "It's not just a job, it's an adventure!" May we truly bring honor to God as his ambassadors in the workplace.

Notes

[1] Knowing how much we desire to be effective at work, and not feeling the need to "reinvent the wheel," I asked permission from my former publishers (DPI) to adapt a chapter on evangelism from Sheila Jones' *9 to 5 and Spiritually Alive.* This powerful book offers counsel on successful Christian living in many aspects of the workday, including a number of chapters on sharing our faith. Afterwards, I will conclude with some of my own suggestions for effective workplace evangelism. Thus chapter 5 is an adaptation of Chapter 5 ("God's Ambassador at Work: Sharing Your Faith") in Sheila Jones' book *9 to 5 and Spiritually Alive* (Woburn, Mass.: Discipleship Publications International, 1997).

[2] Sheila Jones' book has many excellent chapters on evangelism. Most relevant to the subject of *Shining Like Stars* are chapters 5 (on sharing your faith at work, much of which we have just read), 6 (relationships with male coworkers, a great help for all women in the "professional" world), 8 (about how to have an encouraging commute), and 9 (entitled, "What if I do not like my job?").

6
The Goose that Laid the Golden Egg
Campus Evangelism

The Goldmine

Campus ministry may be described as "the goose that laid the golden egg." A large number of leaders in growing churches around the world were met and converted during college years. And many of those not actually converted in college were converted and trained in the ministry by those who were. Yet as time has passed, it is easy to neglect that "precious bird." College ministries tend to flourish when talented men and women devote themselves *exclusively* to that work.

Campus ministry presents a golden opportunity for reaching younger persons—people who may be in their prime in terms of openness to the gospel, who have many years before them, and are well positioned to affect others for Christ by virtue of their placement in the university setting. Tens of thousands have become Christians during their college years, and a great number of these have gone on to enter various fields, including full-time Christian service, and affect countless others.

And yet, although the fruits of campus ministry have been so great, some congregations in university cities are not prioritizing campus ministry. This chapter urges us not to neglect "the goose that laid the golden egg."

Convictions

For ten years I served as a campus minister, heading up outreaches at some twenty universities—in London primarily, but also in Sydney, Birmingham, Stockholm, Philadelphia, and Washington DC. Campus ministry is truly rewarding, for many reasons, including the openness of the students, the relative simplicity of their life situations, and their vibrancy and vitality. My principal convictions about campus ministry are few and simple.

First, students need to flourish academically. While it is true that God in his providence has put them on the college campus to win others to the cause of Christ, they are also there to study. God is not honored by substandard work. This means campus ministry must be elegant and streamlined, not clogged with multiple meetings and complicated programs that interfere with study time. Today's students often have to work part-time jobs as well, which means that a lack of planning on the campus minister's part can make it difficult for them to succeed.

Second, students need good communication with their families. In an era when so many family relationships are already distant or strained, we do students a disservice when we fail to encourage them in relationships with parents, who have often sacrificed so much for them to study. Christian students should be the most grateful students on campus!

Finally and obviously, students need to grow spiritually. Just as discipline is crucial for academic life, discipline is crucial for spiritual life as well. In my experience, I see that students deeply desire to live sacrificially; they admire those who embody the high ideals of Christ in their lifestyle.

When young men and women receive encouragement and support from their leaders in these areas – academics, family relationships, and spirituality – they will flourish evangelistically as well. Students love to hold discussions, and Christian students will find the urge to talk about Jesus Christ irresistible.

As I look back through the years, I realize how much I have learned from my mentor in the ministry, Douglas Arthur. (Once a television program described us as "accomplices": I prefer the term "partners.") Maybe one reason I am such a big believer in campus evangelism is that I became a Christian while a college student. In fact, Gary Knutson and Douglas Arthur knocked on *my* door only a day after I entered university! (I think God knew I was ready. Only seven weeks later, I was baptized into Christ.) Just as I have learned a tremendous amount from Douglas, let me invite you to do the same. The rest of the chapter is the evangelistic strategy this man taught me in our campus years together, especially in Boston and London.

In the beginning

The beginning of the year is perhaps the most critical time in the life of an academic ministry. If it is handled well, it can ensure lots of evangelistic personal Bible studies—and hence a good number of new Christians throughout the year. If it is handled badly, opportunities will be lost that can never be recovered.

Since this is such a crucial time, you need to begin your work before the beginning of the academic term.

Before the Beginning

One good idea is to have a college leadership planning session before the year begins. Ideally, have a mini-retreat; go somewhere overnight as a group. Establish such things as:

- Who will be in which group Bible study.
- Where and when group Bible studies will meet.
- Special activities for the campus ministry (retreats, play days, etc).
- Make sure all the students are involved in good one-another relationships (prayer partners, discipleship groups, etc).
- Have a time of Bible study, prayer and fellowship with a view to developing unity among the leaders of the campus ministry.
- Getting into the dormitories around the campus at the earliest possible opportunity is also good strategy. Frequently, dorms and other facilities are open several days before the first day of classes. Christian students might move in early, get themselves settled and then begin helping others, building friendships through serving.

Two terrific weeks

Many college ministries limit themselves to slow growth by mishandling the first two weeks of the year. During those precious few days virtually everyone is looking for new friends. There is an openness to new relationships that will soon begin to fade dramatically.

Christians must resist the urge to spend large quantities of time with one or two apparently receptive people. Meeting the masses is the need of the hour. Some students will benefit from setting personal goals for making new acquaintances. (E.g., "Today I will reach out to ten new people.") It is terribly difficult to keep track of all those new names and faces, so keep some kind of record. Lots of good evangelism time can be wasted by lack of good record keeping.

In your first few minutes of conversation, mention the Bible discussion that you attend. If people are receptive they will pick up on it immediately. In this way you may get many visitors coming without issuing a single invitation. Take special note of those who seem open and try to see them daily. The key in the first two weeks is not spending a lot of time with them, but making the time you do spend exciting.

Be creative in devising ways to double up on your appointments. For example, if John in Room 14, Frank in Room 62 and Sam in room 53 seem open, plan on meeting them all from 9:00-9:30 for a grand Star Wars competition or the "Minnesota Fats" grand pool championship of the dorm.

Keep the interactions short, sweet and consistent, and continue to meet at lots of new people each day. During the first week don't take time to study personally with people; just get them to the Bible studies or Christian activities. In the second week, study only with the most responsive people and keep on meeting new people. By making the most of these precious days you will surface the maximum number of open contacts.

Halls of Residence

If the Garden of Eden was the paradise for mankind, then dormitories are the Christians' evangelistic paradise. They provide the best environment imaginable for seeking and saving the lost. Next to having a campus minister, having students in the dorms is the most obvious asset a campus ministry can have. Often students are encouraged to live off campus, to get out of the dorms. I think this is often bad counsel. (In my own university years, I lived eight of my eleven years in the dorms—the payoff was enormous.)

The apostle Paul was not afraid of leaders in his society and neither should we be. The resident advisor, or R.A., is the most immediate symbol of authority most dorm residents face. It is important that Christians develop good relationships with the R.A. before the Bible studies begin. Then if anyone complains, you'll be seen as a friend and not as "that religious nut" in Room 18. Moreover, do not be intimidated by the R.A.s—countless times they have turned out not only to be "allies," but also have become Christians. Respect their authority, just as you strive to cultivate good relationships with all authorities in your life. Most residents get to know few people outside of their dorms, classes, and clubs. In the university setting, you will typically encounter a number of small cliques, with only shallow interaction between groups. Our challenge is to get to know people in as many groups as possible, thereby expanding the number of people we can invite in a personal way.

Clubs, student government and sports are good ways of developing friendships, but you must be careful not to flood your schedule with activities that may be evangelistic "dead ends." Ideally, you want to find a number of varying activities on a casual basis. The challenge is to become genuinely interested in things that interest other people, while never losing sight of the fact that the activities are tools and not ends in themselves.

Meals

Everyone likes to eat. Fortunately, in a university setting people are generally eating together with dozens, and often hundreds, of other people. Mealtimes are superb evangelistic opportunities. Regardless of how hectic the pace of life becomes, we must all take time to eat—which means that *everyone* has time to meet people, at least while we eat. Even during final exam times we keep our evangelism going by simply scheduling our meals with other people. The key is planning, and not just doing whatever comes most easily. Whether it is two or three meals you eat each day, plan to make them count. If you don't have someone to sit with, you can look for a group of people that you have never met before and join them.

The classroom

Everyone has a favorite place to sit in a classroom. Many will sit in exactly the same seat for the entire term. Many Christians deny themselves that luxury; through the course of the semester they move around the room, getting to know all the little groups in the classroom. It is a bit like "Dungeons and Dragons"; you enter various chambers, and in some you'll find beasts and in others princes or princesses looking for what Jesus came to offer.

There is much to be said about your example in the classroom. Here are some suggestions about how to increase the brightness of your light.

Come early to class—a person rushing in late is a nuisance to everyone. If you are early you can chat with other students before class.

Do your homework—confused Christians make for timid ambassadors. Gain people's respect academically and they will listen to you about more important things.

Initiate with professors—this will help you learn the material and feel more confident in class. It will also give you a chance to invite them to church.

Be joyful—Demonstrate the peace that passes understanding—let people see your joy even in hard times and they will begin asking "Why?"

Community/Commuter Colleges

In this situation, most students do not live in dorms (halls of residence); some colleges do not even have housing available. That does not stop the work; it simply redirects it. It means that the focus of evangelism shifts to the classes, cafeterias and common rooms. The group Bible studies may take place at lunchtime as well as in the evening, in classrooms or in the homes of Christians who live near the campus. Becoming a recognized student organization is very helpful in all college ministries, but it is especially important in a commuter college setting.

Conclusion

College campus ministry is a challenge and an opportunity like no other. It's a challenge because you stay under constant scrutiny. There is no retreating—only shining like stars all day, every day. It is an incredible opportunity for the same reasons. Never again will you have such easy access to so many people on a consistent basis. Not only that, but you are reaching out to a people who may well be at the height of their receptivity to the gospel.

If you're a student, rejoice and enjoy it. If you're a leader in the church, find men and women to devote themselves to this most fruitful of harvest fields. Whatever your situation regarding college ministry, make the most of it. Let us not neglect the goose that laid the golden egg.

On to more challenging arenas

Having considered three principal evangelistic arenas (communities, workplaces, and universities), in the next three chapters we will explore some rather more challenging arenas.

All of us want to win our own families. We yearn to make an impact on the world. And we would give anything to have the boldness and confidence of Jesus in the presence of the "ultra-religious." Accordingly, chapters 7 to 9 will cover evangelism at home, with foreigners, and with the extremely religious.

7
Reaching Our Families
Relational Priorities

"And whoever does not provide for relatives, and especially for family members, has denied the faith and is worse than an unbeliever" (1 Timothy 5:8 NRS).

Reaching our families

This chapter is primarily focused on reaching our children for Christ, although the principles also apply generally to sharing the gospel with other family relations. If we are going to reach our families, we are probably going to have to rethink relational priorities.[1] To help you think about the subject, please think through the following short exercise. Take a moment to reflect on your most important relationships. Consider the following: husband or wife, children, the church, the lost (those who do not yet know God), and of course the Lord. Arrange them into their order of importance—that is, starting with the most significant relationship. (Single parents, in this exercise, for simplicity, do *not* include your former spouse/partner.) In terms of your God-given Christian responsibility, which feels most important.... next most important... and so on?

1. _____
2. _____
3. _____
4. _____
5._____

It may come as a surprise to some that there actually is a divine order of relationships. Did we perhaps think that all relationships are equally important, apart from our relationship with God? They aren't.

Divine Order

We harm our families, and the church family, when we disregard God's wisdom, his divine sequence. Let's begin with what we all agree, on paper at least, to be our most important relationship. We are pretty confident that you placed the Lord in the number one position. And this is right:

> [4]"Hear, O Israel: The LORD our God, the LORD is one. [5]Love the LORD your God with all your heart and with all your soul and with all your strength" (Deuteronomy 6:4-5).

If we love him with all our heart, there can be no one we love more. Both testaments agree that the Lord God is to be the ultimate recipient of our love and devotion. (In the New Testament, see Matthew 22:37, Mark 12:30, and Luke 10:27.) Are we really loving God with our whole heart? And do our children see us putting God first? Don't think they aren't watching. They know whether father and mother really believe what they claim to profess at church. The kids know what we really love most. And if we are reaching out to parents or older relatives, we must not be confused. They can tell whether our religion is skin-deep, or whether we are really living out what we profess.

Clearly, God comes first, according to scripture, and this has big implications for how we spend our time. Failure of husband or wife (but more typically the husband) to actively seek the Lord has a detrimental effect on the children. How can the family be godly if the leader of the family is taking them in an ungodly direction (Luke 6:39)? Yes, the Lord is first, and others second:

> "Love your neighbor as yourself" (Leviticus 19:18b—also Matthew 5:43, 19:19, 22:39; Romans 13:9; Galatians 5:14; James 2:8).

Our neighbor, our fellow man, includes family members and non-family members, and it is true that sometimes we have to choose between loyalty to Jesus and loyalty to blood relatives (Matthew 10:34ff, Luke 14:26). God always comes first. And yet even if the Bible teaches that we are to put God before our families, we are still to put our families before all other persons.

One of the most challenging verses in the entire Bible addresses those believers who presumptuously expect the church to take care of their aged relatives when it is in their power to help them:

"And whoever does not provide for relatives, and especially for family members, has denied the faith and is worse than an unbeliever" (1 Timothy 5:8, NRS).

Of all the family relationships, the Bible has the most to say about the marriage relationship. In fact, there is far more about husbands and wives, including marriage principles, than there is about children or parenting advice. As Paul says,

[28]"In this same way [as Christ loved the church], husbands ought to love their wives as their own bodies. He who loves his wife loves himself. [29]After all, no one ever hated his own body, but he feeds and cares for it, just as Christ does the church—[30]for we are members of his body. [31]"For this reason a man will leave his father and mother and be united to his wife, and the two will become one flesh." [32]This is a profound mystery—but I am talking about Christ and the church. [33]However, each one of you also must love his wife as he loves himself, and the wife must respect her husband" (Ephesians 5:28-33 NIV).

This famous marriage passage stretches from Ephesians 5:21 to 5:33. It is thirteen verses long, while the parenting passage that follows is only four verses long:

[1]"Children, obey your parents in the Lord, for this is right. [2]"Honor your father and mother"—which is the first commandment with a promise—[3]"that it may go well with you and that you may enjoy long life on the earth." [4]Fathers, do not exasperate your children; instead, bring them up in the training and instruction of the Lord" (Ephesians 6:1-4 NIV).

Why is there so much more biblical material, especially in the New Testament, on marriage than there is on being a father or mother? We believe that's because the better the marriage, the better the parenting. Part of parenting, after all, is showing your kids how to love the one you promised to love and be faithful to "till death do us part."

Spouse comes before all other human relationships, and that includes children! So often, in the world, once the babies begin to arrive, husband and wife grow distant from one another. But if the Bible makes anything clear, it's that the husband-wife relationship deeply affects the children.

This relationship is prior to and more important than the parent-child relationship. When we favor a child over our spouse, we are undermining the very basis of security that the child needs in order to grow up with a sense of well being, confidence, and trust. Worse, if we are not respectful towards our spouse, that disrespect will affect how our children relate to the opposite sex! Of course we are not saying that we should neglect the basic needs of a defenseless baby in order to see to our marital pleasures and whims. There are those who abuse their children. God will not countenance such sin, and his penalties will surely be severe. Having made this qualification, spouse still comes before children, and the children need to know this.

A secular psychotherapist visited a house church meeting in our home a few years ago. I was very encouraged to hear her response after I asked her opinion about the key to well-behaved children. She replied, "It's the marriage." I nearly said "Amen!" It was reassuring to hear biblical wisdom coming from professional a counselor.

Of course parents naturally take care of their children (2 Corinthians 12:14), so children immediately follow spouse in the divine order. We are to favor our own children over "church friends" and the lost, even though fellowship with other Christians is vital, and outreach to the unsaved is also essential. We would encourage you fathers to spend individual times with your children every week, if at all possible. It may be less necessary for mothers to have scheduled time with each child, as they tend to spend more time with the children in a variety of settings anyway (homework, driving them to activities, and so forth).

So far, based on the biblical evidence, we have arrived at the following relational priorities:

> GOD
> SPOUSE
> CHILDREN.

But what about everybody else—those *not* in your immediate family? We can distinguish between believers and non-believers, not because this is a convenient division, but because the Bible itself makes this very distinction. For example, consider Galatians 6:10:

> "Therefore, as we have opportunity, let us do good to all people, especially to those who belong to the family of believers" (NIV).

Other versions, instead of "the family of believers," read "the household of faith" (HCSB, NAS), or "the family of faith" (NRS). The apostle Paul is referring to the church family.

Who are your church family? They come next in the sequence, *not* the lost. Paul made that very clear. He is certainly *not* saying that we shouldn't try to be a light in the community, share the gospel with others, or "push" ourselves to be outgoing, even to the point of initiating with strangers. What he is saying is that we are to honor our spiritual family—our brothers and sisters in Christ—above outsiders.

Nor is Paul saying that it is okay to ignore the lost in the name of church obligations, any more than it is legitimate to ignore children for the sake of spouse. It is not a matter of cultivating the higher priority relationships and ignoring the others; all must be pursued *simultaneously*. But when push comes to shove, when a decision must be made, the priorities are clear.

Please don't misunderstand. Evangelism is a command of Christ that applies to all believers. *Shining Like Stars*, as a book on evangelism, is well founded, biblically speaking. And yet the New Testament emphasizes relationships with fellow Christians—"one-another relationships"—*far* more than reaching out to the lost. Could it be that if we focused more on our one-another relationships (exhorting one another, speaking the truth to one another, serving one another…), evangelism would take care of itself?

Once again, we are obligated to reaching out to insiders and outsiders alike. And yet there is a ranking: insiders first, then outsiders. Also, as we saw, in a number of passages the immediate family takes precedence over others (1 Timothy 5:8). Another reason the church comes between family and the lost is that the church family is ultimately an extension of our own nuclear families, in all their dynamics and patterns of interaction. A spiritual congregation with strong nuclear families will display a tight knit fellowship. And that is bound to be attractive to outsiders.

Putting it all together, the ladder of earthly relationships looks like this:

1. GOD
2. SPOUSE
3. CHILDREN
4. THE CHURCH
5. THE LOST

Counterproductive counseling

Remember this sequence; it is integral to good parenting and also to good evangelism, both of which respect the divine sequence. Unfortunately, this is not often respected, even though there are loads of scriptures to back it up. For example, instead of focusing *(up the ladder)* on God [1] when my marriage [2] is hurting, I am tempted to pour my life into others *(down the ladder)* [3, 4, 5]. It is usually easier to work a rung or two down the ladder than to focus on the real issues. If anything, an improvement at a *higher* level will benefit relationships lower down. The human tendency to focus *downward* instead of respecting the divine order is counterproductive, and leads to confused and unhelpful counseling when we are trying to advise others.

To illustrate further, our children may be acting out, and through various incentives or disincentives I may try to change their behavior [3], when the real problem is between me and my spouse [2]. Or church relationships [4] may be suffering from disunity, resentment, and gossip. And yet the preacher is mostly concerned with bringing in new members [5]—oblivious, one wonders, about the dysfunctional quality of the fellowship the newly evangelized are joining. There are times, we believe, when we should "clean our own house" before inviting the neighbors over.

The human tendency is to look at the surface, not to go to the source (1 Samuel 16:7 etc). If you are running a high fever, putting ice on your skin is not the ultimate solution. We must probe deeper and understand the cause of the fever. If steam and blue smoke are pouring out from under the hood of your car, the problem is not with the tires or the sun visor—it's somewhere under the hood. In the same way, God's word tells us where to look:

- If the marriage is struggling, look one level *up*. Take an honest look at your spouse's walk with God—and also at your own.
- If the kids are acting out, look *up*—at the marriage!
- If the church is not a happy place, look *up*—at the nuclear families it comprises.
- If the lost are not being attracted to the community of faith, look a level *up*—how are relationships in the body of Christ?

In other words, trying to build an evangelistic ministry is not going to work—or at best, see only short-term growth—unless we appreciate biblical relational priorities. Evangelism without sensitivity to these crucial truths is likely to become mechanical, shallow, and counterproductive!

Summary

We must recognize the basic truths that flow from the divine ordering of relationships:

- All relationships depend, ultimately, on one's relationship with God.
- When children arrive on the scene, couples must make the conscious decision to prioritize their marriage relationship.
- Kids observe the spirituality of and interactions between mom and dad, and are deeply shaped by them.
- The church family is merely an extension of the nuclear families of the church, especially the families of principal leaders.
- While our mission is to seek and save the lost, this must not be raised above the biblical imperative to excel in one-another relationships.

A Word to Those in Special Circumstances

Some of you are single parents and some of you are married to someone who is not a Christian. Let me say a few things about your situation, because I recognize it presents some special challenges. Since single parents have to do the work of two, extra patience is required. The two-parent family is God's ideal, and yet thousands of committed, vibrant disciples have been raised by single parents. In other words, as challenging as your situation is, never accept the lie that the obstacles are insurmountable. A few ideas:

- Pray daily with your children. When possible, join with another family for devotionals.
- If remarriage is a possibility, pray for it patiently. Don't let your frustration affect your judgment.
- Although TV has its place, beware the temptation of letting it become a (much-needed) "babysitter." Instead, encourage your kids to invest in friendships, sports, schoolwork, chores, and reading. Do you really want advertisers and liberal programmers conforming your children to the pattern of this age (Romans 12:2)?
- Do not associate with grumblers and complainers (Proverbs 22:24-25). The world is filled with people who will offer you a false sympathy, one that fosters a critical spirit rather than a Christlike one.
- When you drop off your kids to children's ministry, make sure they already have a positive, giving spirit. Cooperate with their teachers, accepting their feedback. Children's ministry is a privilege, not a right.

- Finally, when you are tired—perhaps after a long day— don't "tune out" when your kids need you. Yes, they need you to go "one more lap." You are serving as both mother and father to them!

As for those whose spouses are not disciples, you face yet another set of challenges. Whether you are a man or a woman, 1 Peter 3:1-5 applies. This passage teaches that your character is more decisive in winning over your mate than your words. A few practicals:

- Resist the temptation to make subtle "digs" at your mate, whether in direct conversation or in your prayers. Don't be manipulative. Pray for a gracious spirit. (The Proverbs will prove faithful friends!)
- When you speak about your spouse to others, be positive. Remember, he/she does not have a "voice"; your brothers and sisters in Christ are likely forming their impressions of your mate through your words. Never, ever speak ill of your spouse in the presence of your children. (This would undermine their respect for you.)
- Strive to coordinate schedules as much as possible, giving advance notice whenever possible. Sometimes this means that where there have been sudden changes in plan, you will need to stand at your spouse's side (e.g. the last-minute prayer meeting or church party).
- Never, ever argue, raise your voice at your spouse, or lose your temper. Your mature example in Christ, not childishness, will change his/her heart.
- When you do sin, be quick to confess and ask for forgiveness both from your spouse and your children. Show them that you know you need God's grace and are grateful for it.

For both single parents and those without Christian spouses, character issues are of the essence, more than external behavior. Pray for a pure heart (Proverbs 4:23).

Other Family Members

Some of us are not old enough to have children (or grandchildren) of our own. If this is the case, it is more likely that we have a number of relatives still living: siblings, parents, uncles, aunts, cousins and perhaps grandparents. To win them, here are a few valuable principles.

- Family members cannot be rushed. A stranger may become your friend and make his decision for Christ in a period of weeks or months. With family members, who know your weaknesses (and strengths) well, months and years are often the time units we should be thinking in.
- Keep up regular communication with them, whether by mail, telephone, email or personal visit, depending on the relationship and the time of year. The exact frequency of contact is probably less important than its consistency. Keep them up-to-date with what is happening in your life!
- Forgetting birthdays and special occasions in the lives of our family members can make them think they are not important to us anymore since "finding God." This impression is to be avoided! Write down the key dates in your calendar, and remember them.
- If they are religious, seek opportunities to pray with them. There is no harm in it, and it not only shows your heart for God but also brings you closer together emotionally.
- Very often it will be less awkward if an outsider studies the Bible with your relatives, especially siblings and parents. Though the message may be the same, it will be heard differently, with less defensive ears. Choose someone you trust and be helpful, yet resist the temptation to interfere.
- Ask them for advice. Your relatives are trained professionally as accountants, chefs, business people—each has an area of expertise. People feel special when their counsel is solicited. But do not limit the advice to just the professional—ask for feedback (more than input) in the area of family and marriage. For example, ask "How do you think my children are doing? What do you see in their characters?" Or perhaps, "Dad, when you were at this stage in your life, how did you feel when Mom...?" "Do you have any tips for me?"
- Introduce your friends to them, not just the ministry staff of your local church. Talk about your friends in their absence. Then, when your family happens to meet them, they will have more of a sense of connection.
- Share with them any books on marriage and parenting you have found helpful. (Not, "Here, you really need to read this," but "I have found this helpful for me. I know I have a lot of things to change. Are you be interested in reading it?")
- Pray for your relatives every day. The persistent prayer (Luke 18) will not fall on deaf ears.

Conclusion

Christians are called to love and serve the people of the world. Above all, this includes our own families. After our spouses, out of all the family members we most long to see baptized into Christ, our children are closest to our hearts and at the head of the list. To win them, to "impress" them, we will need to live differently, to talk differently, to schedule differently. If we follow the priorities laid out in this chapter, we will build healthier churches; our children will not resent us, but rather covet the secret of our joy and spirituality; and evangelism will be enhanced as outsiders enter the happy and emotionally healthy[2] family of believers.

Whether you are counseling others (Romans 15:14), sharing your faith with outsiders (Colossians 4:5-6), or simply enjoying Christian fellowship (Philemon 7), keep the "ladder" of relationships in mind. It will help us better love our spouses, parent our children, and build godly families and godly churches.

Of course merely reading this chapter will not change anything. You have got to have your own conviction. So, what decisions have you recently (say, in the last ten or twenty minutes!) made about family evangelism?

Notes

[1] This chapter is an adaptation of chapter 5, "Relational Priorities," in *The Quiver: Christian Parenting in a non-Christian World* (Newton, Mass.: IPI, 2005), which itself is an adaptation of chapter 7, "Impress Them on Your Children," in the millennial (3rd) edition of *Shining Like Stars*.

[2] Highly recommended: Peter Scazzero's *The Emotionally Healthy Church* (Grand Rapids: Zondervan, 2003), ISBN 0-310-24654-7.

8
All Things to All Men
Foreign Evangelism

God's will is that all nations will receive the gospel through Jesus Christ (Galatians 3:8). This means world evangelism. World evangelism can take place "here" (wherever you live) or "overseas"—that is, where indigenous churches will reach out and make a difference. This chapter concerns not so much the need to take the gospel to foreign lands as the need to reach foreigners who happen to be in your own country.

My wife and I have a deep love for things international. When we go out to eat, we rarely eat at a "western" restaurant (I'm talking about American or Continental food, not Texas fries or buffalo burgers from the "chuck wagon"). We prefer Asian—and the spicier the better! Our children were born in three different countries, none in the country where we now live. We have many friends from Africa, Australia, and Latin America. My love of languages naturally draws me to any country where English is not spoken (which is *most* nations). We quickly turn to the international news section of the paper before any other section. (For me, even the crossword has to wait for the international news!) And in our marriage, it is not clear who is the "foreigner" —is Vicki (the Briton) the foreigner, or am I (the American) the outsider? To tell the truth, it depends on where we are at the time, as we have relatives on both sides of the Atlantic.

From the perspective of the citizens of some two hundred nations, it is *you* who are the foreigner! We all tend naturally to view our own nation as the center of the universe, don't we? Most maps are drawn with the nation of production of the map squarely in the center. The Chinese called their land the "Middle Kingdom"—all others were outside. Similarly, the ancient Romans named their primary body of water the "Mediterranean" —from *media* (middle) and *terra* (earth)—meaning the water in the middle of the earth. For the ancient Greeks, those outside the kingdom were barbarians—simply because they weren't Greek! This is the human tendency.

Part of being a citizen of the heaven (Philippians 3:20), in my opinion, is overcoming this natural form of geographical prejudice. At the end of this chapter I will give you some ideas on how better to retain an international focus and awareness. For the time being, our concern is the evangelization of foreigners in your own country. I have personally studied with people from nearly one hundred nations, and the Lord has enabled me to bring many of them to a saving knowledge of the truth. Part of this I attribute to evangelism and prayer, part of it to my genuine interest in things foreign. Do you have a love for "foreigners"?

The evangelization of foreign nationals is of crucial importance as we labor to win the world for Christ. Many countries do not allow foreign missionaries, but it is harder to prevent their own citizens from sharing the gospel with their countrymen. While it is true that churches ought roughly to reflect their geographical setting demographically, it is also true that we must not ignore the alien in our midst. Through our study of the scriptures and our outreach to these people, we have discovered several invaluable principles of effective outreach.

In the following pages, we will discuss the language barrier, the importance of friendship, the need to ascertain motives, "counting the cost," and our own need to be more aware of the world we live in.

Language

Revelation 7:9 describes a truly "international scene":

> "After this I looked and there before me was a great multitude that no one could count, from every nation, tribe, people and language..."

God has never intended for language to be a hindrance to people who are seeking to know him. Today God has provided his written word in almost every language known to man. A "language barrier" should never be an excuse for not reaching out to people from other countries.

When evangelizing foreign people, it is important to realize that most of them know some English, at least enough to find their way around. Foreigners usually understand more English than they can speak, so you should not be afraid to speak to them in English. The most helpful thing you can do is to speak *slowly*, clearly articulating each word (especially the consonants), and avoiding rare idioms and difficult words. And be patient—they will take a little longer to understand what you are saying.

In reaching out to foreigners, it helps to know a few phrases of their language, and to be willing to learn more. Foreigners are elated when they meet someone who can speak a bit of their language. Phrases like "What is your name?", "My name is...", "Where do you live?" and "Hello, how are you?" are great icebreakers in starting conversations. It is well worth learning these phrases in the languages of the main national groups in your own city. A learner's attitude on your part is also very helpful as you begin studying the Bible with those for whom English is a second language. Your interest and humility in leaning their language will, in turn, encourage their interest and humility in learning about God.

In studying with people who know little English, it is important to get them a Bible in their own language. Contact your nearest Bible Society or Christian bookshop. This gives them a greater trust that what you are teaching them is correct (Acts 17:11). It also allows them to do their own personal study, which will be essential for them to develop a genuine and lasting faith. When you study with someone who knows little English, be sure to read each passage at least twice. Ask simple, specific questions.

For Luke 13:1-5, for example, don't ask, "Do you comprehend the import of Jesus' utterance? Is damnation the ineluctable result if one neglects the precepts of the Almighty?" Come down to earth! Use simple vocabulary. Try sentences like "What happens if you don't change?" Frequently ask the question Philip put to the eunuch: "Do you understand what you are reading?" (Acts 8:30). As you study, use fewer scriptures than usual in each study, but spend more time carefully explaining each passage. If you are thorough, much of the language barrier can be overcome.

It is exciting to know that open people will respond even if they understand only a little English.

Friendship

A second consideration is friendship. "A new command I give you," Jesus said. "Love one another. As I have loved you, so you must love one another. All men will know that you are my disciples, if you love one another" (John 13:34-35). As we have discussed, it is important to deal with the language barrier as we reach out to foreigners. Yet we must never forget the most powerful tool Jesus gave us for bringing people to him: love, the universal language.

As we study God's word, we can see that loving friendship is the key ingredient in God's plan for reaching foreigners. We can see this in John 4 as Jesus befriends the Samaritan woman, in Luke 7 as he dines with Simon the Pharisee and in Luke 19 as he meets Zacchaeus. Jesus was known as "a friend of tax collectors an sinners" (Matthew 11:19). When we love people in a way they have never been loved before, then they will know that there is a God who loves them. If we are to win foreigners to Christ, we must be their best friends.

The magnitude of the decisions to be made makes this event more important. It is amazing to think that within a few weeks or months after meeting someone, you may be challenging him to give up smoking, drinking or sexual immorality, or to change his job, schedule or travel plans. You will probably be challenging him to leave behind his family's religious beliefs, no matter how devoutly or sincerely held. These are hard decisions for anyone to make, especially for someone hundreds, or thousands, of miles away from home, facing a strange land and culture, and perhaps with little or no previous exposure to the gospel. We need to be people's best friends so that we can encourage and persuade them to make these kinds of decisions.

Friendship is also important because foreigners tend to form close-knit communities or cliques when away from their home nations. Deep friendships with Christians are crucial in helping them stand up against opposition.

Friendship is vital for winning foreign students, because often they are in the West on scholarship from their own countries, and easily feel much more pressure to please professors and parents than to seek God. Only through a close friendship can you persuade a very busy student to make time in his schedule to consider becoming a Christian.

Generally, foreigners are quite open to friendship, once you have gained their trust. There are several ways to do this. You need to show a willingness to listen to them and understand their problems. Be willing to take time to get to know them. Keep up with current events in their country. Try to learn a little bit about their country and culture. These are excellent ways to start building common ground.

Sharing a meal together also can do wonders for a friendship, especially a home-cooked one. And, yes, be prepared to try any exotic cuisine. Quite often foreign styles of cooking are not only edible, but delicious! And even if they aren't, you are sure to win points by making an effort to try them out. Let us strive to "become all things to all men."

Playing sports or games they enjoy, or going to a film, museum or cultural event can be very helpful, too. And genuine compliments about home, clothing, appearance or personal strengths can be encouraging, as well. Basically, being a friend to people from other countries is not much different from being a friend to anyone else. You need to love them and treat them as unique, special individuals.

Motives

As we have said, we must do all we can to bring people to Christ. Yet in reaching out to people from other countries it is important to guard against wrong motives. This is a tricky enterprise, since "motives are weighed by the Lord" (Proverbs 16:2). It is quite possible for us to think that someone from another culture is interested in Jesus, when in reality his interest lies elsewhere.

Jesus, of course, was a master at reading men's hearts. He did not need man's testimony about man, for he knew what was in a man" (John 2:25). Jesus had that special ability to look into men's hearts and see what was really there. The same Jesus who compassionately forgave the adulterous woman left speechless the proud men who accused her (John 8). Jesus brought salvation to humble Zacchaeus (Luke 19) but stiff challenge to Simon the Pharisee (Luke 7). After feeding the five thousand he told the people that they were more concerned with miracles than truth (John 6). Jesus was continually evaluating the motives of all those he came into contact with. He knew people, and in the same way we need to be wise, especially when evangelizing foreigners. (Admittedly, we will not have the confidence and accuracy of Christ.)

All of us have had the experience at one time or another of reaching out to someone whose interest in Christianity sprang from impure motives. When dealing with people from cultures and backgrounds completely different to ours, we must be sensitive to the possibility that they might have mixed motives for becoming Christians. Improper motives reveal themselves in a variety of ways. Some people are interested in financial gain or solutions to their money problems (1 Timothy 6:9). Many foreigners have large debts to pay or families abroad to support, and some hope to find in the church an easy source of short-term cash. A warning sign that someone may be motivated by money is when he asks for financial help soon after meeting the church. In some cases this may be an expression of legitimate need, in others an indication of hidden and less-than-noble agenda.

Sometimes people come to church hoping to make contacts to help them find accommodation, locate a job, acquire a visa, or sort out personal problems. If, after exposure to the gospel, they still seem more concerned with their problems than with God, we need to re-examine their motivation.

Foreigners may be more interested in learning English than in learning about Jesus. Study at a slow pace with people like this, and see if they are consistent in their personal prayer and Bible study, church attendance and changing their lives. Strong challenges generally sift out the people who are not serious about following Jesus.

Other times people come to church looking for relationships with the opposite sex. If you think this could be the case with someone you are reaching out to, challenge him.

Still other times people come to the church not because they are willing to serve God, but merely because they are lonely and want friends.

Ultimately, the way to deal with impure motives is to teach people Jesus and the message of the cross. As people learn, they will either fall in love with him and change their motives, or they will reject him.

Counting the Cost

Surely part of "counting the cost" (Luke 14:25-34) with anyone is asking them to ask themselves *why* they want to follow Jesus. Don't rush. Ask about relationships in other countries. I once studied with a single man and baptized him. I found out weeks later that he had a fiancée. "I asked you before if you had a girlfriend, and you said no!" I remarked. "You asked about whether I had a girlfriend, not if I was engaged," he came back. Was this a result of a language gap, or a touch of deceit? Hard to judge!

Another helpful idea is to have someone from his home country—preferable Christians currently *in* that country—to have a conversation with him, even to "count the cost." Sometimes this costs me financially. I remember studying with one fellow, a dentist in his 30s, who desperately wanted to be baptized but insisted that his "old pastor" in his home country taught accurately about conversion. "Be my guest," I said." You can phone him, I will pay." He took me up on my offer. Ten minutes and $50 later (time and money well invested), he said, "Douglas, you were right. I am in shock. He reacted just as you said he would. When I go back to my country, I need to help my pastor, too." This man was baptized into Christ soon after, and is a strong, effective, married Christian to this day.

The main reason to let someone else assist you in your study with a foreigner is that you are at a distinct disadvantage. You think differently, use a different language, and lack the background necessary easily to enter the world of the man or woman you are sharing your faith with. Be humble. Don't just assume you understand.

The world we live in

In addition to considerations of language, motives, and so forth, you will enhance your ability to "connect" with foreigners by becoming more aware: internationally, geographically, and culturally. In closing, here are some suggestions towards those ends:

- Re-study your geography! Christians need to be strong in this area if they are effectively to visualize and pray for the nations of the world. I have a large map in my study, with pins inserted in cities I have visited or spoken in. At my website I feature a different nation each week, as a "prayer point." When I read of a land or city I am not familiar with, I look it up! There is a perpetual opportunity to learn. Maybe a new map or globe is the birthday or Christmas present you should pray for!
- Newspapers, magazines, and news broadcasts can be helpful. Avoid only local news. The horizons of the disciple of Christ need to be broad. As the people of God, charged to pray for rulers and those in authority (1 Timothy 2:1), we will do well to become more aware internationally.
- Be more daring! Visit that Ethiopian restaurant. Befriend your neighbor from the Caribbean. Learn a few words of Japanese. Read a book about Mexico. One morning, pray for all the nations of the world! Reach out to an "alien." "Remember, at one time we too were foreigners and aliens…" (Ephesians 2:19)

Conclusion

As we reach out to foreigners, we must be prepared to meet their special needs. We must overcome the language barrier through patience and study. We must love them even more than we love ourselves. And we must test their motives. Yet we must always remember that with everyone we reach out to, it is God who gives the increase (1 Corinthians 3:6-7). With his power at hand, we can convert foreigners and equip them to evangelize their own countries. The alternative: we can go there ourselves!

Let's truly become all things to all men (1 Corinthians 9:22)!

9
The Ultra-religious
Those Who Have a "Hotline to God"

Ultra-religious!

The ultra-religious[1] claim they have a personal hotline to God. They receive direct guidance from the Lord, whereas the rest of us carnal, unenlightened individuals must fumble around in the darkness. They may "speak in tongues," have "visions," or "prophesy." They are convinced, and this conviction includes a way of looking at the world that must be partially dismantled before the light of the Gospel can enter.[2]

Assumptions

Before starting, a couple of comments are in order. I have had a fair amount of experience studying with extremely religious people. Many of the principles in this chapter I have learned through the "school of hard knocks." I have made many mistakes, and I do not desire that you repeat them. Also, many personal Bible study topics are named, assuming you are familiar with them. I realize that the study series, *Guard the Gospel,* is not detailed until chapter 11, so in a sense this chapter is out of order. Yet because it deals with one of the more challenging evangelistic arenas, along with family and foreign evangelism, I prefer to include it here.

Going on the defensive

Many times Christians are on the defensive when talking with the ultra-religious: our adrenaline surges, our voice level rises, our arguments become hurried and emotional—in short, we come on far too strong. We may behave this way because we lack experience in studying with this sort of person, or because their questions seem impossible to negotiate, or because we feel personally threatened. Perhaps we are unsure of the reality of the Spirit in our own lives. People sense such intimidation. It does not give the impression that we are confident of our position, and this can easily reinforce others' false sense of security. The solution:

know your Bible, relax, be friendly and trust God. Realize that God is on your side if you are on his.

No one is saved by virtue of his claims to religious experience. False theology, false doctrine, and false living put us into a precarious position in the sight of God. Don't kid yourself; sincerity does not make one justified in God's sight (1 Corinthians 4:4). If a person has not met Jesus on Jesus' terms of salvation, he is not prepared to meet his God. But if you have the truth, why be on the defensive? Why be intimidated?

Avoiding the cardinal insensitivities

In our attempts to be confident, it is easy to be insulting. This is not wise, nor will it commend your position to the ultra-religious. Here are some of the "cardinal insensitivities":

- Arguing against experience. This is not only insulting, but illogical, since there is no way to prove that someone has not really had the experience he claims. The interpretation of the experience may be open to debate, but never the experience itself.
- Making fun of the ultra-religious position. Comments like, "If you are supposed to have the gift of healing, how come you still wear glasses?" are not likely to win points. Moreover, there were a number of people in the New Testament with the gift of healing whom God did in fact leave unhealed, or without the ability to heal certain others. Paul left Trophimus sick in Miletus (2 Timothy 4: 20), told Timothy to drink wine for his stomach illnesses (1 Timothy 5:23), and himself had a thorn in the flesh that God would not remove even after three prayers for healing (2 Corinthians 12:8).
- Harsh or sarcastic comments about the religious person's views. Sometimes believers bring out of the arsenal such retorts as: "You people are just like the Jonestown group. They were so gullible, they would believe anything. And look where they are now—the same place you're going!" Other times over-generalizations can be just as damaging: "Hey, remember that vision of the nine-hundred feet tall Jesus Oral Roberts saw and told him to ask for more money? I bet your church just wants your money, too!"
- Prematurely judging a religious person not to be a Christian. Informing someone of your assessment that he is lost before you have studied the Bible together and have a good relationship is a common but foolhardy move. First,

it is likely to backfire. Second, you have no right, especially in his eyes, to say such a thing to a fellow believer who has neither been tried nor found guilty. Third, you will undo all the good you may have done and will prejudice him against the things you still plan to study out.

- Denying the work of God in his life. God works in the lives of *everyone*, whether or not they are true disciples. One of the worst errors we can commit is to ascribe good deeds and sincere religious experience to the devil. One of my most haunting memories is turning away a sincere "charismatic" from baptism. We had studied many passages, and he was beginning to surrender many of his ultra-religious interpretations. He had come to the midweek service with a towel and a change of clothes. I asked him whether he still thought God had been working in his life. He replied, "I know I'm lost, but I just can't believe that God never had anything to do with me." David might well be a disciple today if I hadn't turned him away with my judgmental, *too* black and white attitude. God *can* and does work in everyone's life (Matthew 7:7, Acts 14:17, 2 Kings 5:1-15). David, forgive me.

Let us realize that, in the face of the insincerity of the religious world, we have more in common with many of the ultra-religious than we do with most other religious people. This kinship, so to speak, should be capitalized on. Remember, "reckless words pierce like a sword" (Proverbs 12:18). At all costs, let us avoid the cardinal insensitivities.

The friendship factor

Without a solid friendship, you will convert only the most pure-hearted. Unfortunately, not all of the ultra-religious persons are not "Ethiopian eunuchs." The truth is hard to swallow, especially when your entire approach to spirituality is wrong and you are seeing that your friends are lost. Love and gentle instruction go a long way (2 Timothy 2:25). We need to apply verses like 1 Thessalonians 2:8 to the ultra-religious as much as to anyone else. Friendship begins with mutual respect. You are likely to be respected for your commitment to Christ, and you should particularly respect the rather "hot" religious person for his commitment too. Yet even if you don't respect the ultra-religious person's commitment, you should still respect him as a human being. Ask him to tell you about his religious experiences (meanwhile making careful mental notes for future Bible studies). Ask him to share in a prayer at the end of your study; there is no harm in your praying together, and it is likely to draw you closer.

Work on the friendship, balancing serious studies with more relaxed outings together. Eat together, stay in good touch, and allow the friendship time to grow. You will be surprised at what good rapport you will be able to develop after only the first meeting or two, as your relationship is based on mutual respect, love and (increasingly) Christ.

Finally, introduce your ultra-religious friend to Christians in your congregation who were converted out of a similar background. It will be conducive to their conversion and long-term stability to have more than one good relationship, and the older disciple will be able to help them through any difficult patches which may arise during the studies or afterwards.

If you want your studies with ultra-religious to be fruitful, and not just an exchange of disagreements, remember the friendship factor.

Evangelistic personal Bible studies

The personal Bible studies suggested below are only one possible way to help your friend. The units of the Guard the Gospel series (see next chapter) should be employed as needed, depending on the situation of the person you are studying with:

Jesus Christ—his character and dealing with people
Seeking God—getting serious about finding God
The Word of God—its absolute authority
Discipleship—with special emphasis on evangelism
Sin—specific sins and separation from God
The Cross—the motivating power in the Christian life
Repentance—a radical change in life
Baptism—New Testament baptism
False Doctrine—the implications of N.T. baptism and false doctrines
The Church—the need to be totally invested in the body

Keep in mind the following principles if you want to be effective in your studies with anyone, and especially with very religious persons:

- Patience: allow time for concepts to sink in.
- Logical flow: create a sense of continuity in the progression of studies.
- Flexibility: select studies that address the person's individual situation.

Dealing with religious pride

As with all religious people with whom we study the Bible, pride must be confronted. Some important advice:

- Be firm. Jesus was more direct in dealing with proud religious people than he was with "sinners" (John 8:1ff, Luke 7:36ff).
- Temper challenge with friendship (relaxed time together). Play a sport or game with him. This can be very helpful in dealing with pride: Either it provides an *opportunity* to humble him (in something at which you are good), or an *outlet* for his pride (assuming he can beat you)! Play it by ear.
- Initially it may be good to offer to "disciple" the religious person. Teach him what you know about evangelism. Take him under your wing and begin a "discipling" relationship with him, teaching him the basic studies. As the studies progress, he will realize that he has more need of the studies than he thought!
- Offer to take him evangelizing with you.
- Go through a Bible study on self-righteousness with him. Useful passages might include Luke 3:7-11, 5:31-32, 7: 29-30, 18:9-14 and 2 Timothy 2:19.

The issue: repentance

Repentance is the main issue with any non-Christian, no less so with a religious person. Repentance has been watered down in the religious world. Biblical repentance, however, is a radical decision leading to a radical change in one's lifestyle. People who have repented are eager to know God, eager to spend time with others who know God, and eager to help others to know God. If an ultra-religious person claims to be saved but is not devoted to God, committed to reading the Bible, active in sharing his faith, and so forth, it is unlikely he has ever repented. We must not water down the message! Their lives testify to their repentance (Matthew 3:8, Acts 26:20). Ultimately, God is the judge of whether they have repented or not.

Because this the clear biblical focus, make repentance "the issue"—for it is![3]

No baptism without repentance

A classic mistake young Christians make is "blowing away" their friends and family with the Bible's teaching on baptism. Such tactlessness seldom bears fruit, usually hurting the victim's short-term chances of turning to God, and cultivating the habit of using the Bible as a club instead of the fine sword of the Spirit that it is. But many not-so-young Christians make the identical mistake! The mistake, again, is the premature study of baptism. The power is not in the plan of salvation; the power is in the cross of Christ (1 Corinthians 1:17), so unless the message of repentance is clearly understood and responded to first, the biblical teaching on immersion will fall on deaf ears. And on top of all this, by "inoculating" them against the truth, you make it even less likely that they will ever come to Jesus on his terms. And so a fundamental principle emerges: *Avoid the study of baptism with people who have not repented!*

Further advice

Despite the temptation to enter into an involved study of the Holy Spirit with an ultra-religious person in the early stages of your studies with him, *don't!* In fact, you may need to go easy on the Spirit material until he understands he has been mistaught. Also, adapt your studies to ultra-religious, sharing verses or points that will be helpful in the future, once he realizes where he stands before God. Aim to instill *principles*, but do not attack the major issues too early.

When I was a student at the University of London, a very religious man named Mohan, who lived in my dorm, began attending the group study in my room. For several weeks we studied the Bible with Mohan. Mohan, who lived upstairs from me, was a very knowledgeable neo-pentecostal. He spoke five languages fluently—as well as "tongues." He was also a postgraduate student in economics at the University of London, and he wanted *answers*. We met for twelve hours of intense study on the Holy Spirit, but Mohan still remained unconvinced.

One day he walked into my room and asked me if I would like to hear him speak in tongues. "Sure," I said, "go ahead." Mohan then used his "prayer language," hoping to convince me.

"Is that supposed to prove to me that you are saved?" I asked.

"Oh, you're not listening!" a frustrated Mohan said.

"Do you want to hear *me* speak in tongues?" I asked.

"Go ahead," replied Mohan.

"*Korobka dvyer karandashkuya, boomega okno,*" I faked some words of Russian.

"Was that really tongues?"

"More than what you just did," I replied.

"Wow, I'm impressed."

Was this the turning point? No! Hours of Bible study on the Spirit did not do the trick. Nor did impugning his tongue-speaking ability. (I was still learning about the cardinal insensitivities!) What made all the difference? Going back and nailing down the fact that, according to what the Bible teaches on salvation, he was not a Christian. Two days later, Mohan, powerful man of God ministering in India, was baptized into Christ.

The moral of the story is simple: establish the fact that someone is not a true Christian *before* you dive into a study on the Spirit. Otherwise, if he still thinks he is a Christian, he will not be able to make sense of his experiences. (And don't expect him to jettison them all at once.) Once he has accepted his own lostness, he will be looking for—and will need—answers to his questions. Tie up all the loose ends *after* you have covered baptism.

Order of studies

Studies with the very religious may follow the normal sequence until after the baptism study, when it will be time to tie up the loose ends. The *Feelings* study is good to cover early (you will find it in chapter 13), but apart from that there is little need to cover the peripheral Holy Spirit topics. After discussing baptism, one or two studies on the Spirit will be necessary. Many neo-pentecostals will need separate studies on topics like tongue speaking, the purpose of first century miracles, or other themes or difficult passages in the Bible.[4]

Conclusion

There is no magic formula for converting the ultra-religious, but a working knowledge of the Scriptures, a measure of common sense, a lot of love and much prayer can make all the difference. Let's not be intimidated by those whose passion for God—however misguided—takes forms more unusual than that which we are used to. For while their "hot-line to God" is something largely in their own fantasy, God's deep desire for their welfare and salvation is not (Ezekiel 18:32, 1 Timothy 2:4).

Notes

[1] This category includes not only those convinced of mystical, esoteric, and not necessarily biblical experiences, but also those belonging to a number of non-mainstream groups: Jehovah's Witnesses, Mormons, et al.

[2] This chapter is a modification of Chapter 14 of my book _The Powerful Delusion_. The first edition (London Church of Christ, 1987) and second edition (London Church of Christ, 1990) are both out of print. They will not be reprinted. For more information on the working of the Holy Spirit, as well as an exposé of the more common forms of misunderstanding current in our religious world, see my book _The Spirit_ (Newton, Mass.: IPI, 2005).

[3] Did you know that there may be more people in the world who have been immersed for the forgiveness of sins than have scripturally repented? Many groups teach immersion for the forgiveness of sins (e.g. Christian Church, Apostolic Church, Mormons, Church of Christ, some Independent Baptist Churches, and a number of independent evangelical fellowships), but hardly anyone teaches repentance as the Bible does. Surely Christians ought to be known for their radical commitment, knowledge of the scriptures, love for others, and love for God rather than for their adherence to any one doctrine (baptism, e.g.), regardless of how central it is in the scheme of things. Keep the focus on repentance!

[4] Here are some possible study sequences with four ultra-religious persons. The first (Mr. Breeze) in interested in little more than the good feeling he thinks the Holy Spirit can give him. The study series is as follows: _Discipleship._

Is that all? Yes, for it turned out that Mr. Breeze, who was not following in the footsteps of Jesus (1 John 2:3-6), refused to admit that he was not a true disciple of Christ. He became very uncomfortable when he read the verses on evangelism and saw that he hadn't ever really given his life to the Lord. In fact, in the middle of the study Mr. Breeze felt "led" to leave the room, and was never heard from again. (Not all people sort themselves out so easily, however, as we shall see.)

The second (Mr. Gust), another very religious person (though not living for the Lord) was impressed by the Bible knowledge of the Christian, and after admitting that he "could be doing more" to spread the Word and live as a disciple, consented to study the Bible. Here is the series covered with Mr. Gust: _Discipleship, The Word, Feelings, Sin, Repentance._

Alas, things were going well, but then Mr. Gust found it impossible to accept that he (and his ultra-religious friends, whose Christian life was no more active or devout than his own) were not true disciples. In fact, at the end of the _Repentance_ study he saw that he himself was lost, but became completely silent as the implications dawned on him. Then he changed his mind and said he was saved after all. He heartily thanked the Christian for helping him to "grow spiritually" much, and said he would like to continue the studies in the future—which he has yet to do. (The Christian wisely resisted the temptation to study baptism with Mr. Gust, who would have made that the bone of contention instead of repentance, and gone away feeling justified.) From time to time they pass each other in the street, and their relationship is cordial. Perhaps one day Mr. Gust will rethink his decision and seek out the Christian again.

The third ultra-religious individual, Mr. Wind, was a very sincere, very committed individual. He initially got caught up in the excitement of speaking in tongues, but after a year or started to have some doubts. As far as he can see, however, there is no alternative to his ultra-religious fellowship, which has much more to offer than the dead denomination in which he was brought up. He met the Christian while the Christian was inviting people in the streets, and was interested in getting to know him better. These are the studies the Christian covered with Mr. Wind: _The Church, The Word of God, Feelings, Sin, Repentance, The Cross, Baptism (two studies), The Holy Spirit, Discipleship._

As you have supposed, Mr. Wind became a Christian after about four weeks of studying the Bible. The Christian started with _The Church,_ making the study very convicting, and challenging the ultra-religious to get involved in a church where everyone seriously studied the Bible and shared their faith. From then on, Mr. Wind started attending all the services of the local church, which significantly accelerated his decision for Christ.

After the study of *The Word,* Mr. Wind was still talking about what he *felt* the Spirit was saying to him, and so the Christian thought the *Feelings* study would be appropriate. After *Sin* and *Repentance,* Mr. Wind realized that he was lost, and so the coast was clear to proceed toward baptism. To make sure his motivation was pure, however, the Christian first studied *The Cross* with him. *Baptism* was a welcome solution, and after one long study on *The Holy Spirit,* and another on *Discipleship* as a wrap-up, he was immersed. Now the Christian and Mr. Wind are doing some more in-depth study on the Spirit, so that Mr. Wind will be able to reach his religious friends.

The fourth man is Mr. Gale, who, shall we say, has been strongly influenced by the ultra-religious ideology. He speaks in tongues, feels he has been healed of a tumor, and is thought to possess the gift of prophecy, which he exercises on occasion. Mr. Gale was actually the one who invited the Christian to consider Christ! They hit it off from the start, but it was clear that Mr. Gale was not going to be easy to convince. These were the studies the Christian and Mr. Gale covered over a four-month period: *Discipleship, Feelings, The Word, Faith and Works, Sin, Repentance, Baptism (two studies), The Holy Spirit, The Miraculous Gifts, The Church, Speaking in Tongues, The Cross.*

From the very start, the studies were challenging. There was no tip-toeing around, because Mr. Gale was serious about his commitment to Christ. It wasn't until the *Faith and Works* study, which cleared up a lot of misunderstandings in Mr. Gale's mind, that he was prepared to visit church with the Christian. (He was involved in his own church five evenings a week, and felt that, even if they were "drooping" in their discipleship, they needed him, and that was where the Lord wanted him.)

Mr. Gale really appreciated the thoroughness of the *Sin* study. When the time came to study *Repentance,* however, the Christian was afraid that because he was so committed, he would not be able to see that he wasn't saved. But Mr. Gale had a pure heart, and thought that although he had not fully repented, he very much wanted to and asked the Christian to pray for him. After the *Baptism* study, everything fell into place; Mr. Gale did not put up any fight.

That is not to say that he had no questions, though! It took three more studies on the Spirit to satisfy his curiosity and to make it clear to him why the experiences he and his friends had claimed did not prove they were saved. (After the *Repentance* study, Mr. Gale realized that most of his ultra-religious friends were lost, but there were a few who were very committed, and he was not so sure about these.)

The final study, on *The Cross,* helped Mr. Gale to be urgent in finalizing his decision, and he was baptized the very next day.

Although Mr. Gale would have been an intimidating fellow to many Christians, he was reached because someone saw in him a great potential and cared about him enough to spend hours and hours every week with him. (In the last week of their studies, Mr. Gale and the Christian studied nearly every day. Some of those studies on the Spirit lasted two or three hours!) Praise God that the Christian shared his faith with Mr. Gale, because already he has helped three of his friends to become Christians, and will soon be leading his own group Bible study!

What we must understand is that, although most of the ultra-religious are like Mr. Gust or Mr. Breeze, there are a great number like Mr. Wind and Mr. Gale. If we don't know the Bible, or if we are not willing to make them our friends, they may die separated from God.

PART III

LEADING MANY TO RIGHTEOUSNESS

"Those who are wise will instruct many, though for a time they will fall by the sword or be burned or captured or plundered...Those who are wise will shine like the brightness of the heavens, and those who lead many to righteousness, like the stars for ever and ever" (Daniel 11:33, 12:3).

The third section of *Shining Like Stars* contains the bulk of the teaching material—nearly fifty studies you can share with those interested in Jesus Christ, as well as with new Christians. After chapter 10, on how to lead personal Bible studies, you will find three series of Guard the Gospel material. But that is not all! Chapters 14 and 15 contain even more valuable material for the disciple determined to hide the word of God in his or her heart.

As we master the word of God, we will not only instruct—we will, by God's power, lead many to righteousness.

10
Studying with non-Christians
The Biblical Warrant

A set of evangelistic personal Bible studies—does this have any biblical warrant? Shouldn't we just preach the word and leave it to the Lord to bring our friends to faith (John 16:8)? Is there any reason it shouldn't be done in a single session? And the whole notion of "studies"—might be this not be a humanistic approach to evangelism? These are the kinds of questions dealt with in this chapter.

Expecting too much?

If we expect people to go through a study series and make specific changes in their lives, are we not teaching salvation by works? Is this not "performance theology"? Not necessarily.

I do not doubt that it is tempting for us to "raise the bar" too high—to require more than the Lord himself requires.[1] But this is no better than expecting too little—or nothing at all, which is not uncommon in modern-day Christianity. A useful study is to examine the ministry of John the Baptist. What did he require before anyone was baptized? Did he ever turn anyone away?

Actually, yes. Though we won't go into the scriptures at this time, please look them up and come to your own conviction. In Luke 3 many persons came to John for baptism, including the religious leaders. Before he baptized them, they confessed their sins—not necessarily exhaustively, but not vaguely, either. When they asked him what they needed to change, John was quite specific, with special challenges appropriate for the various people who sought baptism. And yet one group apparently did not feel comfortable with such specific admission of guilt and need of repentance: the Pharisees. Although they were present in Luke 3, read Luke 7:29-30. Here we read that they rejected God's purpose for themselves; they were not baptized by John. The Baptist, after all, would have expected specific repentance. Many Pharisees had great difficulty seeing, and admitting, this need (Luke 5:32). Biblical speaking, it is wrong to expect too much, but it would also be wrong to expect too little.

One-shot approach?

The traditional "one-shot" approach of exposing someone to the "whole counsel"[2]—everything needed in order to become a Christian—has an abysmally low success rate. We must discipline ourselves not to rush in our Bible studies with non-believers, but rather be patient. Most likely it will take time to bring them to an accurate understanding of the truth. (The one-shot approach does not allow time to internalize the new concepts or process the far-reaching implications, which normally dawn on those studying the Bible for the first time. See Acts 17:2.)

One-day conversions?

"What about Pentecost?"—someone is sure to ask. "Didn't these people become Christians in a single day?" Now I am pretty sure there were "first-timers" in the audience, and yet Peter speaks to them as persons who know the facts about Jesus Christ (Acts 2:22). They know about Jesus' miracles and even about his death. It may have been their first time to hear an apostle speak, but it was hardly their first exposure to the gospel. These persons[3] have Judaism in common—which is a huge head start on many people in our modern secular society. Many may have stayed over in Jerusalem after Passover, which took place just seven weeks previously. And what about the preparatory work of John the Baptist? And the ministry of the Twelve, and of the seventy-two? Jesus himself had spoken to countless thousands (Luke 12:1) during his approximately three years of public ministry. If I had to hazard a guess, I would say that most of the Pentecost crowd knew quite a bit about Jesus Christ, even before Peter began speaking.

As for the Ethiopian (Acts 8), this is a better example of a "one-day conversion." As a "god-fearer" (a Gentile attracted to Judaism, yet who had not submitted to circumcision—and in his case, one who never would!), he had previously been exposed to Judaism and had faith in God. He was reading, after all, in the book of Isaiah the prophet. He was seeking, and he was receptive. Philip preached the word, and the Ethiopian was baptized the same day. What was it that he needed to hear? He needed to hear about Jesus, and that is who Philip presented to him. At any rate, here is an example of someone who came to faith quickly. (And we all know many more in our own day.)

As for Saul of Tarsus (Acts 9), he had *plenty* of Christian background—when you consider his acquaintance with the faith he was determined to eradicate, the exposure to Stephen's message (Acts 7), the confessions he must have heard as he tried to force men and women to renounce Christ, the Damascus Road experience, and the miracle of regaining his sight. Saul encountered the Lord personally. In terms of knowledge and experience, Saul of Tarsus was well ahead of many who come to faith in our day.

In short, the "one-day conversions" of the New Testament are rare and exceptional. (And even then, it is clear in each case that God had been at work in their past, preparing them for the moment.) These conversions should not be taken to be normative. In my experience, many "one-day conversions" do not endure. I doubt we do people a disservice by persuading to take adequate time to prepare for the most important decision of their life.

Specific Teaching?

In Ephesians 4:20-24, Paul reminds his audience of their conversion. As we read this passage, we too receive this reminder: that we were *taught*—to "put off the old self" and "be made new." In other words, there was teaching *before* conversion.

> [20]"You, however, did not come to know Christ that way. [21]Surely you heard of him and were taught in him in accordance with the truth that is in Jesus. [22]You were taught, with regard to your former way of life, to put off your old self, which is being corrupted by its deceitful desires; [23]to be made new in the attitude of your minds; [24]and to put on the new self, created to be like God in true righteousness and holiness."

Similarly, in Acts 16:31, it was not enough for Paul just to tell the Philippian Jailer to believe in Christ. He had also to preach the word to him (v.32). This was followed by baptism (v.33), and of course a great deal of joy (v.34), as this man and his family had come to a saving faith.

Now the Lord has not told us *how* to teach the lost, only *to* teach them (Matthew 28:19-20). That means we cannot make a hard and fast rule. The goal is that people accept Jesus as he is, as Savior and Lord (Acts 2:36, Colossians 2:6). This is not likely to take place, for most of us, without some helpful instruction. Perhaps this is why *every* person who becomes a Christian in the book of Acts does so through the agency of a human teacher. No one comes to Jesus on his own; everyone is taught. This is humbling. It also takes time. And it requires that we know our Bibles!

Personal studies

A personal study is a session in which you *share* with a non-Christian. What are you sharing? Three things: the gospel, your faith, and your life (1 Thessalonians 2:8). You will talk about God's word. This is easiest with an open Bible (Acts 8:35, 17:11).

All of us want to lead others to Christ, and we know that our lives will never be more fulfilled than when we are sharing the good things we have received with others. We know that if we "instruct many," it's only a matter of time before we begin to "lead many to righteousness" (Daniel 12). Yet when it comes to studying with non-Christians, how often we fall short, not so much through sin as through ignorance! Some of us specialize in diplomacy, yet the message of Jesus is muddled or missing. Others know exactly what to say, but through errors in judgment invest all their time into people who simply are not willing to make Jesus Lord. Or, worse, turn off prospective converts through sheer insensitivity. This chapter aims at giving concrete help as to "what to say and how to say it" (John 12:49).

When should I set up the study?

The answer is "as soon as possible." For a few people that will be the first time you meet. For most it will be after a few visits to a small group Bible study, or to church, or after a few "spiritual" discussions, perhaps in your home. It is important that the person feel comfortable with the concept of seeking God or at least growing spiritually through Bible study before you propose the idea of studying together. The "Oh, no, she's trying to convert me" reaction should most definitely be avoided. On the other hand, sometimes we let timidity or fear that someone might not be open cause us to delay unnecessarily. Perhaps the easiest time to set up a study is *immediately after* a group Bible study or a church service, or even after a good conversation. It is important not to let it go too long before proposing the study—otherwise he or she may become *too* comfortable in the fellowship. Friendship is also an important element for most people. It helps to have at least the beginnings of a good relationship before you begin studying.

How do I set up a study?

That depends largely on who the non-Christians are. Some people, like the Ethiopian Eunuch (Acts 8), are so wonderfully open that they could not care less how you propose it, and will certainly ask you to study with them if you do not hurry up!

Many religious people are more difficult to approach. You have to tiptoe around their religious pride long enough to win trust and dispel unsound doctrinal positions. It is essential you strike the balance between respecting their knowledge and challenging their life and doctrine. If people are very committed, you might share with them the passages that have helped *you* to share your faith with others. Gradually, the impact of these scriptures on their hearts will, prayerfully, enable them to be more receptive to the things God wants to show them.

Other religious people are interested, but not exactly wide open. Sensitivity is of the essence, as you balance urgency with patience. Capitalizing on meetings or discussions is usually best. "What do you think about that verse the preacher used about seeking God? Maybe we could get together and study more about this topic." Or you might say, "He really got my attention when he was talking about *knowing* you're saved. My confidence comes through knowing the scriptures. Would you like to get together and spend some time looking at some other verses?" Regardless of whom you are setting up a study with, there are three imperatives if you want to be as effective as possible.

- Be confident—never apologize for taking up their time or for your lack of knowledge. People listen to confident teachers—our confidence is not based on ourselves but on the power of the gospel.
- Be relaxed—you know that a "no" answer to the gospel is an eternal mistake, but there is no point in conveying that to them, at least initially. Pray and assume the best, then calmly propose to start studying the scriptures together.
- Be excited—in your efforts to be calm, don't be boring! We should have at least as much enthusiasm as the world does when they invite us to parties or events. Those things bring superficial thrills at best; Jesus brings peace and joy forever.

How many people should be involved in the study?

In my situation, it was one other man studying with me. For many others, two or three others were helped them come to faith. There is obviously no biblical rule here! Often it works well when three persons, including the non-Christian, meet together. That arrangement allows a younger Christian to learn how to study from an older one. The non-Christian also benefits from having more than one close relationship. For some, however, "Two is company and three is a crowd." If that is the case, then proceed with two but encourage one or two other Christians to make special efforts to get to know them.

How long should the study last?

That depends on the topic and the other person. Most studies last thirty to ninety minutes. You want allow enough time to discuss things thoroughly, but not so much that you waste time rambling. Resist the urge to explain the Bible from Genesis to Revelation when a person seems eager. These three tips will help you to keep the time reasonable.

- Give them the verses to read in advance—this will help them to feel secure in their understanding of the passages, as well as minimize the time you spend on basic explanations.
- Stick to the topic—if the topic is Sin, don't get involved in a discussion of Armageddon. If it is the Word, don't get diverted into a debate on baptism. Learn to say, "We can talk about that later; for now, let's get back to our study."
- Let the Scriptures do the talking. Don't plead with your friend to accept your views about repentance; have the person read Luke 13:5 himself. Avoid the trap of arguments that are really smokescreens for disobedience. 2 Timothy 2:14 and 23-26 will help you. Of course there are legitimate questions, even in the midst of a study, that deserve an answer. Always direct the discussion back to the Word, because that is where the power is.
- Begin and end with prayer. It will be easier for them to accept the truth when they believe that you too are a seeker after truth, someone who is trusting in the Lord in your own life.

How often should we study?

How often can you study? How available is your friend? Once a week is an ideal. If you study less often than that people may absorb the information intellectually but struggle with making changes in their personal lives. Becoming a Christian is an incredible change for anyone. The transition cannot be made on the strength of a commitment that is inferior to that of an average member of a bowling league.

After you have had a number of sessions and the person's urgency is increasing, it may be possible to study every two or three days. Coming to church or group Bible studies is important, yet so is studying together. Aim to keep your friend growing on both fronts.

It is essential that people develop relationships in the local church and become accustomed to the weekly schedule of church meetings. If they are eager to come to the services, then feel free to study as often as they are willing. Discuss the frequency of meeting together after a study on *Seeking God* or the *Word*. I will often say, "Now, we can study as much as you like. I'm available to study a couple of times a week if you want. If you are not quite ready for that, we can do it once a week." Also, you can save a lot of time by establishing when the next study will be at the end of each session together.

Don't be afraid to study with someone every day. This often works out with singles, not so often with marrieds, especially marrieds with children. Yet even if someone is eager to study daily, don't rush. Haste makes waste. Be alert for possible wrong motives, and try to make sure the implications have sunk in.

How do I know if they are open?

Titus 2:14 talks about people *eager* to do what is good. 2 Corinthians 7:8-11 talks about people *eager* to clear themselves. The following is a list of characteristics to look for in an open or receptive person.

1. They are willing to read the scriptures before you meet to study.
2. They deal with sin in their lives; they don't rationalize.
3. They take stands with family and friends.
4. They initiate with you (phone calls, e-mail, etc.).
5. They attend church services.
6. They are beginning a consistent prayer life.
7. They are willing to spend time together outside of "study time."
8. They confess sins and struggles; they don't conceal them.
9. They change opinions when confronted with Scripture.
10. They understand the difference between your own opinions and the word of God itself (1 Thessalonians 2:13).

When do I strongly challenge?

This is another one of those delicate issues that call for perception and sensitivity. The biblical ideal is to challenge people with severity proportionate to their knowledge. Jesus was exceedingly strong with the Pharisees, calling them "hypocrites," "sons of hell," "snakes" and "blind guides," to name just a few epithets. Yet with those theologically less informed, such as the centurion (Matthew 8) and Zacchaeus (Luke 19), he was quick to reassure them of their place in the kingdom.

Some people never really need strong challenges. A simple encouragement or admonishment brings about immediate repentance or redirection. Others of us, in fact most of us, are not nearly so tenderhearted. We need a more dramatic form of correction. We must be friends like Jesus. He loved people and told them what they needed to hear (Mark 10:21). The best policy is to handle people with tender loving care, using as little force as necessary. If someone makes a mistake out of ignorance, that is one thing. It is an entirely different matter when people "deliberately keep on sinning" (Hebrews 10:26). Our style ought to reflect the teaching of Jesus (Luke 12:47).

When do I "shake the dust?"

Jesus said, "If anyone will not welcome you or listen to your words, shake the dust off your feet when you leave that home or town" (Matthew 10:14). Jesus was unmistakably clear—there is a time to walk away. He mentions two very specific reasons that indicate it is time to part.

- "Will not welcome you"—this one is easy to identify but sometimes hard to accept. When family or close friends are totally closed we must resist the urge to keep "blasting away" until they "break." Invariably, our blasting causes them to harden rather than crack. If people are not willing to accept the word, don't hurt their future chances—move on to others who are searching for the message.
- "Will not listen to your words"—there is a difference between listening and hearing. Virtually everyone can *hear* what we are saying, but fewer are prepared to *listen*. It can be difficult discerning when a person has stopped listening and has only begun to hear. One revealing sign is the inability or refusal to be consistent. People begin saying things like: "I know unless you repent you'll be lost, and I definitely haven't repented…but I'm still sure I'm saved"!
- "Back-tracking" is another clear indication. People begin doubting the authority of the Word, the divinity of Jesus and even the existence of God, when previously these were not issues. We must try to help people through these difficulties, but if they persist we must be willing to walk away.

We must trust that God is in control and that people go through some stages in their lives when they are more open than at other times. "Shaking the dust" does not mean you have stopped caring or that you will never try again. It simply means that in this situation your time is better spent helping others who are searching. We err if we allow dozens to die lost who might have responded if given a chance, yet no chance was given because we stubbornly insisted on "casting our pearls before swine" (Matthew 7:6, Jesus' own strong words).

And yet always leave the door open. People change, and many times they come back months, even years later. So keep up the relationship. We mustn't only be interested in "quick" conversions. Some people take years. Yes, I have studied with people who became Christians in a week or less, and even in a day or two! But others have required years to become Christians. (And two men took ten and fifteen years, respectively!) In short, treat people nicely on the way out, for they will certainly remember on the way back in!

When do I study baptism?

Many a soul has been lost due, in part, to a premature study of baptism. Sadly, some of us have developed a reputation for "preaching baptism instead of preaching Jesus." Ironically, if by magic, starting today, baptism were completely optional and totally unrelated to salvation, that would affect the eternal destiny of less than one person in a thousand. The other nine hundred and ninety-nine would still be lost on the basis of the Bible's teaching on sin, repentance and discipleship.

We must teach people that the road is narrow, not because of Acts 2:38 but because of Deuteronomy 6:5 ("Love the Lord with all your heart, soul...") and Luke 13:3 ("Repent or perish..."). Loving God and repenting of sin are far more intuitively obvious requirements for salvation than baptism. Don't rely on a baptism study to show people they are not yet forgiven. If you establish their need for forgiveness beforehand, you will turn baptism into a joyfully simple solution rather than a doctrinal technicality of "your church."

How do I count the cost?

Jesus was confronted by the perfect convert (Luke 9:57), who said, "I'll follow you wherever you go." Jesus said, in effect, "Count the cost!" Jesus compared becoming a disciple with building a tower and said explicitly "sit down and estimate the cost" (Luke 14:28). Counting the cost is biblical and essential to strong disciple making. It would be unethical to preach "Jesus is Lord" without spelling out in no uncertain terms what that confession really means. We must not bind unnecessary loads on people, but it is equally wrong to dilute the call to discipleship. The overriding question is *"Are you ready to make Jesus your Lord?"*

Once again, before anyone is baptized into Christ, it is our responsibility to follow Jesus' instructions in making disciples, as well as to keep our conscience clean. While we cannot judge the motives of the heart as God (alone) can, it is nevertheless our aim to help prospective Christians to truly repent. Without repentance, the baptism is not scriptural (Acts 2:38, 3:19). Jesus did not want people following him who weren't willing to count—and meet—the cost (Luke 9:57-62, 14:25-35, John 6: 60-61, 66).

Following are a number of areas that may be helpful to cover as you "count the cost" with those considering baptism. Every person is different, and what needs emphasis with one person may not with another. Select from this list what applies to the person you are reaching out to, based on his or her unique situation and needs.

Conversion: He must be able to explain clearly to you how to become a Christian. Ask him about the "good Hindu"—does he understand that no one can go to heaven outside of Jesus Christ? (Or the "good churchgoer"…)

Obstacles and challenges: Ask him what he thinks the biggest challenges could be. Ask specifically about the temptations you covered in the *Sin* study (sex, worldly parties, laziness, selfishness), as well as aspects of commitment you know he may find difficult.

Implications of repentance: Ask, "What is the greatest difference you see between real Christians and others who are less committed?" He should answer, "The commitment, repentance, discipleship, evangelism," or something like that. Make sure he sees how very few believers really teach or practice Biblical repentance.

Implications of baptism: Ask about the false doctrine of "praying Jesus into your heart." Although the Bible never specifically says that someone must understand all the implications in order for baptism to be valid, people who have never followed through intellectually on the implications of the gospel will probably struggle, and are more likely to leave the Lord.

Purpose and mission: He should understand that while his purpose is to have a relationship with God and go to heaven, his mission is to seek and save the lost and to help the needy. Evangelism is for every Christian. Make sure he understands persecution is the inevitable result of preaching repentance (Acts 26:21, Luke 6:22-23, 2 Timothy 3:12). If the person about to be baptized hasn't done much evangelism or feels apprehensive, be encouraging. Share how it was difficult for you at first, and how the Lord strengthened you. Explain that God gives us all time to grow, and more is expected of "older" Christians.

New Testament church: Explain that we must attend only a church, which follows the Bible. This means a church whose mission is to bring salvation to the world; a church which practices baptism as taught in the New Testament; and a church that correctly teaches repentance.

Attending church services: Make sure he knows what the regular meetings of the church are. Explain the expectation to attend additional meetings (retreats, harvests, devotionals, etc.), which usually means a few extra days a month. Talk about arriving punctually—really wanting to be at the meetings. (You get out what you put in.) Emphasize the need to be devoted to the "fellowship" (Acts 2:42), not rush off as soon as services are over. Christians who miss meetings do poorly spiritually, and most of those who quit have been compromising on the services. Make sure he sees that the church is God's plan for Christians to stay strong, grow spiritually and joyfully fulfill God's purpose for their lives.

Dating and marriage: Since we can marry only followers of Christ (1 Corinthians 7:39), it stands to reason that we should date only disciples. The term "believers" in the New Testament always refers to true Christians, not persons with a nebulous, vague faith. A believer is a disciple of Christ. Dating non-Christians messes up our motives and theirs, and is extremely unwise. Since this is one of the areas in which the world has destroyed lives the most, we must be open to lots of input. God must be the center of our marriages. (See the follow-up study on Christian Marriage in chapter 16.)

Giving: All Christians are expected to support the work of the church (salaries)—Matthew 10:10, 1 Corinthians 9:14, Philippians 4:14-19. This is nothing to apologize for; be sure to mention it. All Christians are also expected to give to the poor (Mark 14:7, Matthew 6:2, 1 Corinthians 16:1-2, 2 Corinthians 8-9). Proverbs 3:9 says we are to honor the Lord with our money. The money is God's; we are only stewards, and must manage the Lord's money well. Many people you study with have been undisciplined in their budgeting and spending; you will need to teach them to be responsible.

One-another relationships: Make sure he has one-another relationships, and there is someone who will be "teaching him the ropes," especially during his or her first couple of years in Christ. Explain that there are follow-up studies you will want to do over the next few months. Stress the need to be open to advice.

Taking a stand with family and friends: Does he understand where his family members stand before God? Is he ready, like Cornelius, to reach out to them (Acts 10:24)? Is he willing to firmly (and lovingly) take a stand, share his faith with them, and hold to his conviction? Ask him how he would react if they opposed him. In the case of university or college students still officially living at home or receiving support from parents, it will usually be wise to make sure they have already phoned parents and know how the family feels about the decision. For minors, hesitate to baptize them if parents are opposed.

Sacrifice and service: Jesus left us an example of service (John 13). Service takes time, is humbling and often goes unnoticed (Luke 17:7-10). Are we willing to be servants? There are many opportunities for service, like (a) serving older members, especially those with families; (b) volunteering for work parties as needs arise around the church; (c) helping with the children's ministry, ushering, or whatever other duty we may be asked to assist in; look for other opportunities to serve—even when we have not been asked. Emphasize the importance of coming to church ready to give (Acts 20:35).

Lifelong decision: Explain that it would be better not to be baptized than to take the step and then fall from grace (2 Peter 2:20-22). We "put the hand to the plow" for life. Explain that the confession made at baptism "Jesus is Lord" means just that!

Pray for wisdom so that you may effectively "count the cost." Again, this is just a rough guide to help you cover most areas. You will find some people with special backgrounds and problems, and for them Jesus becoming Lord will entail other issues not listed above.

How many studies should I have?

That depends on who you are and where you are in life. If you are a mother of two small children, then probably one or, perhaps, two is a Herculean effort for you. If you are a working man with family responsibilities, you may also be limited to one or two studies with your friends. An undergraduate student will probably find the time for two or three ongoing studies through most of the academic year. Graduate students differ enormously in regard to their available time. When I was studying theology I often had five or more studies going at any one time. A close brother of mine was doing doctoral work in biochemistry and was in the lab eighty hours a week. I was constantly challenged as he insisted on maintaining at least one study at all times and consistently led people to the Lord.

I generally establish a pool of relationships, investing time and prayer in them all. Some people I meet on airplanes. Others I meet in the neighborhood, or in the gym, or through my children. With a number of men I am reaching out to, there are always people to share my faith with, and some of these are open to studying the Bible with me.

"I don't have time to share my faith" is perhaps the most glaring admission that we are not seeking his kingdom—that our priorities are completely out of line. If you are too busy to seek and save the lost, it's not time that you need, but forgiveness! Jesus described it as "desires for other things" (Mark 4:19) that choke our relationship with God. The question is not "Can I study with people?" but rather "How may I make the best use of the time the Lord has given me as I strive to have an impact on others?"

Guidelines are guidelines, and ultimately only you can make that decision as to how to share your faith. Before deciding, however, you would do well to arm yourself with a deep love for the lost, a sacrificial attitude, and a realistic appraisal of how much time you have. The number of studies you can "carry" at any one time can and will change.

When is best not to study?

When do you become a "Bible basher"? When is the double-edged sword more lethal than life-giving? It is when you become more concerned about getting through your teaching material than you are about getting through the person's heart. There are times when the best thing you can do is say, "Let's not study today; let's just play some backgammon / go for a walk / have an ice cream..." This may especially be the case if every time you meet with your friend it is only for a "religious discussion." Have people into your home. Hospitality—sharing your life—is an integral part of evangelism in the New Testament. As the old saying goes, "People don't care how much you know until they know how much you care."

Oftentimes people simply need to know you can empathize with what they are feeling. Christian workers tend toward one of two extremes. They love either to have fun and hate the challenge of Bible study, or they love the "turn or burn" passages and see relaxation as a waste of God's valuable time, as the earth teeters on the brink of damnation. We must remind ourselves to strike the proper balance. When people feel burdened they need the most support and encouragement. Some of the things that cause people to be burdened are (1) negative reactions from family or friends, (2) feeling overwhelmed about repentance, (3) emotionally battling the implications of conversion, and (4) fear of not measuring up as a Christian. These are some of the most common obstacles people face, and we must be there to help them through.

Answering questions

Questions inevitably arise in the course of studying the Bible with another person. In fact, be a little suspicious those who have no questions, who blithely agree with everything you say. Anyone who interacts and wrestles with the scriptures will be confused, puzzled, or even shaken by certain aspects and teachings of the Bible. The following are seven ways in which Jesus responded to questions:

- With an assignment (Matthew 9:13). Sometimes he gave his questioners "homework." Often the true answer to a question is only be grasped through personal involvement with the subject.
- With illustrations (Matthew 9:14ff). Here the Lord provided a series of great illustrations for his hearers to take away and think over.
- With a scripture (Matthew 12:3). Having a ready recollection of God's Word (both testaments) will enable you to defend the truth, refute error, and proclaim the good news.
- With a question (Matthew 19:17, 21:25). Questions, "hitting the ball back into their court," make them think!
- With a tightly reasoned argument (Matthew 22:41-26). Here Jesus reasons from premises to (implied) conclusion using logic, a familiar but misunderstood Old Testament passage, and the presuppositions of his hearers. (In this case, the conclusion is inescapable: the physical descendant of David is divine!)
- With silence (Matthew 26:63). Sometimes there is nothing to be profited by answering, at least for the moment.

- With a moral challenge (John 8:9). Jesus answered their question in a way that sent them away thinking profoundly on the condition of their own souls
- As always, with gentleness and respect (see 2 Timothy 2: 14, 23-26, and 1 Peter 3:15)!

Conclusion: the key to effectiveness

What is the key to evangelistic effectiveness? It isn't your style. It's not your perception. It isn't even your Bible knowledge. It's God working in the hearts of the men and women you are studying with (1 Corinthians 3:16). We are God's co-workers, but God makes it grow!

Prayer is the secret. Pray for wisdom for yourself (James 1:5) so that you may know how best to meet their needs. Pray for open hearts, because all the good logic in the world will not reach a single hard heart. We must become the best waterers and planters that we possibly can. But we must never forget the simple fact that God makes it grow. This realization is the secret to a joyful, productive life evangelistically.

Notes

[1] As Edward Stillingfleet, Dean of St Paul's London, eloquently put it in 1659, ""It would be strange indeed the Church should require more than Christ himself did, or make other conditions of her communion than our Savior did of discipleship... Without all controversy, the main inlet of all the distractions, confusion, and divisions of the Christian world hath been the adding of other conditions of Church-communion than Christ hath done."

[2] Acts 20:27, RSV. At Miletus Paul reminded them that he had shared with them everything they needed to know—but over a period of several years, not in "one shot"!

[3] Incidentally, since the Jewish counting system regularly numbers men only, it is a fair assumption that the three thousand were men only (see also Acts 4:4). This is not to say that women were not baptized on the first day of the church, only that the usual method of counting, in both testaments, was to focus exclusively on the men.

11
Guard the Gospel
Series A

Guard the Gospel[1] is a collection of personal Bible studies you can use to instruct your non-Christian friends. The lessons are also suitable for sharing with believers. This collection has been designed with three aims in mind:

- To provide a set of teaching materials for conveying the gospel to non-Christians.
- To instruct the young disciple in how effectively to teach the gospel to others.
- To confirm young Christians in their faith by reviewing the basic doctrines of Christianity. The series more or less follows the course of study they may have been taught when they became Christians.

The basic idea of the gospel message is easy enough to grasp, but it isn't always easy to teach the scriptures to others. A sense of natural progression through the studies and the diplomatic touch take time for the young Christian to learn. In fact, aren't these areas in which even the most experienced disciple stands a good deal to learn?

Doubtless, through experience gained in bringing others to Christ, you will perfect your own method. That is good. These studies are intended only as *model* studies, and new believers, less skilled in effectively teaching the Bible, appreciate a working model. Later on they can branch out and re-tool the studies in accordance with their own personalities, preferences and insights. This series has ten units:

Jesus I

Seeking God

The Word of God I

Discipleship I

Sin I

The Cross

Repentance I

Baptism I

False Doctrines

The Church

Note: the Roman numerals following some of the titles do not mean the study is somehow incomplete without a "Part II." They indicate only that there are further studies available in Series B and C.

Scriptures for suggested memorization are given with each study. Scripture memory is one of the most useful things we can do to put the word of Christ into our lives (Colossians 3:16). And yet it is not just for young Christians! Memorization is helpful for all Christians. (The clearest passage recommending scripture memory is probably Proverbs 22:18.)

A number of "tips" follow each compact study. This material fleshes out the study "skeletons" at the head of the unit. Some passages ("extra passages") are not found in the box but may still prove useful, and are provided to increase the scriptural information at your fingertips. (In theory, the study could be shared *only* with the verses and points in the box.)

1
Jesus I: Jesus the Only Way

Who was Jesus? What was he like? What did he say? Most people today do not know the answers to such simple questions as these, because they have not been taught from the Bible. The impression they have of the Son of God is a sketchy and distorted one. The following study, taken from John and Hebrews, will blow away the fog and reveal the truth about Christ.

• John 1:14	God became man in Jesus (the incarnation). Jesus is God in nature.
• John 6:35	Jesus is the bread of life.
• John 8:12	Jesus is the light of the world.
• John 14:6	Jesus is the only way to the Father.
• Hebrews 4:15	Jesus was also human, tempted as we are, qualified to relate to us.

Tips

John 1:14—Tie this verse in with 1:1 to show that Jesus is God!

John 2:3-17—Extra passage. Clearing the temple, Jesus shows us the burning passion for the righteousness of God that we should have. (See Psalm 69 to understand the reaction of the early disciples to Jesus' conviction.) Do you have this level of conviction about the Lord?

John 3:1-10—Extra passage. Jesus teaches the teachers!

John 6:35—Jesus was not just a teacher of truth; he pointed to himself as the source of spiritual nourishment. Could any other man make those claims about himself? (This is one of the "I Am" statements.)

John 8:12—Jesus is light. Jesus taught truth from God so that we can see the way we should go. In the world there is disagreement about basic moral questions, and it is unfashionable to take a strong stand. Without Jesus we are truly in the dark.

John 11:25—Extra passage. Jesus promises eternal life to his followers, because it is his to give. Later, his resurrection proved this to be no empty claim.

John 14:6—Jesus is "exclusive." This makes sense, because the only way *to* God is *through* God—through Jesus. But don't all paths lead to God? No! Why would God want to confuse us with a tangle of different, convicting and contradictory "ways"? (P.S.: No *other* founder of a major world religion ever made such claims.)

Luke 4:1-13—Extra passage. Jesus was tempted. We imagine Jesus to be a superman, invulnerable and gliding through life with perfect ease. But Jesus was tempted like us: desires of the flesh (4:3-4), materialism (4:5-7), pride (4:8-12). This was not a one-time temptation for the whole of Jesus' life (v.13). He lived a life of struggle with Satan (Hebrews 5:7).

Hebrews 4:15-16—Jesus is a sympathetic savior. Jesus understands our problems, because he both faced and overcame them all.

Hebrews 2:17-18—Extra passage. Having suffered all that we suffer, Jesus is merciful. He not only understands, but also *helps* us.

Hebrews 1:3—Extra passage. This passage sums up all we have learned about Jesus: he really is the "exact representation" of God's being.

2
Seeking God

Seeking God is a useful first study. In doing this study, you are essentially asking people if they are open to a change in their lives: to putting God first. A person's reaction to this study reflects his (current) openness to God. (You will probably want to skip this study in the case of someone who is already seeking.)

- Matthew 7:7   Seek and you will find.
- Matthew 7:13-14   The way is narrow, and only a few are seeking.
- Matthew 6:33   The only effective way to seek is to seek God first.
- Acts 8:35   Let another person help you understand the Bible.
- Acts 17:11   Do your homework!

Tips

Matthew 7:7—This is a great promise. God is a loving father, and he wants you to find him!

Matthew 7:13-14—If only a few *find* the way to eternal life, then only a few are truly seeking. How should we seek, then?

Matthew 6:33—Ask what sorts of things keep us from making this our top priority. (Friends, family, social life, job, studies, worry.) Now let's look at some good examples of people seeking God.

Acts 8:26-40—the Ethiopian is an example of someone "seeking first.
- Important man, very busy, yet still made time for God (Jerusalem trip).
- Seeking in the right place (Scripture).
- Was humble (asks for help).
- When he finds, he does not continue to "seek." It is time to act. It has been said, "When a sincere seeker finds what he has been looking for, either he stops seeking or he stops being sincere."
- He is a truly happy person afterwards; he has come to know God.

Acts 17:11-12—the Bereans are another example of people "seeking first."
- Noble character—integrity.
- Enthusiastic.
- Seeking in the right place (the scriptures)
- Read daily.
- Not naïve (healthy skepticism).
- Respond to the truth and become believers.

Matthew 13:44-46—Extra passage. Man in field stumbles across treasure. (Most of us are like him—not actively seeking truth). Three results: joy (the result of finding); sold everything (commitment); obtained the treasure (as always happens when people seek first.) Merchant looking for fine pearls. (Some of us are like him—actively seeking the truth). Similar results.

Conclusion

Close with an invitation to regular Bible study, encouragement to study the Bible daily, and the challenge to start attending church regularly.

3
The Word of God I

This study is absolutely foundational. Anyone who truly accepts it has an excellent chance of becoming a Christian. Aim: to establish confidence in the Bible as the perfect and authoritative Word of God, and to create an obedient spirit.

- Hebrews 4:12-13 — Relevant (living) and active (dynamic). Surgery and pain.
- 1 Tim 4:16 — Life and doctrine both important. Then why are there so many opinions?
- 2 Tim 3:16-17 — Everyone will not accept the Bible, and apply it.
- John 12:47-48 — Rejecting the Word=rejecting Jesus and salvation.
- Acts 17:10-11 — Right reponse: Read Enthusiastically, Asking questions Daily

Tips

Hebrews 4:12-13—The Word penetrates like a sword. Studying the Word is penetrating; like the penetration of any sharp instrument. This means that at times it may "hurt." Don't shy away from the challenges.

1 Timothy 4:16—Life and doctrine are important. Ask, "Why have people come up with so many interpretations?" Consider some of the reasons:

- Ignorance of the word—Matthew 22:29, Hosea 4:6
- Personality cults—1 Corinthians 1:12, Acts 20:30
- Twisting scriptures—2 Peter 3:16, Genesis 3:1
- Personal convenience—2 Timothy 4:3, Isaiah 30:10-11
- Traditions of men—Mark 7:6-9, Colossians 2:8
- Additions to the word—Proverbs 30:6, Revelation 22:18
- Unwillingness to obey—John 8:31-32, John 7:17

Then ask whose fault it is that there are so many differing interpretations—God's or man's? The word of God *can* be understood, and agreement can certainly be reached on the fundamentals of the faith.

2 Timothy 3:16-17—The Word is both inspired and useful.[2] The following acronym provides even more reasons on why men have departed from the Word and exited the narrow road: **E**asy way (2 Timothy 4:2-3, Isaiah 30:10-11, John 8:31-32), e**X**tra teachings (Proverbs 30:6, Deuteronomy 4:2, 12:32, 1 Corinthians 4:6, Revelation 22:18-19), **I**gnorance (Matthew 22:29, Hosea 4:6, Isaiah 1:2, 2 Timothy 2:15), **T**raditions (Matthew 15:6-9, Mark 7:6-9).

John 12:48—Remember taking exams? What if the examiner handed out the test early for all the candidates to study? Would you read it? Would there be any excuse for failure? Emphasize God's generosity and fairness in revealing the standard for judgment.

Conclusion:

Acts 17:11—For those approaching the Bible for the first time. The Bereans were eager to learn, and they trusted the scriptures, not just Paul. Do you have such a noble character? Challenges:

- **R**ead every day (suggest what to read: the gospel of John, for example).
- Do so **E**nthusiastically.
- **A**sk questions; don't just believe what anybody tells you! (Healthy skepticism.)
- Study that Bible **D**aily. Make the scriptures your foundation.

2 Timothy 2:15— Extra passage. For those already studying the Bible and excited about it. Are you lazy in your Bible study? God says, "Do your best!" God wants skilled, reliable workmen. Time to step up your Bible study!

4
Discipleship I

Discipleship may come earlier or later in a study series, depending on the person. For someone from a Bible-oriented background, it will often be one of the earlier studies; for a less active person, wait until faith and commitment have grown. Try not to come on too strong, too soon. "Tiptoeing" around the pride of someone claiming to be "born-again" but lacking the attitude if Christ is the opposite error.

Discuss evangelism with your non-Christian friends as soon as they are able to understand it. It is only fair to bring up the subject, since evangelism will characterize their Christian lives when they make the all-important decision to follow Jesus Christ (Mark 1:38, Luke 19:10). Another reason to bring it up is that people are looking for mission in their lives, something to which they can fully and unreservedly devoted themselves.

The study on discipleship can be used at different stages in a course of studies, according to the needs of each individual:

- Early on, with religious but uncommitted people.
- Early on, with committed people who need the challenge.
- With people who are progressing, but don't show keenness.
- As a wrap-up for everything else for less religious people.

• Acts 11:26c	A disciple is a follower of Jesus.
• Mark 1:17	Jesus came to save souls
• Matt 28:19-20	Chain reaction: disciples making disciples making disciples=church!
• Luke 9:23	Self-denial at the heart of discipleship. Willing to push yourself?
• Luke 14:33	Count the cost: our closest relationships, total surrender...

Tips

The Call to Discipleship:

Acts 11:26c—The word "disciple(s)" occurs over 200 times in the New Testament, whereas the word "Christian" occurs only 3 times. The religious world prefers the "easier" term, doesn't it[3] And yet in the Bible there is no double standard! [3] There are numerous terms for a follower of Christ in the N.T. (disciple, believer, friend, brother, Christian, saint). Can you find any more?

Mark 1:16-20—"Follow me" means Jesus came to save souls (Mark 1: 38) and as we follow Christ we learn to save souls. Evangelism was for the apostles, but is it for every disciple today?

Matthew 28:18-20—the Great Commission.
- Baptism for those who want to be disciples.[4]

- "Obey everything" implies teaching them to obey the "Great Commission" = Chain reaction!
- This collective of people is the church.
- "I am with you always"—in the Great Commission. (Otherwise, is he with us? See 2 Chronicles 15:2.)

The Result of Discipleship

Extra passages—the result of effective discipleship is seen in the explosive growth of the New Testament church: Acts 2:42, 47; 4:4; 5: 14; 6:1,7: 9:31,42; 11:21, 24, 26; 12:24; 13:49; 14:1, 21: 16:5; 17: 4, 12; 18:8, 10; 19:10, 18-20, 26; 21:20. This is what happens when the church obeys the great commission. Stress that his picture of the church is *normal,* not exceptional or ideal. (Skimming through all these passages need not take too long, and is very impacting and convincing. Alternatively, study Acts 8:1-4 and select just a few from the list.)

The Cost of Discipleship

Luke 9:23-26—Some things that may need to be sacrificed through the cross: independent spirit, self-indulgence and softness, impulses and feelings, food, sleep, etc. If we're ashamed to share about Jesus, he will be ashamed of us at the judgment. This is a matter of *salvation.* (End with a focus on verse 24.)

Luke 9:57-62—Extra passage. Must understand cost, priorities (9:57-58); God comes first! (9:59-60); don't look back (9:61-62).

Luke 14:25-33—"Total unconditional surrender"! If necessary, explain what it means to "hate" your family. The best clarification of 14:26 is 16: 13. (*Not* Matthew 10:37, which is similar but with a different emphasis from Jesus' strong words in Luke 14).

Concluding Challenges

- Decide to put the Lord first in your life.
- Give the person you are studying with some evangelistic invitation cards.
- Make a list of whom to invite: friends, family, work-mates, etc.
- Start evangelizing!

Further perspectives

It is common for people who have not shared their faith before to feel that for them it is impossible. An encouraging study to overcome this is "Discipleship II: Excuses and Fear" (chapter 12).

Making the *Discipleship* study convicting:
- Be firm that there is no "double standard" in Christianity.
- Share about your own progress in evangelism—overcoming timidity, learning how to start conversations, the reward of knowing you have done the right thing, and especially of seeing your friends come to Christ.
- Share about your own congregation and its aims in evangelism.

5
Sin I

The Sin study is a highly personal discussion. Most men and women will be much more open if this is a one-on-one as opposed to a two-on-one study. Everyone has sinned, and without specific conviction and specific repentance, there can be no conversion. The human tendency to rationalize and blame-shift must be confronted in love.

By the time you study sin with someone, you should have built up a good relationship—essential at this stage, because many of the things covered in the Sin study are challenging and personal.

It is tempting to go to one of two extremes when doing the sin study: too severe, or too soft! It needs to be convicting (John 16:8), but it mustn't become an interrogation session (1 Peter 3:15)! Don't say, "I'd better challenge his socks off, just to make sure." On the other hand, we must be careful that in our efforts to be diplomatic and considerate we do not tread too lightly, afraid to offend. God is not pleased with those who are soft on sin (Jeremiah 6:14). The right balance takes a lot of practice. If you are dealing with a person whose faith needs building up before making his decision, or with someone who likes the church but is not eager to change, a premature study of this subject could turn him off completely, or encourage him to rush into baptism without the faith and repentance to make the decision solid and lasting. The aims of the *Sin* study are to help people to:

- See themselves as God sees them: sinful.
- Realize they need forgiveness.
- Identify sins specifically, to enable them to repent.

• Romans 3:23	All have sinned, fallen short.
• Mark 7:21-22	Jesus got specific about sin!
• Gal 5:19-21	Sinful acts are obvious!
• James 4:17	Making plans without considering God is sin.
• Isaiah 59:2	Sin separates us from God.

Tips

Romans 3:23—Everyone has sinned and fallen short. Analogy: Leaping across Grand Canyon—even the best Olympic jumper, though certainly jumping farther than me, still falls woefully short! In other words, no one is good enough to make it to heaven on his own. Most people are willing to admit that they have sinned. This verse provides a palatable introduction to a very confrontational study. Ask him what he thinks sin is. Possible answers: breaking God's law (1 John 3:4), not doing what you know you ought to do (James 4:17).

Mark 7:21-22—We are responsible for our sin. It comes from our own hearts. Personal responsibility, despite upbringing, environment, genes, social pressure. Go through the specific sins. Define terms where necessary. Discuss in detail such sins as sexual immorality (adultery, premarital sex, homosexuality, incest, lust, pornography, abortion, child-abuse…) greed (materialism, selfishness), malice (grudges, refusal to forgive), deceit (lies, deceptiveness, work ethics), lewdness (language, dress), envy, slander, etc.

Galatians 5:19-21—Be as specific here as you need to be![6] Sinful deeds are obvious. You don't need a Ph.D. in psychology to identify sin. Cover such specifics as debauchery, hatred, fits of rage, selfish ambition, and drunkenness. When going through a list, do not feel compelled to go into detail for each item. Tailor the scriptures to the individual. Define "entering the kingdom of God" (going to heaven). "Those who live like this": how many of these sins do we have to be actively indulging in to disqualify ourselves for heaven? Answer: only one.

Ephesians 5:3-7—Extra passage. "Not even a hint": not only the action that is being condemned, but even the very appearance of evil. How do you respond when an off-color joke is told? People will try to talk you out of such a black and white position (5:6), but God expects as radical break from the world (5:7).

2 Timothy 3:1-5—Extra passage (excellent for religious people). Notice all the "lovers": Lovers of themselves, lovers of money, without love, not lovers of the good, lovers of the pleasure, not lovers of God. Ask: What do you love? "Form of godliness": this refers to *religious* people.

Romans 6:23—Extra passage. Though God wants us to enjoy eternal life, the wages of sin is death; we get what we deserve.

Revelation 21:8—Extra passage. Hell is real. Cowardice and timidity are *sin;* lying and deceitfulness can cost us our salvation.

James 4:13-17—"Sins of omission," not just "sins of commission."

Isaiah 59:1-3a—Sin separates us from God, putting us in darkness. We're guilty (3a); our hands are dripping with the blood of Jesus. God is not an impotent old man (arm too short = arthritis; ear too dull = hard of hearing). Draw a picture of a person separated from the light of God by sin, thus putting him or her in the darkness. Ask, "Which side of the wall do you think you are on? Would you be saved if you died tonight? Or course the honest answer is, "I'm in the darkness—I'm lost." If the person says he thinks he is right with God, you may

- Challenge him directly, asking him what makes him sure,
- Hold off, in the case of a very religious person who is fairly committed (and perhaps has even had a "conversion experience" and dealt with the more obvious sins) and convict him in the repentance study, or
- Reply candidly, "I doubt that very much" in the case of someone who is obviously involved in sin. Go back and explain from the verses you studied.

Conclusion

Clearly, man's greatest problem is *sin*; his greatest need is *forgiveness*. Sin is against God—it is personal—and so He must decide to forgive us. Soon we will study the first step in receiving the forgiveness of our sins: *repentance*.

6
The Cross of Christ

Jesus said that once he was "lifted up" he would draw all men to himself (John 12:32). The power of the Cross to transform someone's attitude and life should not be underestimated! The aim: to produce conviction and gratitude for God's saving us in Christ. Note: ask your friend to read Matthew 26-27 in advance.

The heart of our message is lost when we rely on our own human wisdom, make baptism the main issue (1 Corinthians 1:17-18), or fail to focus on the cross. As Christians we should be moved by Christ's death. Make sure you have conviction when leading the study, and don't be afraid to show your emotions.

• Matt 26:39	Jesus had a choice, and he chose to die for us.
• Matt 27:46	We are "Barabbas"!
• 1 Peter 2:24	"Die to sins, live for righteousness" is our response to the cross.
• Medical Account	Read the Medical Account (found in Chapter 15).
• Acts 2:36-37	The cross cuts us to the heart, producing a readiness to obey God.

Tips

Introduction

Christ died for our sins. Analogies:
- Soldier: A soldier dives onto a grenade about to explode. In dying, he saves his fellow soldiers from certain death.
- Train: The little boy was playing on the railroad tracks, unbeknownst to his father. By the time the father noticed him, it was too late: he looked with horror as he saw two passenger trains speeding towards each other from different directions; they were on a collision course! The only way to prevent the collision was to redirect one of the trains off onto another track, where the boy was playing. The father had to act fast—it was only seconds before the collision, but he loved his son! What did he do? He threw the switch, saved the passengers, but in doing so he sacrificed his little boy's life. God threw the switch. It was the only way to save us. He watched his son die for our sins. Yet most of the world carries on along its selfish course, unaware and unappreciative of the sacrifice that God made for us.

Matthew's account (shorter version, Mark 15:16-39)
- 26:36-46: Jesus is dreading the cross—prays for the right attitude.
- 26:66-68: Beaten, mocked.
- 26:69-75: Denied. Have you ever denied Jesus? (Luke 9:23).
- 27:26: Flogged.

- 27:27-31: Mocked, crowned with thorns, spat upon, beaten.
- 27:32: Crucified
- 27:46: Abandoned by God. He bore not only the punishment due us, but also the actual *guilt*. He was separated from God (Isaiah 59:2, 2 Corinthians 5:21).

Matthew 26:36-46—Jesus had a choice: "drink the cup" or not; he chose to die for us.

Matthew 27:46 (27:11-50)— Like Barabbas, we don't deserve to be set free. Jesus bore our guilt.

Medical account—Become familiar with the Medical account, which is found in chapter 15 of this book. If necessary, practice reading it aloud so that when you share it with your friends it will "flow."

Our personal response to the cross:

1 Peter 2:21-25 (extra verses Galatians 2:20, 2 Corinthians 5:14-15). Die to sins and live for righteousness! Share your own personal response (leader of the study).

Conclusion

Acts 2:22-38 (extra verse Romans 5:6)—You are a sinner; you crucified Christ, you don't deserve salvation. The Cross always produces commitment in an open heart. How are you going to respond? How *should* you respond?

7
Repentance I

This is the key study! Do it well and the baptism study will be a cinch. Cover it lightly and you may be in for a long uphill battle! The purpose of the study: to clarify real repentance, clear away fuzzy thinking, and create a willingness to put God first. (Don't go directly into a baptism study! The N.T. teaching on baptism is not intuitive. No one appreciates it without having first come to an understanding of repentance.)

The aim of the study is two-fold: To teach the meaning of biblical repentance, and to make it clear whether the person you're studying with has repented. In order to achieve the second aim, the study focuses on five simple questions that can be posed from the scriptures.

• Luke 13:5	Repent or perish (only two categories of people).
• Acts 26:20	Repentance is a decision leading to a radical change of lifestyle.
• 2 Cor 7:10-11	Worldly and godly sorrow.
• Matt 5:29	Radical attitude.
• Acts 3:19	Times of refreshing come. Repentance is a relief, not a burden!

Tips

Luke 13:1-5—Good alternate passage: 2 Peter 3:8-12.

Acts 26:19-21—Repentance is a change of heart/mind. It is a *decision*. It is followed by deeds—one's life must reflect the change. It can be done in an instant, though the effects last a lifetime. Notice that opposition tends to come from religious people when repentance is preached (26:21).[7]

Question 1:

Have you ever had a significant change in your behavior? A time when everyone said, "What's come over you? You're different"?

2 Corinthians 7:10-11—Analogy: *Speeding.* The officer pulls you over. Worldly sorrow—you're sorry you got caught. Good chance you will speed again. Godly sorrow—you're sorry you have broken the law, endangered lives, etc. In both cases you are sorry, but repentance comes only with godly sorrow.

Second analogy: *Pregnancy*: Your girlfriend gets pregnant. Worldly sorrow: sorry about the consequences. Start to use contraceptives instead. May have an abortion. Godly sorrow: will never be immoral again.

Godly sorrow produces a visible change in one's character (earnestness, eagerness to clear self, indignation, alarm, etc.) Thus you can tell whether one has repented or not.

Question 2:
Are you eager to do the will of God, or do you have to be coerced?

Matthew 5:29-30—Radical attitude toward sin (negative side). Zeal to do the will of God (positive side). Ask: Do you think someone who has repented would study his Bible diligently? Attend the church services? Share his faith with others?…

World's attitude: sin is OK in moderation. God's attitude: sin is wrong—deal with it drastically! Do you have a radically repentant attitude about ____ (be specific)?

Question 3:
Do you have God's attitude towards sin? A radical aversion?

Question 4:
Have repented in accordance with what the Bible teaches?

We are almost always looking for a "No" answer. If someone claims to have repented, ask when. "Yesterday," "a few weeks after I met you," or "just now" are more likely correct answers than "when I was ten years old," or "long ago." Go back over the study again if you need to. Emphasize how narrow the road is. Be sure to ask, for there are extremely few religious people (even the committed ones) who have repented. Question him about his life and about the lives of the religious people he may look up to in his denomination. (Why do they accept *him* as a brother if he has never repented and become a true disciple of Christ?)

Question 5:
How many people do you know who have truly repented?

If someone answers that most churchgoers have repented, he hasn't a clue about what you have just taught him. If he thinks that most people back in his old church have repented, again he has probably missed the point. (After all, did they teach him to obey the Lord? Did they hold him accountable?) Back up until he gets it right! Be sure to ask him about where he thinks his friends and family stand.

Acts 3:19—End the study positively!

Additional comments on Repentance:
Often as Christians grow to understand God's will more fully, or are convicted of sin, there is a tendency to doubt one's initial repentance. Remember: repentance is a change of heart—a decision—and a deepening walk with God in no way implied that one's initial decision was defective.

Although the percentage is extremely small, there are some non-Christians who have repented. Be sensitive and willing to concede that someone may in fact truly have repented. If someone is not actively evangelistic and fervent in his devotion to God, the chances are he or she has never repented.

Sincerity is not enough! A person needs a sense of sin, not Bible knowledge alone. Few have repented.

8
Baptism I

Purpose of the study: To explain how we receive forgiveness for sins and become Christians. *Not* a study for anyone reluctant to repent. Be wise; delay the study until God has prepared their hearts for it!

Sometimes it may be wiser to do a preliminary study before plunging in to the Baptism unit.[8] With a very religious person, the study may need to take place twice.[9]

• Ephesians 4-5	Baptism is a basic Christian doctrine—and there's only one.
• Acts 2:38	Repentance+baptism leads to forgiveness and the gift of the Holy Spirit.
• Romans 6:3-4	Participation, not just a parallel.
• 1 Peter 3:21	Baptism is essential for salvation.
• Acts 22:16	The Bible is clear.[10] What are you waiting for?

Ephesians 4:4-6—The Bible identifies the basic, essential doctrinal areas. Baptism is not one of the peripheral items!

Let's look at baptism in Acts, then in the letters, finally in the gospels. We find in Acts that baptism is how people were forgiven of their sins. Here we see people being saved (present tense).

Acts 2:36-39—Already believed (2:37), but still not saved. Must repent first, then be baptized for the forgiveness of sins. "Every one of you," "for all whom God will call" means no exceptions!

Acts 8:26-38—Extra passage (Ethiopian Eunuch). The good news includes baptism (vv.35-36). "Down into the water" implies more than sprinkling.

Acts 16:33—Extra passage (Philippian Jailer). Belief alone insufficient (16:31): must hear the word (16:32). Baptized in the middle of the night.

Acts 22:16—(The apostle Paul). Came to faith on the Damascus road. Fasted, prayed, alone three days (Acts 9:9). "What are you waiting for?...Wash your sins away..." (Urgency, cleansing).

Next we turn to the letters, which are all written to Christians—those who have already been baptized (past tense).

Romans 6:3-4—"Baptized into Christ" means baptized into (participating in) Jesus' death. Buried with him through baptism (participation), raised (participation).[11] Jesus' death: blood of Christ (Ephesians 1:7). "New life" = being born again.

Colossians 2:12—Extra passage. "Burial" (Romans 6:4)—baptism is immersion. Faith in power of God, who forgives us of our sins.

1 Peter 3:21—Floodwater symbolizes baptism (not vice versa!) The Bible never calls baptism "symbolic." It is not just a bath; the spiritual significance of baptism must be grasped. It is an *appeal* (RSV, Greek) to God for a clear conscience.[12] It saves by the resurrection (Rom 6:4, Colossians 2:12).

Finally we turn to the gospels, where Jesus spoke a few times of how people would be saved under the new covenant (future tense).

Matthew 28:19—Extra passage. Baptism involves discipleship

Mark 16:16—Extra passage. Belief + baptism = salvation

John 3:5—Extra passage. Born again of water and spirit.

Conclusion

Recap what happens at baptism. Repentance must come first, then baptism. Analogy: must put film in (non-digital!) camera first, then take the shot. The result of obedience to God's plan: forgiveness of sins (a right relationship with God) and the Spirit, which helps us to live with and for the Lord.[13]

9
False Doctrines about Conversion

Begin the session with a summary of the New Testament teaching on conversion:

• Hear the message	Romans 10:17, Acts 11:14
• Believe	John 3:16, Acts 16:31
• Repent	Luke 13:3, Acts 3:19
• Confess Jesus as Lord	Romans 10:9, 1 Timothy 6:12
• Be immersed	Acts 2:38, 1 Peter 3:21

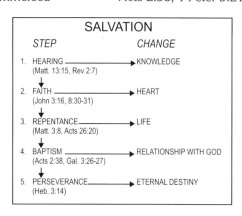

• Gal 1:6-9	False doctrine (teaching) is destructive. No one can alter the Gospel.
• Ezekiel 18:20	"Original sin" is a false teaching.
• Heb 10:26	"Once saved, always saved" is a false teaching.
• James 2:24	Salvation by "faith alone" is a false teaching.
• Rev 3:20	Salvation through the "sinner's prayer" is a false teaching.

Tips

Galatians 1:6-10—We need to take a stand, and not be "people-pleasers" (1:10). No one – religious leader, angel (see 1 Kings 13!), apostle – has the right to "update" the gospel!

Ezekiel 18:20—The false doctrine of infant baptism is refuted by this passage (guilt is non-transferable). Those who advocate infant baptism hold that baptism remits "original sin." Infant baptism is also refuted by Colossians 2:12 and Galatians 3:26-27 (personal, not proxy, faith is key in baptism). Moreover, it is impossible biblically to baptize babies because of the necessity of repentance. This false teaching was not officially endorsed by the Catholic Church until the early 5th century. The sister doctrine of "confirmation" is equally baseless.

James 2:24—The false doctrine of salvation by "faith alone" is explicitly refuted by this verse. John 3:16 shows faith as the basis of our entire response to the gospel. This must not be taken out of context. Consider all relevant passages. Refuted also by John 8:30-32, Hebrews 5:9, Romans 1:5; 16:26.

Revelation 3:20—The false doctrine of "praying Jesus into your heart," or "accepting Christ," of "receiving Christ," was invented on the American frontier in the early 19th century! Examine this passage carefully, and its context! It is spoke to Christians, *already* saved (3:14, 22). "Be earnest and repent" means let Christ back into your life, not be converted initially. The passage mentions nothing about faith, confession, or baptism, as the readers are already converted.

John 1:12—Extra passage. "Accepting" Christ is necessary for becoming a child of God (born again), but it is not sufficient. "Accepting" Christ biblically means accepting the words of Christ, receiving his message (12:48). Nowhere in the New Testament is there a record of anyone just saying a prayer and becoming a Christian!

Luke 23:39-43—Extra passage. The false doctrine of the thief on the cross: "The thief wasn't baptized, but Jesus said he would see him in paradise. What do you say to that?" Here's what you say to that:
- Mark 2:10: Jesus had authority during his earthly ministry to forgive sins in command.
- Romans 6:3-4: Baptism is a participation in Jesus' death, burial, and resurrection. The penitent thief could not have been baptized, as Jesus had not yet died.
- Hebrews 9:17: The new covenant (New Testament) was not yet in force, as Jesus hadn't yet died under the old covenant.
- Still, the passage does show God's willingness to save any and all, even at the "eleventh hour." God is good, and it is ultimately up to *him* (not *us*) to make the exceptions.

Conclusion

Galatians 1:6-9 (once again)—A different gospel is no gospel. (See also 2 Corinthians 11:4). Anyone preaching or following a different gospel is condemned. Doctrine does matter to the Lord! All these false teachings are condemned and condemning.

1 Corinthians 15:1-2—Extra passage. We're saved by the gospel, and must firmly hold to it as it was taught by the apostles. Otherwise we believe in vain.

10
The Church

Aim: To encourage, inspire and teach God's plan for success as Christians. His plan is total commitment to the church, which is the body of Christ.[14]

- Col 1:18   Jesus is the true head of the body, or church,[15] which is his body.
- 1 Cor 12:21   We're members of this body. We need the church; the church needs us.
- Heb 10:24-25   Will avoid "swerving" if we spur others on and make the meetings of the church.
- Heb 3:12-13   Daily encouragement prevents us from becoming hardened by sin.
- Acts 2:42   Time capsule look at the early church.

Tips

Colossians 1:18—The church is not an institution, corporation, building, or denomination, but the body of Christ. Not an *organization*, but an *organism*. As there is only one head, so there is only one body.

Ephesians 2:19-20—Extra passage. The church is not a *building*, but is compared to one because God dwells in his people, the church. It is also a family (1 Timothy 3:15). As with a natural family, you must be born into it. At that time God becomes your father, and every other Christian your brother or sister. The church is the people of God. The church must base itself on the New Testament (N.T. apostles and N.T. prophets [Ephesians 3:5, 4:11]—i.e. their teachings) in order to have a claim to legitimacy. It is through obedience to his word that we submit to Christ.

1 Corinthians 12:12-27—Analogy: church = human body. According to 12:13, we are baptized into the church.[16] According to 12:14, the church needs us, and we need the church. The goal (12:25) is that there be no division in the body, rather equal concern and love for one another.

Romans 12:5—Extra passage. As in an earthly family, each member belongs to all the others. We're not our own! So surrender that independent spirit! We are interdependent, not independent (refusing direction) or dependent (refusing to take responsibility for our own decisions).

Hebrews 10:23-25—To do well spiritually ("hold unswervingly"— analogy of car swerving all over the road) you need the church—this is God's plan. Attend all the meetings of the body you possibly can! Think in advance of how to meet the needs of other members of the body.

Hebrews 3:12-14—Personal involvement in one another's lives, lest sin cause anyone to forfeit salvation. We must persevere to the end (3:14). We are responsible for the spiritual welfare of our brothers and sisters in Christ. This entails openness (Eph 4:24), confession (James 5:16), counseling (Colossians 1:28), and daily encouragement (contact), as seen in many New Testament passages.

Acts 2:42-47—Ask, What are the characteristics of a New Testament church? (If people followed all these principles, what would the church be like?)

- Devotion to God's word, leading to a working knowledge of it.
- Devotion to the fellowship.
- Devotion to communion (Acts 20:7).
- Devotion to prayer.
- A sense of awe and excitement!
- Generous with one another, both with money and hospitality.
- Growth of the body: not only spiritual, but also numerical. In the New Testament, this is the result of daily evangelism.

Conclusion

Urge your friend to keep coming to as many of the meetings as possible. Stress that we will do poorly spiritually if we do not take advantage of the opportunities to grow that God has given us in the church.

In the next two chapters we take this basic series two steps further.

Notes

[1] In the 2000 version of this book, Guard the Gospel appeared in three series (Basic, Intermediate, and Advanced).

[2] Strictly speaking, this passage applies to the Old Testament scriptures (see vv. 14-15), but by extension to all the Bible. For example, 1 Tim 5:18 quotes Luke 10:7 as Scripture. The point is that Paul's and the other inspired writers' view of scripture was not limited to the Old Testament, but included New Testament writings as well.

[3] For example, consider the otherwise positive review of an ICOC publication in *Pulpit Helps of Undivided Devotion* (May 1998): "The writing is very good, and the messages are biblically sound. Many of the writers frequently use denominational jargon such as the word "disciple," a term they use for Christian, or "brother" or "sister," referring to a particular church member. Unless you are a member of this denomination, some of the terminology can get confusing." Christianity has lost sight of its founder when calling one another "brothers" and calling each other to be "disciples" is construed as "jargon"!

[4] The term "Christian" may have been, originally, a term made up by outsiders: Acts 11:26, 26:28, 1 Peter 4:16.

[5] Not to get hung up on semantics, we must still point out that, while one must certainly be willing to live as a disciple in order to be scripturally baptized, it is in one sense incorrect to speak of "baptizing disciples," insofar as baptism is only for the lost. Since we usually use the term *disciple* to refer to a true Christian, saying someone must be a disciple *before* baptism is illogical, as well as somewhat misleading.

John 4:1, at any rate, refers not to Christian conversion but to the pre-Christian baptism instituted by John the Baptist, and which (a) did not confer the Spirit, or (b) bring believers into a covenant with God. John's role (see Malachi 4:1-6) was to prepare the people for the coming of the Lord (Jesus), primarily through getting their relationships right with their fellow man.

[6] Other great passages: Ephesians 5:3-7: "Not even a hint." Not just the action, but the very appearance of evil is condemned. e.g., the club-party scene (1 Peter 4:4). In Revelation 21:8 we see that cowardice and lying are sin. (Not taking a stand, giving in to peer pressure...) 2 Timothy 3:2-5 chronicles the sins of religious people. Luke 18:9-14 is great for confronting self-righteousness. Finally, Romans 1:21-32 and 1 Corinthians 6:9-11 may prove helpful.

[7] Biblical repentance is not Catholic *penance* (something you do to atone for your sin), nor is it Protestant *penitence* (which stresses feelings of contrition over actions). Although true repentance involves feeling (see Psalm 51) and doing (Proverbs 28:13), it is not so much something you feel or do as it is a decision.

[8] A preliminary study on baptism, to get people ready:
a. Time perspectives in the New Testament (this explanation is useful for people who already have knowledge of the Bible):
  • Gospels: look forward to conversion.
  • Letters: look back at the Christian conversion.
  • Acts: shows Christian conversion occurring in the present.
b. Two essential elements:
  • Forgiveness: the "Sin" study shows that man's iniquities separate him from God (recall the diagram showing the wall of sin). No relationship between God and a person can exist until sin is removed (Isaiah 59:1-2).
  • The Spirit: a Christian is someone in whom the Spirit of God lives. No saved relationship between God and a person exists till the Spirit is given (Romans 8:9).

c. The Spirit. Receiving the indwelling of God's Holy Spirit cannot precede the forgiveness of sings (Habakkuk 1:13, Isaiah 59:1-2). Yet similarly, forgiveness comes through the spirit (Titus 3:5, 1 Peter 1:2). A contradiction? No. God forgives someone's sins and gives him the indwelling Holy Spirit simultaneously! Both forgiveness and receiving the Holy Spirit occur simultaneously.

In the baptism study, rather than try to correct false doctrines, focus on the positive work he does in the life of a Christian.

[9] Be wise in studying conversion with a very religious person. We have already warned against the premature study of Baptism. Again, it is *essential* you study conversion only with people who are serious about their repentance. In Luke 3:7-9 we see John the Baptist turning away the self-righteous, insisting on "fruit keeping with repentance" before anyone was baptized by him. When studying baptism with a *religious person,* you may want to split the material between two sessions. First study conversion from the book of Acts (Acts 2, 8, 16, 22). If for some reason your friend does not accept that baptism is essential for salvation, and especially if he thinks he doesn't need it himself, *do not* go on to the remaining passages. Do challenge him to consistently accept the Bible: the scriptures are clear. Study Naaman's healing in 2 Kings 5—which yields some good parallels of the cleansing of baptism.

Focus on repentance, asking specific question about changes made inresponse to the word (righteous living, evangelism, etc). If there is complacency, study repentance again. Only proceed if you are confident there has been a change of heart. Next time you study, cover the remaining passages and talk about the implications.

[10] Further baptism verses: Matthew 28:19, Mark 16:16, John 3:5, Acts 8: 12-13, 9:18, 10:48, 16:15, 18:8, 19:5, 1 Corinthians 1:13-17, 10:2, 12:13, 15: 29, Galatians 3:26-27, Ephesians 5:26, Colossians 2:12, Titus 3:5, Hebrews 6: 2, 10:22.

[11] 1 Corinthians 15:3-4 shows that the gospel is the death, burial, and resurrection of Christ. Thus being baptized is sharing in the gospel.

[12] The NIV rendition "pledge," which reflects evangelical theology, is far from certain.

[13] It may be helpful at this point to "de-mystify" the work of the Spirit. Explain how God does not have impossible expectations; his Spirit enables us to follow him. In Ephesians 3:16 we see that the Spirit brings the power to live the Christian life. Indeed, God lives up to his promise to be with us in our mission to save the world (Matthew 28:20). Furthermore, in John 16:8 we see the role of the Spirit in convicting of sin. Nothing bizarre, however—remember, the Spirit works in our hearts through the word (John 6:63), transforming our personalities to be Christlike (2 Corinthians 3:17-18). God wants us to grow spiritually all of the time. 2 Timothy 1:7 shows that the Spirit helps us in our evangelism.

[14] There is another approach to studying *the church* which is also very effective: tracing the following themes in the book of Acts: (1) Boldness, (2) Persecution, and (3) Growth. For each theme select verses from the book of Acts, proceed straight through for each of the 3 themes, and stress that these are characteristics of God's church.

[15] Church=translation of ekklesia, which means assembly, or congregation. For example, in Acts 19 ekklesia is used three times of the illicit assembly of the enemies of the church! (19:32, 39, 40)!

[16] Moreover, we are baptized in the Spirit when we are baptized in water. The Spirit makes us members of the body of Christ.

12
Guard the Gospel
Series B

Additional useful studies include:

> **Jesus II**
> **Sin II**
> **Repentance II**
> **Obedience**
> **The Resurrection**
> **Grace**
> **Faith**
> **Discipleship II**
> **Baptism II**
> **The Holy Spirit I**

Since this course builds on the material in Series A, several of the studies in Series A find counterparts in this series:

Series B	Series A
Jesus II: Jesus in Action	Jesus the Only Way
Sin II	Sin
Repentance II: Self-righteousness	Repentance
Discipleship II: Excuses and Fear	Discipleship
Baptism II	Baptism

Other studies cover entirely new, but nevertheless important material: *Obedience, The Resurrection, Grace, Faith and The Holy Spirit I*. This last unit finds its counterpart in Series C, which is presented in chapter 13.

The material inside the box is recommended for memorization or identification.

1
Jesus II: Jesus in Action

Whereas the Series A Jesus study is for those without a lot of Christian background, this study especially meets the needs of those who claim to know Christ. It is a challenging study because it focuses on Jesus *in action*. When it comes to describing the manhood and character of Jesus

Christ, there are a huge number of verses giving us a composite picture of the god-man in action.

As we will see, Jesus was a man of power! For first-timers hearing this study, there will be many surprises! (Note: the entire study comes from the gospel of Luke.

- *Luke 24-4-7-11-12-13-23-2 (chapter sequence in study)
- *Agonidzesthai*
- Luke 23:34

Points

Luke 24:19—After his death, people remembered Jesus Christ as a powerful man, not a sissy.

In the following passages we get a mosaic picture of Jesus' life and his power.

Luke 4:1-4—Power to resist temptation! Discuss several specific activities associated with "being a man." Real men don't follow the crowd at parties to show he can "hold his liquor"; real men go against the stream—when it's flowing in the wrong direction.

Luke 4:28-30—Authority! Taking a stand against prejudice, first message to hometown! They try to throw him off a cliff. If twenty or thirty men tried to throw you out the window, could you stop them? Clearly Jesus was no pushover! His authority was felt.

Luke 4:33-37—Speaks sternly to demon. I would have fled in terror!

Luke 4:42—Up early after a busy night. *Packed*, not *wimpy* schedule!

Luke 7:14—Against social convention when necessary. Imagine the guts needed to stop a funeral procession!

Luke 11:37-39, 44-46—Strong talk to religious leaders—as guest at a dinner party! Have you ever talked to anyone that way?

Luke 12:49-51—Jesus was focused and driven! What a radical message!

Luke 13:24—"Make every effort": Greek *agonidzesthai,* contend for the prize (the root of *agonize* in English). To follow Jesus you have to really "go for it"!

Luke 23:34—It takes strength to forgive. Any fool can harbor a grudge or take revenge, but it takes a real man to love and to forgive!

Luke 2:34-35—People reacted strongly to Jesus, because he was such a strong character. Is this the Jesus you want to follow? If so, you are destined to become more and more like him. Watch out!

2
Sin II

This study covers in greater detail than Sin I a number of issues that may arrise in the course of a personal Bible study with a friend. Whether or not all these areas are relevant to the lives of your friend, or even to your own, you will want to gain a mastery of all the material in Sin II.

- Matthew 12:32
- Colossians 3:5-9
- John 6:66
- 2 Timothy 3:2-5
- James 1:13
- Revelation 21:8

Points

1. Alcohol
   - There are cultural differences among countries. Drunkenness is the sin, not drinking *itself.* (Isaiah 5:11, Proverbs 23:29-35, Galatians 5:21.) In other words, though it is a dangerous subtonic, ethyl alcohol is not sinful *per se.*
   - 1 Corinthians 8:9, Romans 14:21—Do not cause others to stumble.
   - In the case of those who have been ensnared, it is probably wisest to counsel abstinence until the sin is under control. For alcoholics, permanent abstinence maly be the best advice.

2. Discos, Drugs, Gambling
   - Titus 2:5, 8, 10—make the gospel attractive. Titus 2:7—be a good example.
   - Discos, clubs, and the like: Ephesians 5:3—not even a hint! No one should get the wrong idea!
   - Drugs: 1 Corinthians 6:20—taking care of the temple.
   - Gambling: Matthew 25:21—responsibility with what we've been entrusted. As an institution, gambling hurts the poor, seniors, and minorities the most. Be careful.
   - Proverbs 3:9—honoring God with our money.

3. Smoking—10 reasons not to!
   - It enslaves (Romans 6:12, 2 Peter 2:19).
   - It is a bad example for others—(Luke 17:1-3a, Titus 2:6-10).
   - The smoker knows it's wrong, and wouldn't recommend it (Romans 14:23).
   - It hurts one's influence (1 Peter 2:12, 2 Peter 2:19): non-smokers, smokers trying to quit, religious people.
   - It violates others' rights (Matthew 7:12, Philippians 2:4).

- It dishonors God with one's body (Romans 12:1, 1 Corinthians 6: 20, 2 Corinthians 7:1, 1 Thessalonians 5:23).
- It takes years off your life (Ephesians 5:16).[1]
- It is a waste of God's money—bad stewardship (Matthew 25:21).
- It's a poor substitute for prayer as a means of dealing with anxiety (Philippians 4:6, 1 Peter 5:7).
- The Surgeon General has determined that smoking causes lung cancer, emphysema and heart disease. (No scripture, see any cigarette packet!)

4. The Occult
   - Condemned in the Old Testament:
     a. Leviticus 19:31—Don't consult the mediums (Isaiah 8:9).
     b. 1 Samuel 28—Saul and the witch of Endor (1 Chron 10:13).
   - Condemned in the New Testament:
     a. Acts 19:19—Word spread as people gave up sorcery.
     b. Galatians 5:12—Witchcraft will keep you from heaven.
     c. 2 Thessalonians 2:9—Satan counterfeits miracles.
     d. Revelation 21:8—A serious sin—Don't play around!

5. Sexual Sin
   - Living together (Genesis 2:24), even if not sexually immoral (Ephesians 5:3).
   - Premarital sex (Genesis 34 [Shechem] and Genesis 29 [Jacob]) wrong under both covenants.
   - Masturbation: address it. Importance of openness, both before and after conversion. Ask, where is the person's mind while he or she is engaged in this act (Matthew 5:28)?
   - Homosexuality: ask about it; don't be embarrassed to discuss. It is dangerous! (1 Cor 6:9, Romans 1:26-27, Leviticus 18:22.)
   - Other useful passages:

Genesis 39:9	Habakkuk 2:15
1 Corinthians 6:9, 18	Hebrews 13:4
Exodus 22:16	Matthew 5:28
2 Corinthians 12:21	2 Peter 2:14
Leviticus 18	Romans 6:19-21
1 Thessalonians 4:3	Revelation 2:21
Deuteronomy 22:20-22	Romans 13:14
1Timothy 5:2	Revelation 21:27
Job 31:1	1 Corinthians 5:9-11
2 Timothy 2:22	Revelation 22:15

6. Materialism
   - Proverbs 30:7-9—Seek the mean between poverty and riches.
   - Ephesians 5:5—Not even a hint of greed!
   - Gospel of Luke –This is one of his special emphases. (over 30 vv.)
   - Recommended reading: *Rich Christians Living in an Age of Hunger*, R. J. Sider.

Theological questions

7. The Unforgivable Sin (Matthew 12:22-37)
   • The healing was clearly of God.
   • The hearts had become evil (vv. 33-37).
   • The unforgivable sin is a (intractably) hardened heart.

8. Original Sin
   • Psalm 51:5 is either literal of figurative. Compare it with Psalms 22:9, 58:3, 71:6—clearly it is figurative. Therefore Psalm 51 does not support the doctrine of original sin.
   • Romans 5:12 (key verse)—if it teaches that all men are born *damned* because of Adam's sin, then 5:18 must teach that all are automatically saved by Christ's death. If so, where is there room for free will? It makes a lot more sense to say that on account of Adam's sin all are *potentially* lost (that is, if and when they sin—"because all sinned"), and that through Christ's sacrifice all are *potentially* saved.
   • Ezekiel 18:20 shows guilt is not passed from father to son.
   • Matthew 18:3, 19:14—children held up as a standard for disciples. Would he have done this if children were guilty and lost?

9. Prayers of Sinners—Are they heard?
   • John 9:31, Psalm 66:18—sin can keep God from answering our prayers, but God will always help us to find if we are seeking. (Matthew 7:7, Acts 10:4)
   • God hears are prayers (nothing escapes his notice [Hebrews 4:13], but obviously a Christian can approach God in a way that a non-Christian never could.
   • Analogy: *servant vs. son.* The master of the house may grant a servant's request, though he certainly has no obligation to, whereas he will freely grant the request of his son.

10. Disfellowship[2], excommunication
   • Matthew 18:15-18—three steps in the case of someone refusing to be reconciled to another (quarrel, leadership problem, marital strife).
   • Titus 3:10—two warnings, then disfellowship in the case of a divisive person.[3] See also Romans 16:17.
   • 1 Corinthians 5:11—on the grounds of such sins as immorality, greed, idolatry, slander, drunkenness, swindling (serious sins).
   • Note: Idleness (2 Thessalonians 3:6-15) is not grounds for disfellowship, though it is grounds for a strong warning.

3
Repentance II: Self-Righteosness

Sometimes a person is not moved by the Repentance study. Simply put, this person seems unable to see himself as a sinner. Repentance II tackles the self-righteousness that characterizes so many religious people these days. (Besides, it is a major theme in Luke's gospel!)

* Luke 3-5-7-13-15-18
* Luke 5:32
* Luke 18:9

Points

Luke 3:7-14—John the Baptist insisted on a serious change.
* Rebuked religious pride.
* Instructed people to repent of selfishness.
* Expected repentance to lead to fruit.

Luke 5:31-32
* In repentance we must see ourselves as lost.
* Jesus always preached against *self-righteousness*.

Luke 7:29-30
* We surrender our way to *God's way* in repentance and baptism.
* John the Baptist *held off* the Pharisees from being baptized—they had not repented.
* They had thus *rejected God's purpose* for themselves: an incredible waste of talent and influence.

Luke 7:36-51
* Pharisaical self-righteousness: "comparative religion"—comparing yourself to others.
* Gratitude, love, and commitment abound when we see ourselves as lost.

Luke 13:1-5 (may omit if already covered in the basic study)
* *Repent or perish*. Any other option?
* It's either one or the other: they either *have* or *have not* repented.

Luke 13:6-9
* God is patient with us.
* Yet he expects change.

Luke 13:22-30
* Make *every effort* (repent).
* Repentance is a matter of *salvation*.

Luke 15—Three parables on repentance: skim over.

Luke 18:9-14
- Are you confident of your salvation? Are you a Pharisee?
- Keeping track of your good deeds?
- Self-righteousness will condemn us!

4
Obedience

Sometimes a person is not moved by the Repentance study. Simply put, this person seems unable to see himself as a sinner. Repentance II tackles the self-righteousness that characterizes so many religious people these days. (Besides, it is a major theme in Luke's gospel!)

- Luke 3-5-7-13-15-18
- Luke 5:32
- Luke 18:9

Points

Old Testament teaching—Let's examine three characters under the old covenant.

Saul—**1 Samuel 15** (selected)
- 15:1-3: Saul is asked to obey a specific command.
- 15:7-9: Saul only *partly* obeys the command.
- 15:12-31: He puts up quite a fight before admitting he has sinned. Rationalizations!
- Conclusions:
  a. Partial obedience is disobedience!
  b. Selective obedience is disobedience!
  c. It's possible to be completely deceived about whether or not we have been obedient.

Uzzah—**2 Samuel 6:1-7**
- God views disobeying his word as serious!
- Sincerity does not remove guilt (1 Corinthians 4:4).
- Does this sound unfair? David thought so too, until he learned what God's word said (See 1 Chronicles 15:12-15).

Naaman—**2 Kings 5:1-15**
- 5:10: God's word is plain and straightforward.
- 5:11: Beware an emotional reaction to God's word.
- 5:11: Surrender preconceived ideas
- 5:12: No, there are *not* any alternatives to doing what God says.

- 5:13: We need friends to help us to be objective and reason things out
- 5:14: God blesses obedience.
- 5:14: *Approximate* obedience is insufficient (five dips in Jordan, or seven dips in Pharpar).
- 5:15: We learn to appreciate and reverence God once we actually begin to obey him.

New Testament teaching: Let' see what Jesus and his followers taught about obedience.

Matthew 7:21-23
- These people were religious, active and possibly sincere—but lost.
- Only those who obey God will make it to heaven.
- It's possible to believe that you have a saved relationship with God yet not be saved at all.

John 14:15, 23-24
- Obedience isn't just part of the old law; Jesus and the New Testament discuss obedience again and again.
- Love and obedience are virtually equivalent.

1 John 2:3-6
- 2:3: You can be sure of your salvation: if you're living as an obedient disciple of Jesus.
- 2:4: If you claim you know him but are disobedient, you are a liar.
- 2:6: We must follow Jesus' lifestyle! Obedience is a central part of Christianity.

Conclusion
As we see, obedience was not rendered optional by the Cross. It has always been crucial for a true follower of God. What has been keeping you from obeying?

5
The Resurrection

This study is useful for bringing people to faith who are open to believing but just need a little "evidence." The Resurrection receives a considerable amount of attention in the gospels and is a major theme in the sermons of Acts.[4]

• 1 Corinthians 15:19	• Matthew 28:13
• 1 Corinthians 15:17	• Acts 17:31
• 1 Corinthians 15:6	• Acts 1:3
• Flow chart (be able to reproduce it)	

Points

An historical event

Opening passage: 1 Corinthians 15:3-8, 11-19, 32. The Resurrection is *crucial* to the entire Christian message. It is "of first importance," as Paul says. Then he insists that Christ *appeared* to many people. He provided "many convincing proofs" (Acts 1:3). As Paul insists, Christianity is an historical religion, based on historical events. The Resurrection is a real historical event, just like the Second World War or the building of the pyramids. The whole Christian faith stands or falls on this single issue. If Christ was not raised:

- Preaching is useless.
- Christians are liars.
- Christian faith is useless.
- Our sins are still unforgiven.
- The dead have no hope of salvation.
- Christians are the most pathetic men in the world.
- We might as well seek pleasure, since life is so short.

Setting the scene

- Read one of the gospel accounts of the resurrection of Jesus (*Matthew 27:26-28, Mark 15:15-16:14, Luke 22:63-65, 23:26-24:12, John 19:1-20:28*).
- Explain that the claims of Jesus stand or fall on the Resurrection.
- If Jesus *didn't* rise from the dead, then what *did* happen? Perhaps you will find the diagram below helpful for your friends. It shows all the possibilities:

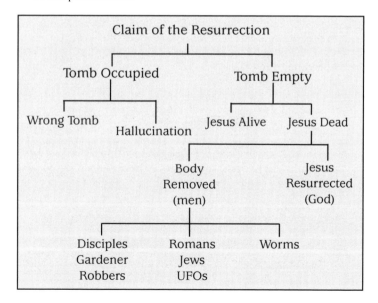

No lazy thinking—You can't just say, "I don't believe it!" and fold your arms. If you deny the resurrection, you must believe that:
- Jesus was buried, and stayed buried,
- Jesus never actually died, or
- His body was removed from the tomb.

Let's see if any of these assumptions hold water:

"Jesus was buried: Jesus stayed buried."—If you think this, you also think that
- They looked in the wrong tomb on Sunday morning, and
- hallucinated the risen Christ.

Taking these one at a time...

"Wrong Tomb!"—Do you really believe that:
- None of the disciples could remember where Jesus had been buried, not even Joseph of Arimathea (he owned the tomb and put Jesus in it himself, by the way).
- The Romans guarded an empty hole?
- Yes, that's what you're claiming!

"Holy Hallucinations"—Their emotions overcame them? Some contradictions in your claim:
- John 20:19—The disciples were not even expecting the resurrection. Thirsty men see water: Yes. Dejected disciples see Jesus: No.
- Acts 1:3, John 20:35—The disciples were skeptical, and needed "many convincing proofs". No hysteria here.
- Acts 2:31—They knew the corpse was the issue. If Jesus' body (and surely it as around *somewhere)* had been shown them, the disciples would have gone back to the fish trade.
- 1 Corinthians 15:6—The "hallucination" appeared to more than 500 people at once?

It is as easy as this to reject conclusively the notion of the "wrong tomb". The actual tomb of Jesus was definitely empty.

"Jesus was just unconscious" (Swoon Theory)—Yes, he felt refreshed after a couple of days in that nice cool quiet tomb. He didn't die. *Really?* Well then, logic demands that:
- Jesus *lied* to his disciples. He tricked them into believing he rose from the dead.
- Jesus survived all this: exhaustion, clubbing, torture, flogging, crown of thorns, beating (by which time he couldn't lift his cross), and crucifixion: around six hours suspended by nails through his wrists and feet, bleeding. Finally, a spear was plunged into his chest, right to the heart. Wrapped in linen and 75 pounds of preservative ointments, he lay in chilly conditions for 36 hours. *Would you like to try?*

- John 19:32—The same executioners who broke the legs of the thieves *mistook* Jesus for dead. and the spear-thrust to the heart was a little too soft?
- When Jesus revived, he was strong enough to get up, unwrap himself, roll away the large stone, overpower the guard, walk several miles on pierced feet, and be calm and casual in front of his disciples.
- (Are you prepared to stand up for these claims? If Jesus didn't die, you *must*. Let's face it: Jesus received enough punishment to kill him several times over. Indeed, *Jesus was dead on the cross.*)
- Someone removed the corpse—The disciples did it, or someone else beat them to it. In other words, you think that:
  a. The disciples were deceitful, or
  b. "Someone else" had both the motive and the means to make off with the corpse.

How likely are these propositions?

- Anxious Apostles: Rather than lose face, the disciples staged the whole thing (Matthew 28:11-15). In other words:
  a. The apostles lied, going against the teaching of their master.
  b. They changed from cowards (John 20:19) to commandos!...
  c. Acts 4:20—They refused to come clean, even when they were threatened and later beaten, and most of them put to death for their deception.

No, the story just doesn't add up. The disciples did not move Jesus' body. Then who?... "All kinds of people (non-apostles) might have done it," you claim? Hold on just a minute. If the body was stolen, then the disciples either lied or hallucinated, and we've already ruled-out those possibilities! We could stop here, but instead let's point the accusing finger at some suspects.

- Guilty gardener: *Motive:* if he was *against* the disciples, he's have given the corpse to the Jews. If he'd been for them, he would have ended their needless persecution. Either way, no motive for a theft. *Means:* He overcame sword and shield with spade and pruning-scissors!
- Thoughtless thieves: *Motive:* Ah! Must be something very valuable in there for a guard to be posted. Even so, is anything worth breaking Pilate's seal and risking punishment? *Means:* Assume they killed Joe Soldier. When disappointed by their find, would they, could they have eagerly stolen 220 lbs (100kg) including ointments≠ of a dead man?
- Rebellious Romans: Christianity turned Jerusalem and the Roman World upside-down! Can you think of any reason why the authorities would want to encourage civil disorder?
- Jealous Jews: Again, what motive would there be? The Jews were the last ones on earth who wanted to be the people to believe the

Christians' "lie." If they had taken the body, they would have been the first to produce it.
- Sorcerous saucers: (Yes, people have claimed this!) Kind creatures "beamed him up" (Scottie). Let's agree that science fiction is exactly that!
- Ravenous worms: Do you get the feeling that we're running out of convincing ideas? Did worms eat the body over a short weekend?

Conclusion: Jesus Rose from the Dead!

In the light of all the evidence, doesn't it take *more* faith *not* to believe in the Resurrection than to accept is as true? Truly, Jesus rose from the dead! This is the only explanation that makes sense of all the facts, including Jesus' repeated prediction that he would rise on the third day. It is also the best explanation for the incredible transformation in the lives of the early disciples, as well as in the lives of his disciples today.

If the resurrection of Jesus Christ from the dead actually took place, then we have "good news and bad news." The good news is, when Jesus returns, you too will be resurrected and have a chance to live eternally with God.[5] The "bad news" is, you have to change. See Acts 17:30-31. The resurrection means we are under the obligation to *repent* – each and every one of us.

6
Grace

A good companion unit to the Obedience study, Grace will be especially helpful for (a) religious people with a twisted understanding of grace, (b) all having difficulty forgiving themselves or letting the past go, and (c) followers of Christ who are flagging in their strength.

The apostle Paul appreciated God's grace perhaps more than any other man of his day, and he tells us that's why he accomplished so much (1 Corinthians 15:10). Since it's essential for us to understand the concept of grace and to teach it clearly, we choose Paul for a balanced understanding of grace.

- Ephesians 2:8
- Titus 2:11
- 1 Corinthians 15:10
- G-R-A-C-E (learn acronym)

Points

Ephesians 2:1-10
- We are dead to God in our sins. When we live the way the world wants us to, or follow our own desires, we become objects of wrath.

- Because of grace (God's love for us), we can be saved. We don't deserve it, but it's free for us as a gift if we accept it.
- It's through our faith in Christ that we're saved.
- God's love motivates us to do good works.

Romans 5:6-11
- Definition of grace: God loving us enough to allow Christ to die for our sins when we were his enemies. Acronym: <u>G</u>od's <u>R</u>iches <u>a</u>t <u>C</u>hrist's <u>E</u>xpense.
- We were lost sinners deserving only punishment, but he sent Christ to suffer in our place.
- Through Jesus' blood we are saved from God's wrath. (Blood must be shed for forgiveness Hebrews 9:22, 28).

Titus 2:11-14
- Grace means salvation for us.
- God's love leads us to purify ourselves from sin; we won't take advantage of God's grace.
- Since grace overcomes passion, it isn't a license for sin (Jude 4). Grace isn't cheap—it cost Jesus his life.

1 Corinthians 1:18-25
- The cross is God's powerful solution for sin.
- Without an understanding of God's love, the message of the cross will be foolishness to us.

2 Corinthians 5:14-21
- Christ's love demands a response! (See 1 Corinthians 15:9-10.)
- Jesus bore our sins to the extent that he became sin, or a sin offering.
- God's love motivates us to live for him, and to speak for him.

1 Corinthians 15:9-10
- Though it is not true that we are saved by working hard, it is true that those most affected by God's grace are God's hardest workers!

7
Faith

Like Obedience and Grace, the Faith study is intended "to comfort the disturbed and to disturb the comfortable." It is also beneficial when studying with an atheist who is tempted to dismiss God and religion because of the "practical atheism" he has seen in churchgoers.

- Practical atheism
- Psalm 14:1

- Hebrews 11:1
- Hebrews 11:6
- James 2:22
- James 2:24
- Martin Luther

Points

Psalm 14:1
- Faith isn't just an option, it's an attitude of the heart.
- You can be religious and yet still be a *practical* atheist. (Do you live as though there's a God?)

Hebrews 11:1
- Faith isn't just "believing in something you know isn't true anyway"!
- It's not just a leap into the dark. (It's actually a leap into the light!)
- It is spiritual *certainty.*

Hebrews 11:6
- It is *impossible* to please God without faith.
- We can and must believe that God exists.
- He is there and we will find him if we earnestly seek him.

James 2:14-26
- Faith without actions is useless.
- Striving to be righteous: deal with sin.
- Striving to have a relationship with God: prayer, Bible study.
- Striving to help others: church, evangelism, caring for the needy.
- Faith is complete only when it is *active* faith.
- Abraham's faith and actions worked together. In Genesis 22, God knew Abraham had true faith only at the moment of obedience (22:12).
- No one is justified by faith without deeds (James 2:24).
- Note: Because of his belief in "justification by faith alone" and "once saved, always saved," Luther (1500s) rejected this passage and many like it.

8
Discipleship II: Excuses and Fear

An excellent follow-on to the basic Discipleship study, this unit removes excuses and inspires prospective disciples to face and overcome their fears. The study centers on five great men of God and how the Lord helped them to become powerful men of God. The study is especially helpful for people who are timid by nature.

- Exodus 4:13
- Judges 6:15
- Jeremiah 1:6
- Isaiah 6:8
- Luke 5:10b

Points

Moses—Exodus 3-4
- 3:10-12: feeling of insignificance
  a. Moses is given an important mission.
  b. Moses thinks God has got the wrong guy!
  c. God is *with us* in our evangelism.
- 3:13: lack of knowledge
- 4:1: fear of rejection
- 4:10-12: lack of eloquence
- 4:13-14: reluctance to obey
  a. This is the real issue!
  b. God is angry with our excuse-making!

(Moses, already eighty years old, goes on to become a bold leader in God's kingdom!)

Gideon—Judges 6:11-16
- 6:11: fearful (threshing in the winepress at a time when God needed men of courage to rise up).
- 6:12: "Mighty warrior": God sees his potential.
- 6:14: "Go in the strength that you have": don't worry, just do your best.
- 6:15: Gideon claims he's too insignificant and unimpressive to follow and obey God.
- 6:16: God will be with you!

(Gideon repents of his fear and excuses and rescues his nation from the enemy–powerfully and bravely!)

Jeremiah—Jeremiah 1:4-8
- 1:5: God has a mission for our lives, too.
- 1:6: Excuse of youth (see 1 Timothy 4:12).
- 1:8: God rejects Jeremiad's excuse
  a. God commands us not to fear.
  b. God is with us! (God plus one is a majority!)

(Jeremiah spreads the word for forty years, even though most people reject him, and becomes one of the greatest prophets of all time!)

Isaiah—Isaiah 6:1-8
- 1:1: He has an awesome vision of the awesome God!
- 1:5: "Woe is me!"

  a. Isaiah sees God in all is glory.
  b. He realizes his own lostness.
  c. He realizes the lostness of everyone else.
- 1:6-7: Experiencing God's forgiveness transforms our lives.
- 1:8: Then and only then are we ready to go and spread God's word.

(Isaiah too goes on to have a tremendous impact on his generation!)

Peter—Luke 5:4-11
- 5:5: Peter is willing to take Jesus at his word.
- 5:6: Incredible result—God's word is powerful!
- 5:8: Peter realizes who he's dealing with; knee-deep in fish he comes to Jesus, realizing his own sinfulness.
- 5:10: Jesus encourages Peter to evangelize.
  a. He commands him not to fear.
  b. "Catching men"—evangelism.
  c. Jesus assures him that he "will" be effective.
- 5:11: We too must pull our fears and excuses up on the shore, and actively obey Jesus Christ!

(Peter ultimately confronts his fears and fulfills Jesus' prophecy of martyrdom (John 21:18-19).

Additional characters: King Saul, Queen Esther, Ezekiel....

Concluding challenge:
  Peter and the others did great things for God because they gave up their excuses and stepped out on faith, despite their fears. You can do the same! God will change you, be with you, and enable you to do great things for him.

9
Baptism II

For the Series A study, see Chapter 11. This unit is a twenty-part mini-reference work, and will supply you with a plethora of angles on, illustrations of, and reasons for baptism!

- 2 Kings 5:1-15
- Hebrews 11:30
- Mark 16:16
- Galatians 3:26-27
- John 3:5
- "Life line"
- Justin Martyr
- Shepherd of Hermas

1. The Life-Line

You can make a "life-line" just before the conversion study, or at least find out the facts ahead of time (when your friend thinks he became a Christian, whether he was baptized, whether he was "saved" before baptism, etc.) Include such items as when he was:

i. converted	*viii. became a Christian*
ii. received Christ	*ix. born again*
iii. came to believe	*x. repented*
iv. forgiven of sins	*xi. confirmed*
v. joined church	*xii. immersed*
vi. infant baptized	*xiii. "Holy Spirit" baptized*
vii. received Spirit	*xiv. truly saved*

Even though many of these items may appear redundant, it is amazing what people will say to you, sometimes placing then all at separate points in time! Draw a time line. Have the person enter the relevant event/experiences, with dates. Then draw your own lifeline. Show that belief and repentance came before your conversion, and that all God's blessings came at the point of baptism (nos. i, ii, iv, v, vii, viii, ix, xii, xiii, xiv).

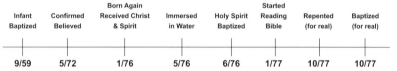

Infant Baptized	Confirmed Believed	Born Again Received Christ & Spirit	Immersed in Water	Holy Spirit Baptized	Started Reading Bible	Repented (for real)	Baptized (for real)
9/59	5/72	1/76	5/76	6/76	1/77	10/77	10/77

The life-line is useful because sooner or later you will need to find out how the religious person views his "conversion." This will prevent him from "revising" his story in light of the new information he will have learned through your study of conversion.

2. Paul's conversion

Paul believed (Acts 22:10), confessed (22:10), fasted (9:9) and prayed (9:11) for three days (9:9), obeyed (22:10-11) and repented, and still was not a saved man. He was *not* saved on the Damascus road, contrary to the teaching of virtually all denominations.

3. "Three lists"

Take a piece of paper and divide it into three columns. Write at the heads the columns:

Infant baptism   "Optional" believer's baptism   "Essential" baptism

Now go through the conversions in Acts and place each in the appropriate column (or two, if more than one view seems tenable from the single passage). The results are striking, with the vast majority of passages falling into the third category. This is not to imply that in the N.T. babies were baptized or baptism was optional – only to show how unlikely the two incorrect interpretations are.

4. Urgency of baptism
  - Acts 16:33—the middle of the night!
  - Acts 22:16—*"what are you waiting for?"*
  - Acts 8:38—"Stop the chariot!"

So why do so many denominations today leave baptism to a convenient time (once a month, annually at Easter, etc)? Because it isn't seen as essential to salvation.

5. Joy

Study the following verses: Acts 2:46, 8:39, 16:34. Joy follows afterf baptism. Why? Because that's when people were forgiven of their sins.

6. "Get up!"
  - Acts 22:16—Paul had been fasting/thinking/praying for several days, but now he was asked to do something. The blessing depends on action!
  - 2 Kings 5:1-14—Parallel: Naaman had been to see the prophet, but wasn't cleansed from leprosy until he did as Elisha instructed.

7. Is the power "in the water"?

No, but it is God's power (Colossians 2:12), and that power becomes available—when? Only when we obey. (The term "baptismal regeneration" is the belief that the faith of the one being baptized is irrelevant, that the true power is "in the water." This, of course, is a false teaching! So if someone asks you, "Do you believe in baptismal regeneration," the correct answer, paradoxically, is "No.")

8. Repentance first!

It is best not to study baptism with someone who hasn't yet repented (i.e., coming to the services, convinced the Bible is God's Word, beginning to share his or her faith, reading the scriptures on his own, without prodding). There are a few exceptions:
  - Someone who is *not religious*, who has no religious preconceptions and no religious friends who might "poison" him (Acts 14:2). In Northern Europe, for example, where faith in God is rare and even going to church is seen as a bit unusual, studying baptism earlier on is fairly innocuous. In the United States, on the other hand, where "churchianity" is rampant, the premature study of baptism only leads to strife, as baptism becomes "the issue"—when it is not!
  - *Religious people* who are highly committed, reasonably knowledgeable, and evangelistic. (We are *not* talking about someone only familiar with the Bible, sharing his faith now and again, even if he attends church regularly.) The Apollos type (Acts 18:24ff) is a rare exception among religious people.

9. "But aren't we saved by faith?"

Yes, we are, but *when* are we saved by our faith? Before that faith manifests itself into action, or after? Excellent example: Hebrews 11:30. The walls of Jericho fell "by faith," but the writer is showing us that *action* was involved. This was a matter of obedience. So it is with baptism.

10. "Isn't baptism a work?"
  - Well, it is something you *do* (so is repenting, believing [John 6: 29], etc), but not in the sense of a work by which you obligate God to save you (as spoken of in Romans 4:4).
  - Some say we cannot be saved by a *physical* act. Yet even the sacrifice of Jesus on the cross was a physical act.
  - Baptism is simply redeeming a coupon, collecting that which God has freely promised anyway. That fact that salvation is conditional on our response in no sense detracts from God's generosity, or from his grace.

11. But don't we *believe* into Christ?
No! In fact, the "into" Christ terminology is only in connection with baptism (Romans 6:3, 1 Corinthians 12:13, Galatians 3:26). Non-Christians are outside of Christ. Christians are in Christ. To get *into* a right relationship with God, you must be baptized.

12. "But I was born again before I was baptized!"
Romans 6:4—the new life begins in baptism. To claim that new life begins *before* baptism (i.e., that we are born again first) is to say that the new creation is put to death! Many groups implicitly teach that we put to death the born-again self, since baptism is a death as well as a birth.

13. Use "baptism verses"
Many, alarmed when studying out what the Bible says about baptism, prefer to turn to verses on *other* topics (faith, God's love, etc) anything rather than baptism! We must help people to be logical. When we study sin, we do not turn to the genealogies of Chronicles to find out what is right and wrong. We turn to passages about sin! When we study baptism, let's look at the verses on baptism. So often people try to sidestep the issue by getting off on a tangent.

14. Difficult verse: Luke 23:43
Three points are to be made concerning the thief on the cross:
  - Mark 2:10—Jesus had the authority during his earthly ministry to forgive sins on command.
  - Romans 6:3-4—baptism is a participation in Jesus' death, burial, and resurrection. The penitent thief could not have been baptized into Jesus' death, since Jesus has not yet died.
  - Hebrews 9:17—the New Covenant (New Testament) was not yet in force, as Jesus had not yet died. The thief died under the Old Covenant.

15. Difficult verse: Romans 10:9-10, 13
This passage is a favorite out-of-context proof of salvation by faith alone. Several things should be noted:
  - The Romans do not need to be told how to be saved. They are already saved. Romans 6 specifies the time of their rebirth, in baptism.

- *Everyone* who calls on the name of the Lord will be saved. In context (Romans 10), "everyone" means Jew and Gentile alike.
- Calling on the name of the Lord is done in baptism (see Acts 22: 16). The passage does not mention baptism, but that does not mean that baptism is somehow optional.
- Paul's argument is that faith/confession, which makes baptism powerful—(Colossians 2:12, Galatians 3:26-27) is something anyone can do, whether or not he is circumcised. We are not saved by works under the new covenant nor were the people saved by works (law) under the old (Deuteronomy 30).
- Paul is discouraging Judaizing tendencies. We must examine Romans 10 in context! This is not written to non-Christians, telling them how to be saved, but to Jewish and Gentile Christians, urging them to accept one another in Christ.

16. Difficult verse: Mark 16:6

Belief plus baptism equals salvation. But why does it not also say "non-belief plus non-baptism equals non-salvation"? Illustration: *He who eats his food and digests it will live, but whoever does not eat will die.* Similarly, baptism follows logically from belief. Furthermore, John 3:18 says that whoever does not believe is condemned *already*! Thus there was no need for Jesus to say "but whoever does not believe and is not baptized..."

17. Difficult verse: John 3:16

It is incredible to think that this verse is often cited as proof that one does not need to be baptized in order to be saved! True, it does not mention baptism. Nor does Mark 16:16 mention repentance. Nor does Acts 2:38 mention faith. Obviously, we have to put all the pieces together, not playing games, picking or choosing the passages that best suit our purposes! A response to the John 3:16 line of reasoning has been suggested:

Christian: "Do you think you have to repent to be saved?"
Non-Christian: "Sure."
Christian: "I disagree. I don't think you do have to repent."
Non-Christian: "Of course you do. What makes you say that?"
Christian: "Well, John 3:16 doesn't say anything about repentance."
Non-Christian: "Yes, but there are lots of *other* passages that make it perfectly clear that you have to repent to be saved."
Christian: "My point exactly!"

18. Linguistic arguments
- Insights from the Greek
  a. *Cheo = pour.* Never used in the New Testament in connection with baptism.
  b. *Hrantidzo = sprinkle.* Never used in the New Testament in connection with baptism. Old Testament sprinkling with blood = background (sanctification).

    c. *Hydraino* = *apply water.* Never used in the N.T. in connection with water baptism—although it would be the ideal word, since it doesn't specify "mode."

    d. *Baptidzo* = *immerse.* This word is the one *always* used for New Testament baptism.

- Insights from the Syriac
Syriac is one of the languages into which the original Greek New Testament was translated. In the Syriac translation, which probably dates from the second century, hamad = *baptize.* (Its derivative, *mamaditho*, appears in John 5:4 and 9:7, and means *pool.*) In secular Syrian authors, *mamaditho* means a *bath* or *baptistery.* Clearly *immersion* is the action of the verb *hamad,* and not sprinkling or affusion.

- Insights from the Latin
Although not the original language of the N.T., Latin is another of the early versions. Often it is said that the King James translators (1605-1611) chose to *transliterate* the word *baptidzo* instead of to *translate* it, in order to avoid embarrassing the king. In fact, transliteration of the word dates back at least as early as the fifth century. The Latin Vulgate translation (completed in 405 AD) of Acts 2:38 reads:

    Petrus vero ad illos: Paenitentiam, inquit, agite, et baptizetur unusquisque vestrum in nomine Iesu Christi... (Peter replied to them, "Do penance, and let every one of you be baptized in the name of Jesus Christ...")

The Catholic Church adopted *baptidzo* into their language (Latin) as *baptizo.* Why? Infant baptism appears to have been first practiced in the second century, although it was rare until the fifth century. By then it was widespread, special thanks to Augustine. In light of this, it is hardly surprising that the Latin church chose to create a new word, *baptizo,* instead of using the normal Latin verb *immergere* (to immerse).

19. Arguments from the Patristic Literature

References to baptism in the patristic literature (early church "fathers") abound! It is extremely clear from a survey of the early writings that for the first few centuries everyone was in agreement baptism was *for the forgiveness of sins,* meant *immersion,* and was the only way to become a Christian. Consider the following examples:

- Justin, *Apology, 1, 61,* c.150-165 AD: "As many as are *persuaded* and *believe* that the things are true which are taught by us... and decide to live *accordingly,* are instructed to pray and to entreat God with fasting, for the *remission of their past sins,* and we pray and fast with them. Then they are brought by us where there is *water,* and are *born again...*"

- Hermas, *Shepherd, IV. iii.,* c.140-150 AD: "...when we went *down into the water* and received remission of our former *sins.*"

- Irenaeus, *Dem. 3.41f, haer. 5.11.2,* c. 180-200 AD: "We have received *baptism for the remission of sins...* And this baptism is the seal of eternal life and the *new birth* unto God..."

- Creed of the Council of Nicaea, fourth century: "...I acknowledge one baptism for the remission of sins..."

Naturally, such evidences from early church history do not stand on an equal level of authority with the Bible, but they do shed light on the understanding of early Christians of what was involved in becoming a Christian. Beyond a shadow of a doubt, baptism in New Testament times was *immersion for salvation*—at least for the first few centuries!

20. Other assorted proofs
    - Combination proofs:
        a. Acts 2:41 + 2:47
        b. Galatians 3:26-27 + 4:6
        c. Ephesians 4:5+ 5:26
        d. 1 Peter 1:3, 23 + 3:21
        e. Ephesians 5:26 + 1 Peter 1:23 (James 1:18)
    - Passages showing death and resurrection in Baptism:
      Romans 6:2-7   1 Corinthians 1:13-17
      Gal 2:20, 5:24, 6:14   Colossians 1:13, 22, 2:20, 3:1, 3, 5
    - Other verses:
      1 Cor 6:11, 12:13   Titus 3:5 (John 3:5)
      Hebrews 6:2, 10:22

10
The Holy Spirit I

Since the Spirit is received at baptism, at least a few verses on the Spirit ought to be covered shortly after, or in connection with, the Baptism unit.

- Acts 5:32
- Acts 8:18
- Romans 1:11
- Romans 8:9
- 2 Corinthians 12:12
- 2 Timothy 1:7

Points

1. Indwelling
    - Received at baptism (Acts 2:38, Acts 5:32, Gal 3:26-27, 4:6).
        a. Hence necessary for salvation (Romans 8:9, John 3:5, Titus 3:5).
        b. Also described as baptism in the Spirit (1 Cor 12: 13).[6]
    - Helps us be transformed.
        a. The Spirit changes us to become more and more like Jesus (2 Corinthians 3:18).
        b. The Spirit makes us fishers of men (2 Timothy 1:7).

- Helps us to overcome our timidity.
- Gives us power to live dynamic life.
- Helps us to focus on others more than on ourselves, and so become more loving people.
- Increases our self-discipline—Every area of our lives comes under the Lordship of Jesus.

2. Miraculous Gifts of the Holy Spirit
    - Passed on by apostolic laying on of hands (Acts 6:6, 6:8, 8:6, 8:18, Romans 1:11, 2 Timothy 1:6, etc).
    - When the generation after the apostles died, so did the supernatural gifts of the Holy Spirit.
      a. There was no one around to transmit them.
      b. The supernatural gifts were a confirmation of the message (Acts 14:3, Hebrews 2:3-4, Mark 16:20), but miracles only confirmed the *spoken* word of God, never the *written* word. Once the New Testament was completed, therefore, there was no need for them any longer. The eventually died out.
      c. Signs, wonders, and miracles were marks of the apostles (2 Corinthians 12:12). Once the apostles completed their work and laid the foundation for the church (Ephesians 2:19-20), the supernatural apostolic ministry was no longer needed.
      d. Conclusion: there are no supernatural gifts of the Holy Spirit today.

3. Are miracles impossible today?
    - God still answers prayer (e.g. James 5:16), so you can't say that God never does anything fantastic anymore.
    - But many "miracles" are of the devil (2 Thessalonians 2:9, Deuteronomy 13:1, Matthew 24:24, Matthew 7:22), or psychosomatic. This is particularly true of the Neo-Pentecostalism.
    - Remember, apparently miraculous activity doesn't prove one's salvation (Matthew 7:22, 1 Samuel 19:18, etc).

Conclusion

The Holy Spirit study in the next chapter (Series C) covers ten difficult questions about the Holy Spirit.

Conclusion to Series B

Well, that's it for Series B. In the next chapter we find yet another round of useful studies. Reminder: This material is meant to be used, not only read. Do something with it! Get out there, let your light shine, and teach anyone who will listen.

Notes

[1] The regular cigarette smoker runs a risk of death from lung cancer ten times greater than the nonsmoker does. Smoking more than a pack a day increases the risk of death from lung cancer twenty times greater than nonsmokers' risk level. Only one out of twenty cases of lung cancer is cured. The death rate from all causes is about 60% higher among smokers as compared to nonsmokers. A pack of cigarettes takes six hours off your life. Nonsmokers may 10 to 15 years longer than smokers. The death rate from heart attacks is three times greater with smokers than nonsmokers. Cigarette smokers between the ages of 45 and 64 miss 40% more work days than the nonsmokers.

[2] Although something you ship is a shipment, there is actually no such word as "disfellowshipment." The opposite of fellowship is disfellowship; the opposite of disfellowship is fellowship, not "fellowshipment." (E.g., "Unfortunately there was a disfellowship at midweek service last week.")

[3] A divisive person is by definition one who is dividing the body of Christ by beginning his or her own group, apart from the body. N.B.: Merely disagreeing with a leader does not constitute "divisiveness." Nor does 1 Corinthians 1:10 forbid differences of opinion. See also Romans 14:1, 1 Corinthians 16:12, Acts 15:39).

[4] There have been many books written on the resurrection, such as Frank Morison's classic *Who Moved the Stone?* and Josh McDowell's *The Resurrection Factor.* If you would like more material but do not have time to read an entire book, you may enjoy chapter 9 ("Miracles and the Resurrection") of my book *True and Reasonable: Reasons for Faith in an Age of Doubt* (Newton, Mass.: IPI. 2005).

[5] This is better news than you may realize. When Jesus returns, we will be resurrected. Without our "resurrection body" (see 1 Corinthians 15) we cannot be taken up to heaven! See how vital the resurrection is? By the way, the order of events biblically, beginning with our own exit from the world of the living, is: death—paradise—resurrection—judgment—heaven. Simply put: No resurrection, no heaven!

[6] For more on this, see *The Spirit* (Newton, Mass.: IPI, 2005), which deals with this intriguing subject. Simply stated, my view is that, just as the new birth involves water and Spirit (John 3:5, Titus 3:5), so baptism is immersion in water (Acts 8:36) and Spirit (1 Corinthians 12:13).

13
Guard the Gospel
Series C

Whereas the Series A and B Guard the Gospel studies are intended to teach you how to bring non-Christians to a positive decision for Christ, Series C goes far beyond the elementary teachings. Its purpose is to meet specialized needs. All the studies are usable by the "layman," but several of the topics in this chapter are more challenging to master.

> The Word II
> Jesus III
> Repentance III
> Calvinism / Once Saved, Always Saved
> Hot-Cold-Lukewarm
> Old Covenant, New Covenant
> Messianic Prophecy
> Premillennialism / The Coming of the Kingdom
> The Holy Spirit II / Feelings
> The Judgment / Is Sincerity Enough?

Notice that several of the units incorporate a second study – for example, the unit on Calvinism includes Once Saved, Always Saved.

1
The Word II

The Series C Word Study (The Word II) will equip you to answer a number of questions commonly arising about the trustworthiness of the Bible. Accordingly, a question and answer format has been followed for this chapter.

- Proverbs 30:6
- Hosea 4:6
- Matthew 22:29
- John 7:17
- Colossians 2:8
- Psalm 119
- Dead Sea Scrolls

1. Do we know anything about Christ or Christianity apart from what the Bible tells us?

- Sources: Tacitus, Suetonius, Thallus, Pliny (Roman sources), Josephus, Rabbinic literature (Jewish sources), New Testament Apocrypha, Patristics (more than 30,000 citations before 325 AD) (early Christian sources), Koran (Muslim source, 7th century AD). Conclusion: the Bible is only one of many sources for early Christianity. Many of these sources will be found in *Evidence That Demands a Verdict*, McDowell, and *Jesus and Christian Origins outside the New Testament*, Bruce.

2. How did the Bible come together?

- "Canonization" was a lengthy and intricate process, governed by God's providence. (*Kanon*—Greek for "reed, measuring rod, cane" Canon is the norm by which the inspiration and or authority of a book is measured.) The earliest written canon we have is probably the "Muratorian Canon," dating from around 180 AD. Doubtless the majority, if not all, of the books of the NT were in circulation earlier than that date. The earliest canon that corresponds exactly to our present NT canon dates from the early 4th century. The OT canon seems to have been settled around the end of the 1st century AD. See *The Books and the Parchments*, Bruce, *The New Testament Documents: Are They Reliable?*, Bruce, *Evidence That Demands a Verdict*, McDowell.

3. Is the Bible accurate?

- Dead Sea Scrolls (1947) show the excellent textual transmission of the OT They date from around 200 BC to 100 AD. See *Second Thoughts on the Dead Sea Scrolls*, Bruce. The DSS were discovered in 1947 in the vicinity of the Dead Sea by a shepherd boy (named Mohammed)! *Before* the discovery of these MSS (manuscripts), which include all OT books except Esther, as well as other materials, the earliest surviving OT MSS dated from around 10th century AD! The most celebrated find is probably the two Isaiah scrolls, one of which proves the excellent textual transmission of Isaiah 53, a key Messianic prophecy.[1]

4. Is the King James version the only "authorized" version?

- It was a good translation for its day (completed 1611), but is now out of date.[2] Never officially "authorized," the KJV did not have access to DSS for OT, or the Greek papyrus finds (19th century) for NT. Furthermore, the English language has undergone many significant changes since Elizabethan times.

5. What about other English versions?

- Be wary of *paraphrases* (Living Bible), exercise caution with *free translations* (New English Bible, Jerusalem Bible, Today's English Version), teach from *dynamic equivalence versions* (New Living Bible, New International Version, Holman Christian Standard

Bible), rely on *stricter translations* (Revised Standard Version, New American Standard). In the English speaking world, the New International Version (dynamic equivalence translation) is now the most popular, and is reasonably accurate.[3] The Holman Christian Standard Bible, in my opinion, is equally readable, and even more accurate.

6. Do we have everything the apostles wrote?
- By no means! See Colossians 4:16, 1 Corinthians 5:9, 2 Thessalonians 3:17, etc. The NT furnishes us with part of what the apostles wrote, but not all. It is sufficient, but not exhaustive—otherwise our Bibles would be very fat indeed! See John 20:30 and 21:25. (There also exist the NT Apocrypha and NT Pseudepigrapha, not to be confused with these. NT Apocryphal writings for the most part date between the second and fourth centuries AD, and contain speculations about the childhood of Jesus, the travels of the apostles, the end of the world, etc. Pseudepigrapha are writings that claim [falsely] to be written by someone other than the true author. For example, men in the fourth century may have written a book and ascribed it to a first century person, such as the apostle Thaddaeus. Such fraudulent works are not difficult to detect.)

7. Are Paul's writings really inspired? Do they have equal authority with the words of Jesus?
- See 2 Peter 3:15-16 (*"wisdom that God gave him," "other scriptures"*). Peter certainly seems to have thought so! Furthermore, Paul's writings were recognized by the early church.
- For a similar line of reasoning, see 1 Timo 5:18, quoting Luke 10:7.
- In 1 Corinthians 7, Paul is *not* saying his views are mere opinion, as compared to the teachings of Jesus. In 1 Corinthians 7:12 he is legislating on a subject the Lord had not addressed (mixed marriages), whereas in 7:10 he refers to the words of Jesus on a subject Paul also refers to (on marriages between Jews), and on which there was no need for him to offer further instruction.

8. Are there other inspired writings in addition to the Bible?
- Galatians 1:6-9, 12. E.g., Mormons: *Book of Mormon* (1827), *Pearl of Great Price, Doctrines and Covenants;* Unification Church: *The Divine Principle;* Christian Scientists: *Science and Health with Key to the Scriptures.* The gospel is non-adjustable, must not be tampered with or added to (1 Corinthians 4:6, Deuteronomy 4:2, 12:32). There is no "latter-day revelation" (Jude 3, 2 Peter 1:3, Ephesians 4:13, 1 Corinthians 13:10-11). The canon of inspired writings was apparently fixed by the late 1st century.

9. What about the Apocrypha?
- Written in the period 200 BC-100 AD, and brought into the Christian Bible c.400 AD, these writings have not been considered inspired

by most Protestants since the 16th century (the Reformation). The Apocrypha had been widely used by the Catholic Church since inception, and until 1546 seem to have been accepted even by Protestants. I would encourage you to study these writings and make your own decision as to their usefulness. They fill in the gap between the end of the OT (late 5th century BC) and the beginning of the New (early 1st century AD). For example, 1 Maccabees (2nd century BC) is of considerable historical value. There are a number of allusions to the Apocrypha in the New Testament.

10. What if people do not believe in the Bible? What should we do then?
    - Get them to read it! (Romans 10:17, John 20:30-31)
    - They must be willing to put it into practice (John 7:17). Following God's word is fundamentally a *moral*, not an *intellectual*, issue.

2
Jesus III: The Great I Am

This study follows the "I am" statements of Jesus in John, and is excellent for beginners, adherents of other world religions, and "enlightened" or liberal thinkers offended by the idea that one single religion might have the truth.

Jesus is "the great 'I am'" (John 8:58). This epithet refers to God himself. In Hebrew, YHWH (the Lord's name) means "I am what I am." The gospel of John is filled with allusions to a well-known OT text— Exodus 3:14, with its overtones of deliverance and redemption.

- "I am" (Exodus 3:14)
- John 6:35
- John 8:12
- John 10:14
- John 11:25
- John 14:6

John 6:35—Jesus is the bread of life.
    - He keeps us going when we are spiritually hungry.
    - God has set eternity in our hearts (Ecclesiastes 3:11). But until a relationship with God fills the empty place in our heart, we will never be truly satisfied.
    - OT connection: Exodus 16 (Manna).

John 8:12—Jesus is the light of the world.
    - "Darkness" involved being unsure where you are going in life, confused, fearful…
    - This is a bold claim! Jesus does not say, "*There* is the light of the world," but *I am* the light…

- OT connection: Isaiah 9:1-2 (Messianic prophecy).

John 10:14—Jesus is the Good Shepherd.
- Sheep (biblically and pastorally) tend to wander.
- We need a shepherd.
- He cares for us sheep.
- OT connection: Ezekiel 34 (the Messiah as a new "David").

John 11:25—Jesus is the resurrection.
- It's not reincarnation that Jesus is offering (Hebrews 9:27).
- Nor is it "afterlife" that Jesus promises (everyone will have that), but eternal life with God!
- Because of Jesus (and his resurrection), we too will be resurrected.
- OT connection: Psalm 16 (prediction of resurrection of Messiah).

John 14:6—Jesus is the only way.
- An incredibly exclusive claim!
- People don't "accidentally" believe in Jesus (without knowing it)! It's a conscious decision (John 3:18.) In the same way, you don't get married by accident. It's by mutual agreement and happens at a specific point in time. If Jesus is right, no other position or religion is valid.
- No wonder Jesus received such opposition!
- OT connection: Deuteronomy 18 (the prophet like Moses who must be heeded).

Conclusion
There are many other "I am" verses we could have looked at (8: 58, 10:7, 15:1, etc.). But this assortment of just five of the amazing statements of Jesus is enough to give us a good picture of how radical a character he was!

3
Repentance III: The Rich Young Ruler & Zacchaeus

This study is a comparison of two men with two different responses to Jesus. The episode of the Rich Young Ruler is found in Matthew 19, Mark 10, and Luke 18. Zacchaeus is found, however, only in Luke 19. What do we see when we compare and contrast these two "would-be" disciples of Jesus Christ? The difference between the two may be just the thing to help your religious friend see where he or she really stands with God.

In addition to Luke 19, for Zacchaeus, choose one of the three parallel passages on the Rich Young Ruler. Begin with the Rich man (the negative example) end with Zacchaeus (the positive example).

- Matthew 19-Mark 10-Luke 18 (Rich Young Ruler)
- Luke 19 (Zacchaeus)

Similarities:
- Both appear to be well-known individuals.
- Both have money.
- Both took the initiative to find Jesus.
- Both "humble themselves" to approach Jesus—the Rich man *down* on his knees, the tax collector Zacchaeus *up* in a tree.
- The Rich man looks better on the outside. He speaks the religious lingo and is impressive to others. Zacchaeus is not; his profession is despised, he is corrupt, and even is physical appearance does not command respect.
- Both need to repent! Each has a major shortcoming, involving wealth.

Differences:
- Only Zacchaeus repents.
- The rich man is unwilling to let go of his "god," his money.
- Zacchaeus responds quickly to Jesus.
- Zacchaeus *volunteers* to make restitution for his sins (2 Corinthians 7:10).
- Paradoxically, the "less likely" disciple finds salvation, whereas the "shoe-in" fails the crucial test.

Conclusion:
    The disciples are shocked when they realize the kind of repentance Jesus is looking for. (See the section following the failure of the Rich Man to put Jesus first.) And yet God's plan is to bless us a hundredfold! Remember, end positively.

4
Calvinism

- T.U.L.I.P. (acronym)
- Romans 5:7
- Acts 13:46
- 1 Timothy 2:4
- Hebrews 10:29-30
- 2 Peter 2:20

Introduction
    John Calvin (1508-1564) was one of the leading thinkers in the Protestant Reformation. He re-taught many of the ideas of Augustine, bishop of Hippo (in North Africa), who lived 354-430 AD. Denominations that follow his thinking are numerous: Baptists, Presbyterians, Reformed,

many Anglicans, even the original "Churches of Christ" (1690-1830). Calvinism is a unified and internally consistent system. The basic teachings are described by the convenient acronym: T.U.L.I.P.:

> Total Depravity
> Unconditional Election
> Limited Atonement
> Irresistible Grace
> Perseverance of the Saints

This is one of the most academic of our studies, and is intended to show the consistent error of Calvinism. (This is also called "Reformed Theology.")

1. Total Depravity
- Doctrine: There is absolutely no good in fallen man. Before he is converted, all his actions and thoughts are sinful and selfish. Therefore there is absolutely nothing he can do to save himself; salvation is completely from God, and man plays no part in it. Only when God's Spirit quickens a man and enables him to believe can he be saved.
- Supporting passages: Calvinists appeal to Ephesians 2:1, Romans 3:12 and many other passages to prove that we are no more able to save ourselves than a corpse can rise up and walk.
- Biblical emphasis: Calvinism stresses the sinfulness and lostness of man. This is an emphasis sadly lacking in the religious world, which prides itself on its good deeds and empty rituals.
- Error: The Bible does indeed paint a dark picture of man's selfishness, but to say that there is no good at all in an unsaved person is going too far. Romans 5:7 and many other passages assume or imply that there is some good in the world at large. Cornelius was a good man (Acts 10:2, 35). As far as salvation goes, Calvinism grossly undervalues the part man plays in accepting the salvation that God offers. To illustrate, we'd all agree that there is nothing a drowning man can do to save himself. But when he is thrown a life preserver, he must *decide* to accept it and then *do something* about it (grab on). Calvinism errs because it denies that man has *free will*.
- Logical link to next section: Total Depravity logically leads to the next of the five basic Calvinistic doctrines, Unconditional Election. Since there is nothing man can do to save himself, God and God alone decides who will be saved.

2. Unconditional Election
- The doctrine: *Unconditional Election*, or *Predestination*, teaches that the decision about who will be saved is 100% God's. He has decided in advance exactly who will be saved. Not only is there no way for us to save ourselves, but *even if we wanted* to be saved, unless God had already chosen us, we would have no chance of going to heaven.

- Supporting passages: God's *grace* saves us, and faith is a gift from God (Ephesians 2:8-9). Acts 13:48 speaks of "those who were appointed for eternal life." Revelation 20:5 mentions the "book of life," in which the names of the saved have been written. Romans 8:29 mentions predestination, so obviously who will be saved has already been determined
- Biblical emphasis: This doctrine emphasizes *God's sovereignty*, another truth missing in our selfish world, where everyone wants to determine the course of his own life. Furthermore, it is true that God is willing to save men and women of *any* race, nation, social class, income bracket or religious background; salvation is unconditional in that sense.
- Error:
  a. To begin with, Ephesians 2:8-9 doesn't teach that faith is a gift from God (though ultimately God does help us to believe, through his Word, Christians, circumstances, etc). Ephesians 2:8-9 says that *salvation* is a gift from God!
  b. Acts 13:48 discusses God's involvement in man's salvation, but Acts 13:46 shows that man is justly responsible for accepting or rejecting the gospel. Again, free will has been overlooked!
  c. Revelation 20:5 mentions the Lamb's book of life, but Revelation 3:5 implies that it is possible for our names to be erased from it. Psalm 69:27-28 is yet another passage shattering the notion that God's book contains only the names of the saved, and that the list is unchangeable.
  d. Romans 8:29 says that Christians are predestined to become like Christ (not the same as being predestined to salvation), but in Ephesians and other books there is a sort of predestination that *is* mentioned. Two analogies may be helpful:
    (1) Train destination: You board a London train, and the destination is clearly marked "Heathrow Airport." This destination has been decided in advance. Heathrow Airport is its "pre-destination." As long as you stay on the train, you are fine. If however you choose to leave the train, you forfeit your "predestination." The train still goes to the airport, but you will miss your flight—unless of course you manage to get back on the train. This analogy assumes, unlike Calvinism, that we have free will.
    (2) Aerial view: From the top of a tall building you are able to view two intersecting streets. Down the first street a speeding sports car approaches the deadly intersection, down the other street zooms a motorcycle. From your vantage point, you can "see" the accident even *before* it happens. But are you responsible for the collision? Foreknowledge does not imply predestination.
  e. 2 Thessalonians 2:14 clearly teaches that God *does* call us, but the call is not arbitrary, or through strange sensations, but through the gospel. There is an inseparable link between the gospel and the "sanctifying work of the Spirit." No one is saved in a vacuum! See also Romans 10:13-17.

  f. Finally, *Unconditional Election* is *unfair*! Imagine the scenario: you are standing before God's throne, hoping to be saved, and hear the sentence pronounced on you: damned! Moreover, God informs you that the deck was stacked against you from the beginning; there never was any hope of your being saved. Would you or would you not be justified in accusing God of unfairness? Calvinism promotes a distorted, negative concept of God. It's not going too far to say that in Calvinism, conversion is a mere formality, since people are saved or damned even before they are born.

- Logical link: Since God does nothing in vain, and since only the few "elect" will be saved, Christ must have died only for those who would be saved. Thus the doctrine of *Limited Atonement* flows logically from *Unconditional Election*, or *Predestination*.

3. Limited Atonement

- Doctrine: Christ's sacrifice on the cross was limited to those who would be saved. In other words, he did not bear the sins of all mankind, only those of the elect.
- Supporting passages: In Matthew 26:28, the blood is said to provide forgiveness of sins for "many," and in Ephesians 5:25 Christ is said to have given himself up for the church. Acts 20:28 teaches that God bought the church with his blood (not the world at large).
- Biblical emphasis: This doctrine enhances the "success" of the crucifixion, and affirms that God does nothing in vain. So many in our world today have no appreciation of the cross, and like to think that, if there is a God, everybody will be saved anyway.
- Error:
  a. The Bible teaches that all men are potentially saved through the cross (Romans 5:18). In fact, 1 Timothy 2:4 says that God wants all men to be saved. If this is God's sovereign will, why did Christ die only for the elect? Thus Calvinism contradicts 1 Timothy 2:4.
  b. Matthew 26:28: Either the word "many" refers to all mankind, or we can say that while the blood was shed for mankind, the "blood of the (new) covenant" mentioned here implies that salvation is only for those in the covenant, not that the blood was shed for a set number of persons.
  c. Ephesians 5:25 and Acts 20:28: the idea that God bought the redeemed with his blood is certainly biblical, but that in no way necessitates that he only shed enough blood to redeem those who would be saved. A good illustration is found in 1 Timothy 4:10: "God… is the Savior of all men, and especially of those who believe." The Bible teaches that *anyone* willing to believe and repent can be saved.
- Logical link: Since Christ died only for the elect, no grace is "wasted" on non-elect unbelievers. So when God's grace, through his Spirit, starts to work in an unbeliever's heart, it cannot be resisted.

4. Irresistible Grace
   - Doctrine: The Spirit of God draws men to Christ, and it is utterly impossible to resist God's grace once this has begun to happen.
   - Supporting passages: John 6:44 says that God the Father draws men to Christ. Acts 16:14 discusses Lydia's conversion, and says that the Lord opened her heart to believe.
   - Biblical emphasis: This doctrine certainly emphasizes the Spirit's power, something we've under-emphasized.
   - Error:
     a. John 6:44 only says God draws all men to himself, not how or on what basis he draws them. Other passages in John make it clear that the people God chooses to draw are those who will accept God on his own terms (1:12, 8:31, etc.).
     b. It is not denied that the Lord opened Lydia's heart, but *how* did he open her heart? *Through the message* (Acts 16:13). As always, faith comes through hearing the word (Rom 10:17)!
     c. Acts 7:51, Galatians 5:4, Hebrews 10:29-30, Hebrews 12:15 and many other passages teach it is possible for people to resist God's grace. How can grace be "irresistible" if so many people *do* in fact resist it?
     d. Calvinism, through teachings such as *Irresistible Grace*, makes humans into robots. Once again, there is no free will.
   - Logical link: Since grace is irresistible, it follows that once saved, you're always saved. In other words, falling away is impossible.

5. Perseverance of the Saints
   - Doctrine: Once a person is saved, it is impossible for that person to become "unsaved." And if someone seems to be saved, but later leaves God, that is proof that he was never saved to begin with. Only the saints persevere to the end.
   - Supporting passages: John 10:29 says that no one can snatch the sheep (Christians) out of the hand of the Shepherd (Christ). And Romans 8:38-39 teaches that nothing can separate us from the love of God.
   - Biblical emphasis: We need to feel secure in our salvation. So many religions and denominations do not offer their members the security of knowing that they are saved. It will be difficult for us to live effectively as disciples if we are always doubting our salvation.
   - Error:
     a. John 10:29 says that no one can snatch a Christian away from his secure position, but it never says that a Christian cannot *choose* to walk away from the flock (and the Shepherd). Isaiah 53:6 says that all of us like lost sheep had gone astray. Even the chosen people, the Jews, were able to go astray, and Jesus told his disciples to go first to "the lost sheep of Israel."
     b. Romans 8:38-39 is certainly a great comfort to real disciples, but Jude 21 shows that we need to do our part to stay in God's love.

c. Ironically, far from providing any real security, Calvinistic teaching destroys it; you can never really know you're saved, since if you give up that means you never were in the elect to begin with! The Bible, on the other hand, says that you absolutely *can* know that you are saved (1 John 5:13—see 1 John 2:3-6).

d. James 5:19-20 (see 1:15) shows that a Christian can wander from the truth.

e. The Bible repeatedly says that we will be saved "if" we obey God or persevere: John 15:6, Hebrews 12:25, 1 Corinthians 15:2, 2 Peter 1:10. Salvation is unconditional in the sense that there is nothing we can do to *earn* it, but it is *not* unconditional in the sense that we *can* lose it.

f. It is often (correctly) said that we are saved by faith. If this is true, what happens when we give up our faith? Will God force us to be saved? Again, where is free will?

g. 2 Peter 2:20 makes it abundantly clear that a Christian can fall away, as do many other passages. (See discussion in Supplementary Study, below.)

h. Moreover, *Perseverance of the Saints* is contrary to experience! There are many men and women who became Christians, were doing well spiritually, bearing fruit and growing in the Lord, but who allowed their hearts to stray and harden. They are not with us today—but that does not mean that they were never saved initially! They most certainly *were* saved, but they have wandered away!

i. Perhaps the gravest error of this doctrine is that Perseverance of the Saints, or Once Saved, Always Saved," is a great disincentive to evangelism and commitment in general:

   (1) Although a noble heart should be eager to do good, discipleship is in fact secondary, or irrelevancy, since our salvation was decided in heaven long before we were born. Not surprisingly, most Calvinists are lukewarm in their commitment.

   (2) Why evangelize the "lost" when there's nothing you can do to save them? If they're damned (not of the elect), no amount of evangelism can help them. And if they are in the elect, sooner or later God will make that plain to hem, but in the meantime your evangelizing them really doesn't matter, since they will be saved anyway! Sadly, but consistently with their system, very few Calvinists try to seek and save the lost.

• Logical link: By now you can see that Calvinism, although it contradicts the Bible over and over, is internally a highly consistent system.

Concluding Thoughts and Strategy

We have studied the five petals of the Calvinistic tulip, and have seen that they do not fit with what the Bible teaches. This is obviously a complex subject, and many non-Christians would be unable to grasp the study as it stands. A helpful alternative is to go through the supplementary study below, which focuses on the fifth petal of the tulip, *Perseverance of the Saints*. Then, refer to the main study *as necessary*. This is probably the best strategy for helping someone to see the error of Calvinism.

On the positive side, we have seen that Calvinism is correct to emphasize the:

> Sinfulness of man
> Sovereignty of God
> Success of the Crucifixion
> Spirit's Power
> Security of grace

However, on the negative side, we saw that there were many faults with Calvinism:

> Too negative a view of man
> The denial of free will
> No salvation "by faith"
> Little incentive for evangelism
> Creation of an unjust God
> Contrary to experience
> Can breed lukewarm commitment
> Refuted by hundreds of verses

Supplementary Study: **Once Saved, Always Saved**

There are literally hundreds of scriptures that demolish the position of those who claim it is impossible, once one has come to know Jesus Christ, to lose salvation.

- Hebrews 10:26-31
- Hebrews 6:4-8
- John 10:28
- Romans 8:39
- 2 Peter 2:20-22

Hebrews 10:26-31—Deliberate sin can cause us to lose our salvation. This is clear, yet some insist this passage applies only to non-Christians, or unsaved churchgoers. But verses 29 ("the blood of the covenant that sanctified him") and 30 ("The Lord will judge his people") show that the writer has in mind the covenant people— who are already saved.

Hebrews 6:4-8—It is impossible to bring certain people back to repentance. Where the "point of no return" is God only knows.[4]

"Crucifying the Son of God all over again" implies they have already shared in Jesus' death and resurrection. (Hebrews 6:7-8 continues the thought.) This is the strongest passage in Hebrews refuting "Once Saved, Always Saved" (see also 3:12-14, 4:1, 4:11, 6:11-12, 10:36, 12:14-15, 13:4). And yet there are hundreds of other verses in the New Testament, which disprove this false doctrine—not even to consider the Old Testament.

John 10:28—This verse is often cited as proof of the impossibility of apostasy. However, it does not state that it is impossible for someone to turn his back on God (Luke 9:62) and walk away, only that it is impossible for external powers to drag away a disciple against his will.

Romans 8:39—Nothing can separate us from the love of God, but it's our responsibility to "keep ourselves in God's love" (Jude 21). Again, there is free will. Most advocates of "once saved, always saved" ("perseverance of the saints," "eternal security"), at some point, deny free will.

2 Peter 2:20-22—This verse clinches the argument. These people have "escaped the corruption of the world," which is possible only through participating in the divine nature (see 1:4). The corruption of the world is vividly symbolized by vomit and mud. It is tortuous to argue that the "washing" applies to a non-Christian. Finally, if they give up on God, they are worse off at the end than they were if they had never become Christians. Clearly it is possible for a Christian to lose his salvation!

Conclusion
    Although at first Once Saved, Always Saved appears to take on an academic point, in fact it strikes directly at the heart of the issue: one's willingness to follow Christ. Properly done, it's quite a challenging study, and makes a good Pilot Study (next section).

5
Hot-Cold-Lukewarm

- Revelation 3:14-22
- Revelation 2:4-5

Revelation 3:14-16 is the text for this basic study.[5] Here are the main points to cover:
- Jesus knows our hearts and deeds. Deeds do matter!
- There are three degrees of commitment: hot, cold and lukewarm.
    a. As in any area of life, for example, sports, a hot person is characterized by fervent commitment. A "hot" person will be characterized by such things as Bible study, prayer, evangelistic zeal, devotion to the church, desire to repent of sin, etc.

b. Cold people are either apathetic or negative. They have no desire to perform the deeds the hot person performs, and probably have no interest in church, reading the Bible, etc.

c. Ask your friend whether he thinks he is hot. If he's honest, he will probably say no. Then ask him whether he is cold. Again, a yes answer is unlikely, so tell him there is only one other category: lukewarm. Don't allow your friend to plead that he is "lukewarm-hot" or "sometimes hot, sometimes lukewarm." Jesus spoke of only three degrees of commitment; there are no half–categories. Make sure he agrees that he is lukewarm.

- Ask him which temperature is most pleasing to God. The answer, of course, is "hot." Then ask him which temperature comes next. The answer, for most people surprisingly, is "cold." And, yes, "lukewarm" is the worst temperature possible.

- Revelation 2:4-5 shows us that all Christians begin "hot"—at a certain "height," and may need, from time to time, to be called back to their original standard.

- Since he has already agreed that he is lukewarm, drive the implications home: his salvation is in jeopardy, if he ever was truly saved. Jesus prefers that we be either hot or cold, but not lukewarm. That makes Jesus sick to his stomach. In the passage, Jesus is about to spit his lukewarm followers out of his mouth. (Do not try to drive home the implications too early, or you will find your friend doing exegetical gymnastics, redefining "hot," telling you "That's just your interpretation," etc.)

- Now that your friend knows where he stands, ask him what he's going to do about it. Set up a study. Get a commitment to come to church, or to accept the "three-week challenge" to attend all the meetings for three weeks. Encourage him or her to start evangelizing. Also commend him for his honesty in admitting where he stands.

6
Old Covenant, New Covenant

Introduction: the Sabbath

Many in the religious world today insist that Christians must observe the Sabbath. Most interpret this to mean that on Sundays Christians should have a day of rest. But what does the Bible say? For one, the Sabbath is the seventh day of the week, not the first. But Saturdays aren't the only Sabbath days, according to the Old Testament. Sabbatical and Jubilee years (Leviticus 25) count too, and thus in a fifty-year span a typical Jew would have observed over 5,000 Sabbath days, as compared to only 2600 for the modern "Sabbath keeper." Moreover, on the Sabbath the people of God had to stay at home (Exodus 16:29). No sports, no visiting friends, and (strictly speaking) no attending church services! Nor may any cooking be done—all food must be prepared in advance (Exodus 16:23-29). All work is prohibited. Finally, the OT teaches that failure to observe the Sabbath is punishable by *death*! (See Numbers 15:35.) Who really observes the Sabbath today? No one!

Obviously, there are parts of the Old Testament that have not carried over into the New Testament (e.g. sacrificing lambs and pigeons). Are we bound by the Sabbath? Or other holy days ("holi-days")? Is there a priesthood today, a clergy-laity system? Is the church building the "house of God"? In short, exactly what *is* the relationship between the Old and New Covenant?

The following study may be done as a group Bible discussion or as a personal study. It is invaluable for those from a ritualistic and traditional background, and even for those from other world religions. Old Covenant, New Covenant highlights the uniqueness of New Testament Christianity, and explains much of the confusion in Christendom today.

- Colossians 2:16
- John 4:24
- Ephesians 1:1
- 1 Timothy 2:5
- Colossians 2:17

Two Covenants
- Hebrews 9:15-17 shows that the new covenant (will, testament) superseded the old covenant. Just as two wills cannot be in effect at the same time, neither can two testaments.
- Although the heart of the law carries over into the NT (see Galatians 5:14, Matthew 22:37-40), the law and its specific commandments were nailed to the cross, invalidated (Colossians 2:13-14).
- Thus Christians are not bound to observe the regulations of the Old Testament.

Double Standards
- If some days are *holy*, the others must be *unholy*.
- In practice this means that people try harder to please God on the special, or holy, days than at other times. *Two* standards of commitment have thus emerged.
- But Christianity is meant to be a daily lifestyle (Luke 9:23, Romans 12:1), not a weekly observance. All *time* is holy!
- These double standards are seen in a variety of areas:
  a. holy time
  b. holy space
  c. holy people
  d. holy things
- Since the Old Testament distinction between holy and unholy has been invalidated, or transformed, now *all* days are holy, *all* space is holy, *all* people are holy.

Holy Time
- Christians are not bound by Sabbath observance (as in the fourth commandment, Exodus 20). This is made explicit in Col 2:16.
- Attempts to be justified by observing special days, seasons, etc. will lead to condemnation (Galatians 4:8-11).
- It is true that the early church often met on Sundays (Acts 20:7, Revelation 1:10), partly in commemoration of Christ's resurrection (Matthew 28:1), which took place on a Sunday, but Sunday is nowhere called a "Sabbath."
- The lesson for us: we should be on our best behavior, striving to be disciples, *all the time*. It is not a *sin* to observe a special day (Romans 14:6), but it is a sin to try to make others do so.

Holy Space
- God cannot be confined to "holy" space (Acts 7:48-49, John 4:24).
- The OT subdivided space, physically restricting access to God (Hebrews 9:1-8—see Matthew 27:51), but the NT does not limit access to God in this way (Ephesians 2:18).
- We worship God wherever we are; our whole lives are our worship (Romans 12:1).
- Although the church is called the "household of God" (Ephesians 2:19, the *church building* is no more a "holy place" than any other building.
- The lesson for us: we should strive to do our best for God *wherever we are.*

Holy People
- There are no "saints," in the traditional sense of the word. All Christians are holy, or "saints" (Ephesians 1:1).
- There is no priesthood today except that of Jesus himself (Hebrews 7:23-28). It is true that all disciples form a "royal priesthood" (1 Peter 2:9), yet no one needs to go through another person in order to reach God, and there is no need for the presentation of sacrifice, as Christ has been sacrificed once for all.
- There is only one mediator between God and man, and that is Jesus Christ (1 Timothy 2:5). Thus praying to the saints and Mary is wrong.
- There is no "clergy" (Matthew 23:9). All Christians are to be equally committed. Christians have different gifts and functions, but *all* disciples are expected to obey *all* the commands *all* the time. All disciples are called into the full-time ministry.
- The lesson for us: nothing could be further from the spirit of Jesus Christ than the clergy-laity system, which upholds a double standard of commitment.

Holy Cow!
- Miscellaneous
  a. Holy foods (1 Timothy 4:3, Hebrews 13:9, Mark 7:19)
  b. Holy altars (Hebrews 7:27, 13:10)

   c. Images and icons (Exodus 20:4, 1 John 5:21)
   d. Vestments, water, censers, medals, relics, languages, formulae, crosses...
   e. The importing of OT categories into the NT simply will not do!

Conclusion: from Shadows to Light

     Colossians 2:17 teaches that the Law was only a shadow of the reality—or that which creates the shadow—which is found in Christ. Yes, there are many parallels between OT "shadows" and NT realities, but the two covenants are distinct. Today the Old Testament is obsolete (Hebrews 8:13), and yet most of modern Christianity resembles OT Judaism more than the original NT faith! Let's leave the shadows of the Old Covenant and come into the light! That's where real freedom is.[6]

7
Messianic Prophecy

This is an Evidences study. *Evidences* is the area of religion concerned with showing the reasonableness of the Christian faith. (Other areas of Evidences, or Apologetics, include biblical archaeology, the existence of God, the reliability of the Bible, comparative religion, philosophical proofs, etc.) *Messianic Prophecy* was a crucial study in the early church (Acts 2:25-28, 2:34-35, 4:11, 4:25-26, 8:32-33, 13:33-35).

- Micah 5:2
- Isaiah 7:14
- Psalm 110:1
- Isaiah 9:1-2,6
- Isaiah 52:13-53:12 (location only)

Prophecies of Jesus' birth
- To be born at Bethlehem (Micah 5:2).
- To be born of a virgin (Isaiah 7:14).
- God to become man (Psalm 110:1, Isaiah 9:6).

Prophecies concerning his ministry
- To be heralded by John the Baptist (Isaiah 40:3-5, Malachi 3:1, 4:5-6).
- To minister in Galilee (Isaiah 9:1-2).
- To be a wise counselor (Isaiah 9:6) and champion of the needy (Isaiah 11:1ff).
- To be the shepherd in the spirit of David (Ezekiel 34).
- To heal the sick (Isaiah 53:4).

Prophecies concerning his death
- To come into Jerusalem on a donkey (Zechariah 9:9).
- To be betrayed (Psalm 41:9).
- To be abandoned by his disciples (Zechariah 13:7).
- Lots to be cast for his clothes (Psalm 22:18)
- To be crucified (Psalm 22).
- To be pierced (Zechariah 12:10).
- To bear our sins on the cross (Isaiah 53)

Prophecies concerning his resurrection and ascension
- Divine rescue (see foreshadowing in Genesis 22).
- Physical resurrection (Psalm 16:10).
- To ascend to God and receive everlasting dominion (Daniel 7:13-14).

A note on different levels of prophecy
- Foreshadowing: Genesis 22:1-18 (nine parallel details between sacrifice of Isaac and sacrifice of Jesus).
- Prophecy: Psalm 22 (finds deeper fulfillment in events surrounding Jesus, but also makes sense in its original context).
- Strict prophecy: Isaiah 52:13-53:12.
- Be careful! Interpretation of prophecy is tricky.

Conclusion

The prophecies are clear and the implications inescapable. Jesus was the Messiah predicted in the Old Testament centuries in advance. There are dozens of other important prophecies about the Christ. This study (intended to be manageable) is, however, a good representation of these remarkable passages. For more on Messianic prophecy, please study the material stored at www.douglasjacoby.com.

8
Premillennialism

"Premillennialism" is hard enough to pronounce, let alone to understand. It is a system of doctrines taught by many denominations today, including most evangelical groups.[7] The first major millenarian group, condemned by the church for taking Revelation literally, dates to about 130 AD. Since premillennial teaching is so prevalent in religious circles, the fully equipped Christian worker must grasp the teachings and gain competence in refuting it.

Whereas the doctrines of *Calvinism* appeal to the mind, the teachings of *Premillennialism* appeal more to the emotions. The basic notion is that we are living in the "last days," under the haunting specter of the second coming of Christ; doomsday is on the way! But for the faithful, it is claimed, great blessings and riches are in store. Since the kingdom of God has not yet arrived (we are said to be living in the "church age"), when Jesus returns he will establish a physical, political, earthly kingdom on this earth. This will come to pass after the "rapture" snatches the saved up to heaven, sparing them the agonies of the painful "tribulation" period which will punish the unbelievers of the earth. Support for these speculations comes from an assortment of Old Testament passages (out of context), Matthew 24 and its parallel passages, and especially Revelation (the favorite book of premillennialists).

Below is the basic Premillennialism study. We will examine five tenets of premillennialism. Afterwards follows a study you can teach on The Coming of the Kingdom.

- "Premillennialism"
- Matthew 24:34/Revelation 1:3
- Acts 2:16
- Revelation 13:17
- Luke 17:20/1 Thessalonians 5:1
- Colossians 1:13/John 18:36

The prophesied end of the world
- The Old Testament is said to prophesy modern political events (Amos 3:7, etc.)
- To support this view, many passages (especially prophecies) are claimed to have "double meanings."
- Matthew 24 (paralleled by Mark 13 and Luke 21) is said to apply to our time, despite the fact that it describes first century Jewish history and Jesus said that all of it would be fulfilled in his generation (Matthew 24:34).
- Revelation is said to describe the awesome events immediately preceding and following the Second Coming, despite the fact that Revelation claims immediate fulfillment (Revelation 1:3).
  a. Daniel had a vision around 550 BC (Daniel 8:1) that was to be fulfilled around 165 BC, nearly 400 years later. The vision was to be fulfilled "in the distant future."
  b. Surely Revelation 1:3, which states that the prophecy of Revelation will be fulfilled in the "near" future, cannot be any further away in fulfillment than Daniel's vision! How then can premillennialists claim it applies (mainly) to events around the year 2000?

The last days
- Although a look at the Scriptures clearly shows that the "last days" began with Christ's first coming (see Acts 2:16, Hebrews 1:2, James 5:3, 2 Peter 3:3), premillennialists believe that the last days began quite recently.[8]
- Premillennialists historically have proposed various dates for the start of the last days. In the 20th century, some popular years guesses were 1901, 1914, 1967, 1987, and 2000.
- Although God's word commands every generation to live in anticipation of the end of the world—be ready!—it simply isn't possible to pinpoint the "end times" of earth's history.

Literalistic interpretation
- When premillennialists say that they take the Bible "literally," they mean that they try to take literally the book of Revelation and other similar parts of the Bible.
- Definition of terms:
  a. *literal:* straightforward, not symbolic at all: Luke 8:26: "They sailed to the region of the Gerasenes:" The word "sailed" means they traveled by boat, a sail being filled and pushed by the wind. It does not mean (figuratively) that they sailed across the sky, sailed in their minds, or that their friends hallucinated their transit.
  b. *figurative:* symbolic, metaphorical, not literal: Psalm 91:4: "He (God) will cover you with his feathers, and under his wings you will find refuge." Here God's "wings" symbolize his concern, care and shelter for his people. God doesn't *literally* have wings (or an arm, ear, mouth, etc.), but that doesn't mean the passage is "incorrect." Figurative passages are normal in Biblical poetry and prophecy.
  c. *literalistic:* taking figurative passages literally. In the previous passage, God would have real feathers: either physical, birdlike feathers or spiritual feathers. This is clearly nonsense!
  d. *face value:* the natural sense of a passage. We are to take literal passages literally and figurative passages figuratively. Taking the Bible "at face value" avoids the confusion of the literalistic approach.
- Thus believing that the Bible is *literally* the word of God doesn't mean that every passage must be taken *literally*.
- The literalistic approach leads to many abuses, particularly with the book of Revelation:
  a. The plagues against the ungodly (which symbolize God's judgment against the sinful world, and particularly against the Roman Empire, who are persecuting the Christians) are taken literally. (Hal Lindsay writes that the torturing locusts of Revelation 9:7-10 are actually Cobra helicopters!)
  b. The pictures of the victorious church (and the glimpse of heaven) at the end of Revelation are literalized (streets of gold, pearly gates, very wealthy Christians!).
  c. Premillennialists expect a literal battle of "Armageddon" (Revelation 16:16).
  d. Endless speculations on the meaning of "666" in Revelation 13:18. (Premillennialists love to play with numbers.)
  e. A typical example is Revelation 13:17, which is construed to mean that every man and woman who does not follow God will have a mark (silicon implant) under the skin of the hand (or forehead) with the number "666," without which they will have no credit. It is a sort of international credit card.

Timetable predictions
- The basic premillennial view of the flow of time divides history into seven 1000-year periods:

a. about 4000 years before the coming of Christ
b. about 2000 years from then until about now
c. and a final 1000 years (Latin *millennium*), predicted in Revelation 20, of the triumphant rule of Christ on earth.

- Yet it is clear from Scripture that "1000" is often a symbolic number (Psalm 50:10, Deuteronomy 7:9, Psalm 90:4, 2 Peter 3: 8), and it's certainly a symbolic number in Revelation.
- Premillennialists find in the Bible "predictions" of persons, dates, times, events. They try to use prophecy as a sort of "timetable." But 1 Thessalonians 5:1 clearly discourages any predictions of the times and dates surrounding the final years of earth's history.
- There is a common pattern to premillennial predictions:
  a. *prediction*: a scripture is taken out of context to "predict" a historical event—usually the end of the world.
  b. *postponement*: the predicted event fails to happen. At first this is rationalized, but soon it becomes an embarrassment.
  c. *depression*: disappointment sets in, morale drops, confidence in the current leadership is lost.
  d. *recalculation*: the date is refigured. The prediction is seldom dropped; after the initial depression has lifted, followers are willing to assume that the predictors made a mistake in calculation, or made wrong initial assumptions. One premillennial group, the Jehovah's Witnesses, has calculated the end of the world over and over and over: 1874, 1914, 1918, 1925, 1941, 1954, 1975...

Physical, political, earthly kingdom
- Premillennialists wait for the Second Coming of Christ to usher in a physical, political, earthly kingdom. It is to be based in Jerusalem, and Christians will become "top nation," so to speak. The faithful expect all kinds of thrills and rewards, and it is obvious that wrong motivations abound where the nature of the kingdom is misunderstood. In the first century, Jews took the prophecies literally and expected an earthly kingdom ruled by a conquering warrior Messiah. But Jesus discouraged these would-be "premillennialists" (John 6:15); they completely misunderstood the nature of his Messiahship and mission.
- Jesus stated emphatically that his kingdom is "not of this world" (John 18:36).
- Premillennialists take several different approaches:
  a. Jesus meant to establish the kingdom, but had to delay it due to opposition.
  b. The kingdom is only partially here. The Bible does speak of heaven as the "heavenly kingdom" (2 Tim 4:18), but premillennialists are looking for an intermediate state between the church and heaven: the millennial reign of Christ.
  c. Some think that the church will convert the entire world, and thus the kingdom will be ushered in through evangelism (total saturation) and (Christian) political legislation. This position is really "millennialism."

- All these approaches fail to deal with the fact that the kingdom of God expressed itself on earth in a unique way through the church (Colossians 1:13).

Major weaknesses of the premillennial approach
- Passages are taken out of context; Bible study tends to become one-track and superficial.
- Disproportionate emphasis is placed on Biblical prophecy.
- Evangelism suffers as many believers are made to feel that the end of the world is the most important thing.
- The Christian message loses credibility in the eyes of non-believers as predictions are shown to be wrong.

Recommended reading:
- Clouse, Robert G., Robert N. Hosack and Richard V. Pierard, *The New Millennium Manual: A Once and Future Guide* (Grand Rapids: Baker, 1999).
- Ferguson, Gordon, *Mine Eyes Have Seen the Glory* (Woburn, Mass.: Discipleship Publications International, 1996).
- McGuiggan, Jim, *Revelation* (Fort Worth: Star Bible Publications, 1976). (800) 481-7809.
- Wright, N. T., *The Millennium Myth: Hope for a Postmodern World* (Louisville: Westminster John Knox Press, 1999).

Supplementary Study: **The Coming of the Kingdom**

This study is a good companion to—and somewhat less complicated than—the Premillennialism study. In some cases you may wish to use this study as an alternate to the basic Church study.

Many O.T. passages discuss the kingdom, which is described as present but also as future.[9] See Daniel 2:31-45 (c. 600 BC).

Kingdom	Substance	Dates
Babylonian	gold	605-539 BC
Medo-Persian	silver	539-333 BC
Greek	bronze	333-63 BC
Roman	iron + clay	63 BC
Kingdom of God	mountain of stone which fills the earth	30 AD

Approach of kingdom in first century AD
- John the Baptist's message—Matthew 3:2, see Malachi 3:1, 4:5 (Matthew 11:11-14).
- Jesus' teaching—Matthew 4:17
- Jesus' disciples' teaching—Matthew 10:7
- Luke 24:49, Acts 1:3-8
- Peter to hold keys to kingdom—Matthew 16:19

Nature of the kingdom
- Not political—John 6:15, 18:36
- Not visible—Luke 17:20-21
- Entered spiritually—John 3:3, 5, 7
- Grows!—Matthew 13:31-33

Day of Pentecost (Acts 2)—Coming of the kingdom: all the loose ends are tied up on that day. (All the prophecies are fulfilled.)

Perspective of the NT: The kingdom is especially manifest on earth in the church (Acts 2:30, Colossians 1:12-13, Revelation 1:5-6, 5:10). Yet we may pray for it to continue to "come" (Matthew 6:9), and we eagerly anticipate the kingdom in heaven, as our citizenship is already there (Philippians 3:20).

Seek first the kingdom! Put God first, and seek to do his will (Matthew 6:33, 7:21).

9
The Holy Spirit II

The format of this unit is, as with the Word II, a question and answer forum.

- Matthew 7:22
- Luke 16:31
- John 7:39
- 2 Timothy 1:6

1. Can God heal today?
   - Few have actually seen "healings." Beware of second-hand information.
   - Most "healings" are frivolous (e.g. colds, short legs).
   - Many "healings" are psychosomatic. Positive attitudes or "vibrations" speed up the healing process.
   - Nevertheless, God does heal through *prayer*, even though there is no supernatural *gift* of healing today.

2. Don't miracles prove one's salvation?
   - Deuteronomy 13:1-5. Even if someone performs a miracle, if he isn't preaching the Word, he isn't right with God. Do not go after him; God may be testing you.
   - 1 Samuel 19:18-21. God enables Saul and others to prophesy. Doesn't prove they were saved. (They were opposing God, and by this point Saul has fallen away.)
   - Revelation 13:13, 2 Thessalonians 2:9. Some "miracles" are of the devil.
   - Acts 19:13. *Jews* are casting out demons.
   - Mark 13:22. False Messiahs.

- Matthew 7:22. Perhaps the most useful passage. Doing the will of God, not miracles, leads to salvation.

3. Doesn't the Spirit lead us today?
    - Yes, but what does that mean?
    - It is not "reading your feelings": Proverbs 14:12, Jeremiah 17:9.
    - Galatians 5:16-26, Romans 8:1-16. Putting the flesh to death; becoming more like Jesus.
    - Psalm 143:10. Being taught by God to do his will—through the precepts of the Word. Ezekiel 36:27. This is a learning process, a matter of discipline. No short-cuts!

4. Didn't people have the Holy Spirit in the OT?
    - No, not in the *indwelling* sense. John 7:39, Romans 8:9. Strictly speaking, there were no Christians before Pentecost, neither in the OT nor in the gospels. And yet many in the OT are spoken of as having the Spirit, or having the Spirit fall on them: Balaam (Numbers 24:2), Othniel (Judges 3:10), Jephthah (Judges 11:29), Saul (1 Samuel 19:18), David (1 Samuel 16:13), Amasai (1 Chron 12:18).

5. Can we nail down the idea that miraculous gifts were passed on only by the apostles?
    - Basic verses: Acts 6:6, 8; 8:6, 17-18.
    - Also 2 Timothy 1:6, Romans 1:11, 1 Corinthians 1:4-7.
    - Paul was in Corinth 18 months, in Ephesus 3 years—a considerable time. They had miraculous gifts because Paul had been there.

6. What about Holy Spirit Baptism?
    - There is only one baptism (Ephesians 4:5), and the "rules" are unchanging (Acts 2:39).
    - John the Baptist said that Jesus would baptize us with the Spirit (Mark 1:8).
    - This baptism is the alternative to damnation ("baptism" with fire).
    - Christian baptism involves two elements: water and Spirit (John 3:5, 1 Corinthians 12:12-13). Both are crucial, and we were all baptized with/in/by the one Spirit.
    - No supernatural abilities are conferred through this baptism.
    - In other words, baptism in the Spirit is simply another way of describing Christian conversion.
    - *For more on this subject, see chapter 24 of my book* The Spirit.

7. Don't we need to be filled with the Spirit?
    - Absolutely, but what does it mean?
    - Acts 6: apostles laid hands on men already filled with the Spirit (v3). "Spirit-filled" has no connection with ability to perform miracles.
    - John the Baptist was Spirit-filled from birth (Luke 1:15), but he never performed miracles (John 10:41).

- Ephesians 5:17-20, Colossians 3:16. Counseling one another, singing to one another, putting the Word into our lives. It's a progressive thing, not just one-time. We should strive to be filled with the Spirit every moment of the day.
- Being "filled with the spirit" means being spiritual.

8. Doesn't the Spirit do things for us beyond what the Word enables us to do?
    - The Spirit convicts of sin, for example (John 16:8), but *not* apart from the Word (Romans 10:17).
    - The Spirit operates through the Word. For example, it
        a. Quickens us (Psalm 119:50)
        b. Strengthens us (Psalm 119:28)
        c. Sanctifies us (John 17:17)
        d. Gives us wisdom (2 Timothy 3:14-15)
        e. Enlightens us (Psalm 119:130)
        f. Allows us to participate in the divine nature...(2 Peter 1:4)
    - All these things are normally attributed to the power of the Spirit, and rightly so. But notice that in these passages it is the Word of God that provides all these blessings.

9. Are there any miracles outside Christianity?
    - Montanism (2nd century AD heretical charismatic sect.
    - Sufis (charismatic Islamic sect).
    - God may answer the prayer of a non-Christian and heal him, for example, just to drive him
    - onward in his search for God.
    - But 99.99% of "miracles" outside Christianity are fraudulent, psychosomatic or exaggerated.

10. Don't we still need miracles today?
    - The historical purpose of the miracles was to confirm the spoken word (Exodus 4:5, 1 Kings 17:24, Mark 16:20, Acts 14:3, Hebrews 2:4). There is no record of confirmation given for the written word (scripture).
    - Luke 16:19-31. If they don't listen to the Word, they won't believe even if someone rises from the dead. The Word is sufficient for anyone with a pure heart (John 20:30).

Further reading
Please see *The Spirit* (Newton, Mass.: IPI, 2005). This book contains an extensive bibliography for further reading.[10]

Supplementary Study: **Feelings**

For a neo-pentecostal, this study is a good prelude to the study of *The Word of God*, although in some cases it may be wise to study *The Word* first. *The Feelings* study presents material you will want to cover with almost all who have neo-pentecostal leanings.

Proverbs 3:5—Trust in God, not your own feelings.

Proverbs 14:12—We'll pay the penalty if we follow our own feelings.

Proverbs 28:26—It is foolish to follow perceptions, hunches, feelings, intuitions...

Jeremiah 17:9—The human heart is deceitful.

1 Kings 13:1-26—The story of the young prophet and the old prophet. Particularly useful because it deals with the issue of ultimate authority.

Galatians 1:6-9—Even if you were convinced that you had received an angelic visitation, or a revelation from an apostle, no one has the right to change the gospel message.

Jeremiah 23:16, 21-22, 25-32, 35-36—False prophets of OT times:
- Claim to speak from God (verse 16).
- Their messages are purely psychological, not from God (verse 16).
- They water down the word of God (verse 22).
- Their dreams (see Numbers 12:6) are delusions, merely psychological (verses 25-26), and lessen the commitment of the people by imparting false hope (verse 27).
- Although they fancy God to be speaking his word through them, he is not; their messages have absolutely nothing to do with the word of God (verses 28-29).
- They borrow "messages" from one another; they exchange "oracles" (verse 30).
- They do not benefit the people (verses 31-32).
- They do sincerely expect the Lord to speak to them (verse 35).
- They suffer terrible theological confusion as God's Word and their word are completely confused (verse 36).
- The end result: they distort God's word (verse 36).

Jude 19—These men confuse natural instincts with the Spirit.

Luke 9:23—Discipleship means denying your selfish feelings, not following them.
- Deny feelings, follow Christ.
- Follow feelings, deny Christ.

Matthew 7:21-23—"Charismatics" and judgment day
- Many will be surprised on Judgment Day.
- God expects obedience.
- True spirituality is obeying God, not just feeling him.
- Are you sure you know the Lord? (1 Corinthians 8:3.)

10
The Judgment

This study is intended to convict, to awaken, to bring a man or woman more quickly to a decision for God and Jesus Christ. The points are very straightforward, and the thrust of the message is clear. Preaching about "the judgment to come" is both powerful and biblical (Acts 24:25, Matthew 3:10, 10:28).

- Revelation 20:15
- Hebrews 10:27
- Luke 12:47
- Luke 16:26
- 2 Thessalonians 1:8

Judgment is universal.
- There are three inescapable facts for all mankind: life, death and judgment.
- Regardless of position, knowledge, race or nation, all mankind will stand before the throne of God. Anyone who has not lived according to God's word will be condemned (Revelation 20:15).

Hell is dreadful.
- It is terrible and to be feared (Hebrews 10:27).
- It's foolish to laugh at fear as an illegitimate motive; it's healthy to have a fear of dark alleys, high voltage, too close to the edge of a tall building, etc. How much more should we fear hell!

Punishment is proportional to knowledge.
- God is not an ogre: he wants everyone to be saved (Romans 2:4, 2 Peter 3:9).
- Nevertheless, there will be punishment for everyone who sins (Romans 3:9-20).[11]
- The severity of punishment after death will vary individual to individual, depending on knowledge (Luke 12:47).
- (This is not to say that anyone who has never understood the gospel can be saved—John 3:18.)
- One thing is sure: if we reject the gospel (understanding it), our judgment will be the most severe!

Hell is irreversible.
- In life, some choices have irreversible consequences: suicide, arson, murder, etc. Hell, too, is a choice (we choose to go there by persisting in living by our own standards instead of God's) which cannot be reversed.
- Once we have died, there is no purgatory, no "upgrading," no second chance (Luke 16:26).
- Since the decision to obey God is so crucial, and the consequences are irreversible, we must choose to put God first as soon as possible—before it's too late.[12]

The only hope is the Gospel.
- There is hope, but only those who obey the gospel will be saved (2 Thessalonians 1:8).
- Jesus died in our place; he bore our sins (1 Peter 2:24). Sin must be judged and punished, but Jesus has already borne the penalty.
- Paradoxically (since no self-righteous person can go to heaven— Luke 18:14), in order to go to heaven we must believe that we deserve to go to hell.

- Worried that God will let someone slip through the crack? Anyone who seeks God's kingdom with all his heart can be saved (Matthew 6:33). But we must take the good news to them! If they listen and obey—even though they don't deserve it—they will be saved. (But if they do not obey the gospel, whether or not they have heard the Word, they will be forever lost—also what they "deserve.")
- Sin is that serious! Sin is so horrible, and God is so loving, that he gave his Son to die for our sins.

Supplementary Study: **Is Sincerity Enough?**

This study is a good companion to – and somewhat less complicated than – the Premillennialism study. In some cases you may wish to use this study as an alternate to the basic Church study.

Many O.T. passages discuss the kingdom, which is described as present but also as future.[1] See Daniel 2:31-45 (c. 600 BC).

- 1 Corinthians 4:4
- Romans 10:1-2
- Romans 9:1-3

1 Corinthians 4:4—Sincerity is not enough. A clear conscience does not mean you are in the clear. Analogy: *fuel gauge.* You may not be aware that your gasoline/petrol gauge indicates you are on empty, but that does not change the fact of the matter. Someone who has not heard the gospel, or someone who has been mis-taught, is not saved if sincere. Ignorance is not bliss.

Romans 10:1-2—Sincerity and commitment in religious people are not sufficient for salvation. Paul's fellow Jews were very "zealous." Yet, as Paul says, they are lost ("that they may be saved").

Romans 9:1-3—Paul was deeply disturbed by the lostness of the religious person. Yet for him this wasn't just an academic question, or a matter of doctrinal irritation. He was willing to contemplate trading places with these people, for, like Moses (Exodus 32:32), he loved them.

Ask, "If you became convinced that your religious friends/those how have never heard/all the people in the world were lost, would you be *willing* to go and take them the message?" If the answer is no, your friend's objections are not entirely sincere. If yes, then challenge him to embrace the teaching of the Bible, regardless of how painful personally it may be.

For sincerity is not enough.

Conclusion to the Series C

The Word of God is powerful (Jeremiah 23:29)! If we learn to communicate it effectively, there is tremendous potential for good! But if we are lazy, we'll wield it wildly and unwisely. God is calling each of us to a deeper knowledge of his Word in order that we may equip ourselves to take the Word to an unbelieving and skeptical world. It is to this end that all the Guard the Gospel series was designed.

Conclusion to the Guard the Gospel Series

Let's never grow content with our level of Bible knowledge, whether we've been in the Lord's church for a long time, are just starting out on our Christian walk, or (especially) if we are serving as Christian leaders. For, as the Hebrew writer says, many of us "by this time...ought to be teachers."

Notes

[1] For more on this, see *How We Got the Bible* (Newton, Mass.: IPI, 2005). This is a four-part audio set with notes.

[2] The KJV was completed in 1611 and revised in 1629, 1638, 1762, and 1769. See Jack P. Lewis, *The English Bible from KJV to NIV: A History and Evaluation, 2nd ed.* (Grand Rapids: Baker Books, 1991) and Adam Nicolson's *God's Secretaries: The Making of the King James Bible* (San Francisco: Harper Collins, 2003).

[3] In the United States, the NIV has, since the early 1990s, outsold the veteran KJV more than two to one. (The NT translation was completed in 1973, the OT in 1978.)

[4] The Bible distinguishes between those who have "wandered away" (James 5:19) and those who have "fallen away (Hebrews 6:4). For those in the first category there is hope; for those in the second, none. Incidentally, when Jesus predicts that his apostles will, on the night of his arrest "all fall away" (NIV mistranslation), this is a different verb to that normally used for "falling" or "falling away." (To illustrate, the verb in connection with these predictions is consistently translated "be offended" in the KJV.) Hence we must distinguish between stumbling and falling.

[5] Note: the root cause of the Laodiceans' lukewarmness, in the context of the passage (Revelation 3:14-22), is *materialism*. Lukewarmness is a symptom of misplaced priorities, not a root sin in itself. The same holds with the lives of true disciples. Urging them to "get fired up" when there are significant root problems (relationship strains, major disappointments, unconfessed sins, unanswered [serious] doctrinal questions, marriage problems, and so forth), is bound to backfire, even to encourage the habit of feigning zeal. Deal with the heart (the internals), not just the externals.

[6] The abolition of the various OT categories does not mean that we should downplay our "priestly" responsibility to bring others to God, or to behave irreverently when gathered for worship. Sometimes in the name of "freedom" we can lose our sense of "reverence and awe" (Hebrews 10:28) – which was *not* nullified at Calvary!

[7] Strictly speaking, the term applies to an interpretation of Revelation which holds that Christ's second coming will come before the establishment of his thousand-year reign on earth. Postmillennialists assert the second coming follows the millennial reign. Millennialists believe through our words and actions the people of God will bring about the "kingdom" on earth. Amillennialists deny that there is any such "millennium."

[8] A worthy consideration is that the Last Days are the last days of Judaism, particularly the forty-year period between 30 AD (Pentecost, as Peter declares in Acts 2) and 70 (the Destruction of Jerusalem).

[9] For more material on the kingdom, see Jim McGuiggan's *The Reign of God: A Study of the Kingdom of God* (Fort Worth: Star Bible Publications, 1992) and *The Kingdom of God and the Planet Earth* (Fort Worth: Star Bible Publications, 1978). Or order by phoning (800) 433-7507).

[10] In addition, you may enjoy the tape series *The Spirit: The Work of the Spirit in the Life of the Disciple* (Woburn, Mass.: DPI, 1998).

[11] The Bible teaches that punishment for the lost commences after death. However, this is not the same as hell (the lake of fire), which follows the Last Judgment. The two possible sequences of events after death, then, are:
• For the lost: Sin—Death—Hades—2nd coming—Resurrection—Judgment—Hell
• For the saved: Salvation—Death—Paradise—2nd coming—Resurrection—Judgment—Heaven.

[11] For an intriguing exploration of the nature of hell, please see the article on Terminal Punishment at www.DouglasJacoby.com.

14
Old Testament Guard the Gospel
Sharing your faith from the "O.T."

How well do you know your "OT"?

"OT" does not mean occupational therapist, overtime, or on time, but it's—*about time* we raised our standards when it comes to knowledge of the "OT," or Old Testament.

Most of us who have been around church for a while are very familiar with the New Testament. We may describe ourselves as a "New Testament" church. We hear many lessons from the New Testament (henceforth NT), do much of our personal Bible study in the NT and have done most of our scripture memory from the NT. But what about the OT? Although we may have read the NT through five, ten, or more times, few of us have completed the OT even once! Considering that the OT is the basis for the NT (and is about four times the length of the NT), shouldn't we make a serious effort to master the Old Testament? Are you convicted about your Bible knowledge?

The Bible of the Early Christians

For the early church, the Old Testament was their Bible! Probably the earliest NT writings date from around the mid-40s AD, and the NT was certainly not completed until the latter part of the first century. And even this does not guarantee that everyone had the same gospels and letters – that did not occur until around the latter part of the second century!

When Jesus rebuked the Sadducees for their defective Bible knowledge (Matthew 22:29), he was referring to the OT (certainly not 2 Peter or Philippians!). When Paul urged Timothy to devote himself to scripture reading (1 Timothy 4:13), he is referring primarily to the OT (See 1 Timothy 5:18 for a possible exception.) Even the much beloved 2 Timothy 3:15-17 refers to the Old Testament (though by extension the principle applies to the new as well).

Recreating the Scene

Imagine that you are living in the middle of the first century! Very few NT books have been written or become available, although from time to time your leaders may read aloud a letter from Paul – before it is sent by special courier to sister congregations (see Colossians 4:16). How would you study with those interested in the new faith?

The fact is that virtually everything we teach our non-Christian friends could be taught from the OT. We surely get a clearer picture of

Jesus in the NT (1 Peter 1:10-12) than in the OT, but most of the great NT doctrines are first found in the OT.

First Principles Class?

How do you think the first century church patterned their instruction for prospective members? Topics were evidently arranged and studied out (Hebrews 6:1-2, Ephesians 4:21-24, Romans 6:17). Scripture memory may have played a part (Proverbs 22:18). But all of the material in the beginning, at least, must have come from the Old Testament.

Do you know your OT well enough to come up with five or ten passages for every great theme of the faith? Whatever evangelistic approach you are most familiar with, hopefully you are competent to share them with your non-Christian friends.

A Fresh Approach

The following course series comes completely from the Old Testament. Each study is arranged in one of many possible arrangements of the verses. For example, in our New Testament series, the *Word* class uses such scriptures as Hebrews 4:12-13, 2 Timothy 3:16, and Matthew 22:29. Instead of Hebrews 4:12, which compares the Word to a sword, try using Jeremiah 23:29, which compares it to a hammer. A possible illustration: "Have you ever been hammering in a nail and the hammer slipped? God's Word is powerful, and although we may feel pain (challenge) at times, we must press on." Instead of 2 Timothy 3:16, which discusses the inspiration of all scripture, how about Psalm 12:6? Good alternates to Matthew 22:29, which explains that ignorance of God's Word is a major reason why the religious world is in such a muddle, might be Hosea 4:6, or Jeremiah 8:7.

To get the most out of the material, I encourage you to take out your Old Testament (right now!) and study each topic in your own Bible. What are the major points you would come up with? How about your illustrations?

Seeking God	Sin	The Kingdom
Isaiah 1:2	Ecclesiastes 7:20	Daniel 2:31-45
Jeremiah 29:11-14	Leviticus 18	Isaiah 2:2
Proverbs 4:7	Leviticus 19:1-18	Isaiah 4:2
Psalm 10:4	Ecclesiastes 4:4	Genesis 49:10
Psalm 42:1-2	Genesis 4:7	Isaiah 40:3
Psalm 63:1	Proverbs 6:16-19	Malachi 3:1
Psalm 62:1	Isaiah 59:1-3	Malachi 4:1-6
Psalm 61:2	Psalm 26:1-2	

Messianic Prophecy
Isaiah 52:13-53:12
Genesis 22:1-18
Psalm 16:8-10
Psalm 2:7
Genesis 3:15
Genesis 12:3
Deuteronomy 18:15
Micah 5:2
Isaiah 7:14
Isaiah 9:1-2
Isaiah 9:6

The Cross
Isaiah 53
Psalm 22
Zechariah 9:9
Zechariah 11:12-13
Zechariah 13:7
Zechariah 12:10
Deuteronomy 21:23

Evangelism
Exodus 19:6
Isaiah 49:6
Zechariah 8:23
Proverbs 11:30
2 Kings 7:3-9
Esther 4:14

Repentance
Ezekiel 18:30-32
Lamentations 2:14
Psalm 139:23-24
Job 42:5-6
2 Samuel 11:1-12:13
Psalm 34:18

Commitment
Deuteronomy 6:5
Leviticus 19:18
Malachi 1:10
Isaiah 6:1-8
Jeremiah 48:10

Baptism
Proverbs 30:12
2 Kings 5:1-15
Leviticus 14:1-7
Isaiah 1:18-20

Decision
Deuteronomy 30:11-20
Joshua 24:14-15
Ezra 10
Psalm 84
Daniel 3

The Word
Jeremiah 23:29
Hosea 4:6
Jeremiah 8:7
Psalm 12:6
Proverbs 30:5-6
Deuteronomy 4:2
Psalm 119

Grace
2 Sam 11-12
Psalm 102
Psalm 103
Isaiah 30:18-19
Jonah 2:8

Concluding Challenge

The challenge is clear: to do our best to become familiar with the whole Word of God (2 Timothy 2:15). For most of us, that means a renewed determination to learn how to teach the OT (Ezra 7:10). That is the only way we will be like Philip (Acts 8), who "began with that very passage of scripture and told him the good news about Jesus." Some of you may even take up the challenge to study with a man or woman exclusively from the Old Testament!

Just as Jesus did his best to master God's Word, let us all determine to do our best to master the Old Testament.[1]

Notes

[1] Recommended: *Foundations for Faith: Old Testament Survey* (Newton, Mass.: IPI, 2004).

15

A Medical Account of the Crucifixion
Simplified and Amended[1]

Hanging, electrocution, knee-capping, gas chamber: these punishments are feared. They all happen today, and we shudder as we think of the horror and pain. But as we shall see, these ordeals pale into insignificance compare with the bitter fate of Jesus Christ: crucifixion.[2]

No one is crucified today. For us the cross remains confined to ornaments and jewelry, stained-glass windows, romanticized pictures and statues portraying a serene death. Crucifixion was a form of execution refined by the Romans to a precise art. It was carefully conceived to produce a slow death with maximum pain. It was a public spectacle intended to deter other would-be criminals. It was a death to be feared.

Sweat like blood
Luke 22:24 says of Jesus, "and being in anguish, he prayed more earnestly, and his sweat was like drops of blood falling to the ground."[3] His sweat was unusually intense because his emotional state was unusually intense. Dehydration coupled with exhaustion further weakened him.

Beating
It was in this condition that Jesus faced the first physical abuse: punches and slaps to the face and head while blindfolded. Unable to anticipate the blows, Jesus was badly bruised, his mouth and eyes possibly injured. The psychological effects of the false trials should not be underestimated. Consider that Jesus faced them bruised, dehydrated, exhausted, possibly in shock.

Flogging
In the previous 12 hours Jesus had suffered emotional trauma, rejection by his closest friends, a cruel beating, and a sleepless night during which he had to walk miles between unjust hearings. Despite the fitness he must certainly have gained during his travels in Palestine, he was in no way prepared for the punishment of flogging. The effects would be worse as a result.

A man to be flogged was stripped of his clothes and his hands tied to a post above his head. He was then whipped across the shoulders, back, buttocks, thighs and legs, the soldier standing behind and to one side of the victim. The whip used – the flagellum – was designed to make this a devastating punishment, bringing the victim close to death: several short heavy leather thongs, with two small balls of lead or iron attached near the end of each. Pieces of sheep's bone were sometimes included.

As the scourging proceeds, the heavy leather thongs produce first superficial cuts, than deeper damage to underlying tissues. Bleeding becomes severe when not only capillaries and veins are cut, but also arteries in the underlying muscles. The small metal balls first produce large, deep bruises which are broken open by further blows. The fragments of sheep's bone rip the flesh as the whip is drawn back. When the beating is finished, the skin of the back is in ribbons, and the entire area torn and bleeding.

The words chosen by the gospel writers suggest that the scourging of Jesus was particularly severe: he was certainly at the point of collapse when he was cut down from the flogging-post.

The mocking

Jesus was allowed no time to recover before facing his next ordeal. Made to stand, he was dressed in a robe by jeering soldiers, crowned with a twisted band of thorny twigs, and to complete the parody, given a wooden staff as a king's scepter. "Next, they spat on Jesus and struck him on the head with the wooden staff." The long thorns were driven into the sensitive scalp tissue producing profuse bleeding, but even more terrible was the re-opening of the wounds on Jesus' back when the robe was torn off again.

Further weakened physically and emotionally, Jesus was led away to be executed.

The crucifixion

The wooden cross used by the Romans was too heavy to be carried by one man. Instead the victim to be crucified was made to bear the detached crossbar across his shoulders, carrying it outside the city walls to the place of execution. (The heavy upright portion of the cross was permanently in position here.) Jesus was unable to carry his load – a beam weighing around 75 to 125 pounds (approximately 35-55 kg). He collapsed under the burden, and an onlooker was ordered to take it for him.

Jesus refused to drink the wine and myrrh offered him before the nails were driven in. (It would have dulled the pain.) Thrown down on his back with arms outstretched along the crossbar, nails were driven through Jesus' wrists into the wood. These iron spikes, about 6 inches long and 3/8 inch thick, severed the large sensorimotor median nerve, causing excruciating pain in both arms. Carefully placed between bones and ligaments, they were able to bear the full weight of the crucified man.

In preparation for the nailing of the feet, Jesus was lifted up and the crossbar fixed to the upright post. Then with legs bent at the knee, a single nail was used to pierce both feet, one foot being placed over the other. Again there was severe nerve damage and the pain caused was intense. It is important to note, however, that neither the wounds to the wrists or feet caused substantial bleeding, since no major arteries were ruptured. The executioner took care to ensure this, so that death would be slower and the suffering longer.

Now nailed to his cross, the real horror of crucifixion began. When the wrists were nailed to the crossbar, the elbows were intentionally left in a bent position so that the crucified man would hang with his arms above his head, the weight being taken on the nails in the wrists. Obviously this was unbearably painful, but it had another effect: It is very difficult to exhale in this position. In order to breathe out, and then take in fresh air, it was necessary to push the body up on the nailed feet. When the pain from the feet became unbearable, the victim would again slump down to hang by the arms. A terrible cycle of pain began: hanging by the arms, unable to breathe, pushing up on the feet to inhale quickly before again slumping down, and on and on.

This tortured activity became more and more difficult as Jesus' back was scraped against the upright post,[4] as muscle cramps set in because of the inadequate respiration, and as exhaustion grew more severe. Jesus suffered in this manner for several hours before, with a final cry, he died.

Cause of death

Many factors contributed to Jesus' death. A combination of shock and suffocation killed most victims of crucifixion, but in Jesus' case acute heart failure may have been the final trauma. This is suggested by his sudden death following a loud cry, after only a few hours: a quick death, it seems (Pilate was surprised to find Jesus already dead). A fatal cardiac arrhythmia, or perhaps cardiac rupture, are likely candidates.

The spear wound

Jesus was already dead as the executioners broke the legs of the criminals crucified alongside (in order to speed their deaths). Instead, we read that a soldier pierced Jesus' side with a spear. Where on his side? The word chosen by John suggests the ribs, and if the soldier intended to make Jesus' death certain, a wound to the heart was the obvious choice.

From the wound came a flow of "blood and water." This is consistent with the spear blow to the heart (especially from the right side, the traditional site of the wound). Rupturing the pericardium (the sac surrounding the heart) released a flow of watery serum, followed by blood as the heart was pierced.

Conclusion

The detailed accounts given in the gospels combined with the historical evidence on crucifixion bring us to a firm conclusion: modern medical knowledge supports the claim of the scriptures that Jesus died on the cross.

Notes

[1] This is a simplified medical account of Jesus' crucifixion (an adaptation of the well-known Truman Davis version). Other medical reports have been written – all useful but usually rather technical. This account aims to be readable to the average reader. I made this adaptation, with the assistance of Alex Mnatzaganian, in December 1989.

[2] Highly recommended: Martin Hengel, *The Cross of the Son of God* (London: SCM Press, Ltd: 1981).

[3] The original version of our version of the Medical Account of the Crucifixion included these sentences: *"Haematidrosis* – bloody sweat – is rare, but well documented. Under great emotional stress, capillaries in the sweat glands can break, mixing blood in with the sweat. Luke's account is consistent with modern medical knowledge: Jesus was in emotional torment so intense that his body could not bear it." However, Luke only says that Jesus' sweat was *like* blood as it fell to the ground, not that it *was* mixed with blood. As disciples we must be careful not to overstate the case. There is no evidence that the early Christians preached the gore of the cross in an effort to sicken or shame those they were trying to convert.

[4] In some locations, trees were plentiful, while in others upright posts needed to be fixed into the ground. It is quite possible that in the place where Jesus was crucified there was an abundance of trees, in which case the patibulum he and Simon of Cyrene carried was simply attached to a tree. Of course, whether Jesus was killed on a tree literally, or on a tree by metonymy (on the wood of a tree) is incidental to the point of the crucifixion.

PART IV

Ever Brighter

"The path of the righteous is like the first gleam of dawn, shining ever brighter till the full light of day" (Proverbs 4:18).

Entering the kingdom of God is amazing, yet there is so much more still to come! After our friends have become Christians, they need to be grounded in the faith (Colossians 2:6-7) and continue the learning process begun before conversion (Ephesians 4:20-24). The light has dawned. May this passage in Proverbs describe our Christian walk: "shining ever brighter."

The fourth division of *Shining Like Stars* contains a number of follow-up studies, useful for instructing new believers. In addition, you will find two chapters about leading group Bible discussions, which have proven to be very effective forums in attracting seekers.

16
Grounding New Christians in the Word
Thirteen Follow-up Studies

We understand the imperative, methods, and urgency of evangelism. We teach it, preach it, and know what it means to be a "minister of reconciliation." And yet we have a chronic weakness. Too often we see conversion as the end of the process of evangelization, rather than as the middle. What, the *middle?* Yes, the middle! Our work is certainly not even *half* finished when we have when we have influenced someone to obey the gospel (Romans 1:5, 16:26, 2 Thessalonians 1:8). Obedience to the gospel is an *ongoing* process. Spiritual maturity (Ephesians 4: 16) cannot be achieved in just a few Bible study sessions. In fact, to lead someone to the point of faith, repentance, and baptism without ongoing study and discipleship is terribly careless (2 Peter 2:20-22)! The result of this weakness: a poor retention rate, as people come into the church through the front door and just as rapidly exit out the back door. Certainly we will want to do all that we can to keep faithful those who have confessed Jesus as Lord.

These studies have been designed to do something about that, to be used *after* baptism. The order in which you make use of them will vary from person to person. Perhaps you will want to come up with your own studies. In the meantime, take these as a suggestion, as a model. To aid you in bringing the principles to life, several practical suggestions have been added to most of the studies.

I. THE BASIS: Relationship with God
1. Prayer: speaking to God
2. Bible study: listening to God
3. Faith, works and grace: the balance

II. THE CHURCH: The Body of Christ
4. Relationships in the body
5. The New Testament Church
6. One-another relationships: God's plan

III. THE WORK: Becoming like Christ
7. Hindrance: the heart
8. Laziness, idleness, discipline
9. Evangelism, boldness and tact
10. Service with a smile

IV. OTHER NEEDS: Following God's Way
   11. Academics: obstacle or opportunity
   12. Christian marriage: cord of three strands
   13. The Christian Family: parents & children

I. THE BASIS: Relationship with God
1—Prayer: Speaking to God
   What could be more natural between two people who love each other than to communicate? Surely one would expect to see an enormous amount of communication between a man and the God he loves with all his heart, soul, mind and strength. And yet this is far from what we observe! Communication of this sort is not natural; it must be learned. There are many hindrances all of which Satan will gladly use in his campaign to keep us off our knees. Yet they can all be overcome, if we are willing to rely on God and give prayer the priority it deserves.

Priority
   • Mark 1:35—Jesus, a *busy* man, finds time to pray.
   • He finds a *place* free from distraction.
   • He finds a *time* free from distraction.
   • Suggested: Psalm 42:1, 63:1, Luke 6:12, Hebrews 5:7.

Learning process
   • Luke 11:1-13—It's *not* natural (even Jesus' apostles had to be taught).
   • Develop *structure* in your prayer life.

Hindrances
   • 1 Peter 4:7—Lack of concentration. May wish to pray aloud.
   • Psalm 66:18—Lack of personal righteousness.
   • Luke 18:1-8—Lack of persistence.
   • 1 John 5:14—Prayer contrary to God's will.
   • Mark 11:24—Lack of faith.
   • Suggested: Matthew 6:5, John 9:31, 14:13-14, Ephesians 6:18, Colossians 4:2-4, James 5:16-17.

Conclusion
   • Philippians 4:6-7—Cast your worries upon God.
   • Jeremiah 20:21b—God is looking for people who will devote themselves to be close to him. Take up the challenge!
   • Psalm 5:3—Have a *daily* prayer time.
   • Suggested—1 Thessalonians 5:17, 1 Peter 5:7, 1 John 5:14.

Practicals
   • Set a time and length to pray every day.
   • Write out a prayer list.

Fasting
- Often associated with prayer in the Bible.
- Matthew 6:17-18—shows that this is expected of Christians
- Suggested: Nehemiah 1:4, Isaiah 58, Joel 2:12, Acts 14:23.

2—Bible Study: Listening to God

Assisting young Christians to become rooted in consistent and productive personal Bible study is one of the top priorities of those helping them to mature in Christ. This is an excellent way to take our stand against Satan and his schemes, wielding "the sword of the Spirit" (Ephesians 6:18). Let us listen to God's voice.

Introduction
- Matthew 4:4—"Every word." Comparable to physical bread, therefore essential. If you don't stay in the word, you won't stay in the faith.

Work at your Bible study
- 2 Peter 3:15-16—Possible to distort scriptures to own destruction. Tremendous responsibility on us personally to stick with the truth.
- Yes, some passages are difficult to understand—but not impossible! (2 Corinthians 1:13). Strive to comprehend them yourself first, before asking others what they mean.
- 2 Timothy 2:15—Becoming a well-equipped workman (3:17), not being ashamed, developing competence in teaching God's word to others.
- 1 Peter 3:15—Equipped for evangelism: not just Bible knowledge, but being able to answer questions, helping others, gently and respectfully.
- James 1:22-25—It is useless to study the Bible without making the applications to our lives.
- Suggested: Psalm 1:2-3, 119 (entire), Ezra 7:10, Isaiah 66:2b, Matthew 24:35, Romans 15:4, 1 Corinthians 10:11, Colossians 3:16, 2 Timothy 2:7.

Practicals
- Have a set time to study your Bible daily. Spend daily time in the word (Joshua 1:8, Acts 17:11, Deuteronomy 17:18-20).
- Write down the convicting points and pray about them.
- Do well in church classes; make the most of any available local teaching programs.
- If you're reading the Bible for the first time, don't try to read straight through. Focus on the NT until you are quite familiar with it, then venture out into OT.

3—Faith, Works and Grace: The Balance

One of the greatest travesties in the church today is that new Christians are taught to depend on self, to struggle up the road of salvation by works. This attitude may be created before he/she comes to Christ, in the Bible study setting. But more often this is an acquired deficiency, learned through observation of "older" Christians. Such an orientation undoes the work of the cross. Equally sad, however, is the school of thought that prides itself on having arrived at a true understanding of grace, only to condone and even encourage lukewarm commitment to our Lord Jesus Christ. Clearly we must strike the balance—hence this study.

Faith
- Hebrews 11:6—We need faith to please God, but what is faith?
- James 2:14-16—Faith is more than intellectual belief—it results in action. Compare verses 20-24 with Genesis 22. Note the interrelationship between faith and obedience.

Works
- Ephesians 2:8-10—The Bible clearly teaches that we are not saved by our own effort, but this doesn't mean that God doesn't expect anything from us. It is an unearned gift, but it is conditional on obedience (2 Kings 5:1-15).

Grace
- Titus 3:5—We're saved not because of our righteous deeds, but by his mercy.
- Grace is unmerited favor or mercy. But the fact that we do not earn or deserve it does not mean that we can do as we like (Jude 4).
- 1 Corinthians 15:10—Grace will have its effect.
- Titus 2:11-14—It is because of grace that we strive to live self-controlled, upright and godly lives.

II. THE CHURCH: The Body of Christ

4—Relationships in the Body

When one enters the community of the redeemed, relationships are radically transformed! Instead of having ourselves as the centre of our focus, we are to "consider others better than ourselves" (Philippians 2:3). However, implementation of these biblical principles will never occur as long as we retain a defective concept of fellowship and the body. Church is not something we attend; it is an opportunity to tend to needs. And there are many needs to be tended to! If young Christians are not grafted into the body in a functional way, they may well be reclaimed by the world. And if that is what happens, we are failing (1 Corinthians 2:12-15). The most crucial time for integrating the young convert into the local congregation is the first few weeks—and even days.

Why different from the world's relationships?
- John 13:34-35—Jesus commands us to love each other as he has loved us. This quality of love is what makes us distinct as Christians.

- Mark 3:35—We are Jesus' brothers and sisters if we do God's will. Because of this common purpose, Christian relationships transcend even blood relations.

How are they different?
- 1 Peter 1:22—Our love for each other must be sincere and from the heart.
- 1 John 3:16—Jesus is our example. Our love for others can be measured by how much we are willing to sacrifice for them.

What does this mean in practice?
- 1 Thessalonians 5:12—Different people have different needs.
- 1 John 3:17—Look after each other's material needs.
- Colossians 1:28—Let's be concerned about each other's spiritual well being.

Conclusion
- Ephesians 4:29—Be edifying.
- Ephesians 5:21—Be submissive not only to leaders (Hebrews 13:17), but also to each other (Ephesians 5:21).
- Suggested: Acts 2:42-47, 4:32-35, Romans 12:5, 1 Corinthians 12:12-27, Hebrews 10:24-25, 13:1-2, James 1:19, 3 John 5.

Practicals
- Make it a point to phone and email other Christians.
- Spend time with other believers in order to build relationships (Hebrews 3:12-14).
- Pray for each other daily.
- Introduce yourself to at least one new person in each service for next month.
- Write notes and cards to your brothers and sisters.

5—The New Testament Church: Three Aspects
We demand book, chapter and verse for all our doctrines and practicesand rightly so. Hearing our Restoration Pleas, how does a young Christian respond when he sees practices he may never before have seen in his life? He is not used to *weekly* communion, and certainly not to *sacrificial* contributing. And what about the strange custom of "going forward"? This study provides scriptural explanation for these three practices in the New Testament Church.

Communion (Lord's Supper, Eucharist)
- Matthew 26:26-29—Passover supper (Jewish background). Bread is the body of Christ, wine is blood.
- 1 Corinthians 11:23ff—Jesus instituted the Lord's Supper. It is a proclamation of the Lord's death until he comes. Examine yourself before eating.

- Acts 20:7—Christians came together in order to break bread.
- It appears from the evidence of the NT and that of early church history that the Christians broke bread together at least once a week.
- Suggested: Exodus 12 (historical background), Mark 12:12-26, Luke 22:7-20, John 6:48-58, Acts 2:42.

Contribution (for needs of the church)
- Matthew 6:21—Your treasure is where your heart is.
- Matthew 6:24—Cannot serve both God and money, so make sure that God is first.
- Proverbs 3:9-10—Are you honoring God with your money? Give him the "firstfruits" of your income. Be responsible when you are away; leave your contribution behind (church needs it)
- 1 Corinthians 16:1-2—Taking up a collection to meet the needs of the poor is biblical.
- 2 Corinthians 8:1-15—Advance planning.
- 2 Corinthians 9:6ff—Good material on sacrificial giving...
- Suggested: Exodus 36:6-7, Mark 12:41-44, Luke 6:38, 1 Timothy 6:5-10, 17.

Confession of sin (e.g. coming forward in response to the preached message)
- James 5:16—Public confession. No private "confessional" in the Bible. Ask spiritual people to pray for you. Their prayers will be effective.
- Proverbs 28:13—You will not prosper if you keep sins inside.

6—One-another relationships: God's Plan

Although you will not find a doctrine of "discipling partners" explicitly spelled out in the New Testament, it is indisputable that the scriptures teach the necessity of one-another relationships. The importance of ongoing discipleship should be clear to someone before he makes Jesus Lord. This study aims to cultivate an attitude of openness on the part of the young Christian to input, as well as to remind him that, in the final analysis, it is the responsibility of the one who has confessed Jesus as Lord to persevere in his Christian growth.

Discipleship is not a human expedient; it is a clear command of God (Matthew 28:19).

Levels of discipling
- Hebrews 3:12—Others disciple us.
- Hebrews 4:12—The Word disciples us.
- Hebrews 5:12—We disciple ourselves.
- Hebrews 6:12—We are discipled by the faithful examples of biblical figures.
- Hebrews 12:12—The Lord (through circumstances requiring patience) disciples us, too.

Being discipled
- 2 Timothy 2:2—The teaching process: a chain reaction.
- Colossians 1:28-2:1—The goal is maturity/completeness/perfection. There will be difficulties in any one-another relationship, but try to realize that the challenges you receive are made in love. This is hard work.
- Proverbs 10:17—Attitude of openness to correction. If you have the wrong attitude, you will lead others astray.
- Proverbs 11:14—Ask for advice.
- Proverbs 12:15 and 15:12—Cherish challenge and initiate with the one helping you.

Discipling yourself
- Hebrews 5:11-14—Don't be slow to learn. By constant use (habit), train yourself. Ultimately, you are the one responsible for how you do spiritually. You cannot blame your failings on others.

Practicals
- Arrange a regular time to meet together each week with an older, more mature Christian.
- Strive for daily contact.

III. THE WORK: Becoming Like Christ
7—Hindrance: The Heart
The Bible speaks of the heart as the governing center of the whole man—intellectual, physical, and psychological, and thus a man's heart makes him what he is and gives rise to all his thoughts and actions. It is imperative that a young disciple be taught to guard his heart, to keep it sensitive and open to God's word.

Introduction
- 1 Samuel 16:7—God looks at the heart.

Problems of the heart
- Jeremiah 17:9—Deceitfulness: in the sense of feelings and impulses. Deceitful with regard to discerning the truth, or what is best.
- Mark 7:21—Sinfulness: the heart is the source of sin, as well as evil desires.
- Hebrews 3:12—Hardening: hearts can become hard, become unbelieving (doubt) and turn away from God.

The remedy
- Jeremiah 29:13—*Seek* God with all our heart. This verse is not just for non-Christians!
- Psalm 51:17—Cultivate a penitent, *contrite heart,* which responds quickly to God's Word.

- Psalm 119:11—Hide *God's Word* in our hearts.
- Proverbs 3:5-6—*Trust* in the Lord with all our hearts.
- Ezekiel 11:19-20—The Lord has placed his Spirit in our hearts to lead us in the right way.

Conclusion
- Proverbs 4:23—Above all else, guard your heart! It is the source of our spiritual life.
- Suggested: Genesis 6:5, 2 Chronicles 16:9, Psalm 51:10, Proverbs 14:12, 28:26, Ezekiel 18:31, 1 John 3:20.

Practicals
- Pray for a pure heart.
- Confess sin; be humble.
- Write out Bible verses that pertain to your heart.

8—Laziness, Idleness, Discipline

How many of us have had great dreams for how God was going to use us—how he would mold us into what he wanted us to be—and just when the going got rough, and the process became painful, we resisted, and perhaps even took a couple of steps backwards! Few of us are naturally disciplined; discipline must be learned. And yet without it, how do we suppose we will really grow? Surely that is fantasy! Discipline, therefore, must be built into our Christian lives from the earliest moment.

Introduction
- 1 Timothy 4:7—Train yourself to be godly. Physical training (sports) is of limited value, but spiritual training is immeasurably valuable. The Christian life is a process of training in righteousness.

Laziness
- Hebrews 6:12—Don't become lazy. Laziness is a constant threat to the life of every Christian, young or old. Imitate those who are patient, faithful and disciplined. Look for good examples; learn from them. Realize laziness is a sin!
- Suggested: Proverbs 12:1, 24:30-34, 26:13-16.

Idleness
- 1 Thessalonians 4:11ff—Be constructive members of society and of the church. Hard-working people win the respect of others. Try not to be dependent on anybody (do not go into/remain in debt). Both unemployment and underemployment can be detrimental to spiritual growth.
- 2 Thessalonians 3:3ff—Follow the example of disciplined people. Don't be a "busy-body"—appearing busy but not really achieving anything.

Discipline
- Heb 12:11-12—No discipline pleasant, but it yields a more satisfying life. Make your life count!
- Suggested: 1 Corinthians 9:24-27, 2 Timothy 2:4-6, Heb 5:14.

Practicals
- Make a timetable of how you use your time. Get some suggestions.
- Set some goals.
- Spend time with a disciplined person and learn from him or her.
- If you are not a punctual person, make an effort to be early.
- Suggested: *The Disciplined Life* by Richard Taylor and *The Seven Habits of Highly Effective People* by Stephen Covey.

9—Evangelism, Boldness, Tact

When it comes to evangelism, few young Christians possess both boldness and tact. We are tempted towards one extreme or the other: so tactful we say little, if anything, or so bold that tact is thrown to the wind. Boldness comes via prayer, and tact is developed through observation of those who are diplomatic. In view of the crippling effect of fear on new Christians—and old—and considering the number of tactical errors that are made by all, why we need a separate lesson on this important subject.

Evangelism
- 2 Corinthians 5:10-21—Because we know and fear God, we try to persuade others. We are Christ's ambassadors and God has given to us the ministry of reconciliation. It is not an option.
- Acts 8:1, 4—The early Christians were evangelistic—not just the leaders!
- 1 Peter 2:9-10—We are *all* a royal priesthood. There is no "clergy" today!

Boldness
- Romans 1:16-17—The gospel is nothing to be ashamed of because it has the power to save.
- Luke 9:23-26—If we are ashamed of Jesus and his words, he will be ashamed of us.
- Acts 4:29-31—Pray for boldness! God will answer your prayer.

Tact
- Matthew 10:16—Need to be wise/shrewd in our evangelism.
- *Negatives:*
  Proverbs 12:18—Beware reckless words.
  Proverbs 25:17—Avoid *too* frequent contact.
  Proverbs 27:14—Don't come on too strong.

- *Positives:*
  1 Corinthians 9:20-23—Accommodate yourself to your hearer.
  Titus 2:10—Make the gospel attractive.
  1 Peter 3:15-16—Show gentleness and respect.
- Suggested: Matthew 7:6, 2 Timothy 2:23-26.

Practicals
- Push yourself to be friendly and start conversations wherever you go. The Lord will use this.
- Invite people to come to church with you.
- Work on improving one area of your life in order to make the gospel more attractive.

10—Service with a Smile

When Jesus came to the earth, he came as a suffering servant (Mark 10:45). And he is still a servant, since he always lives to intercede for us (Hebrews 7:25). In following the Master, this is one area that we dare not play down, no matter how unglamorous it may seem. For, as Jesus taught us, the road up is the road down.

- Matthew 20:26-28—The way up it the way of service, opposite the way of the world. Jesus came to serve, not to be served.
- Philippians 2:3-8—Do nothing out of selfish ambition or vain conceit. Consider others better than yourselves—then you'll look to see others' needs met. For Jesus to come to earth was the supreme act of self-humiliation. We need to imitate this selfless example in our everyday lives.
- Luke 17:7-10—When we have served, our attitude should be that we have only done our duty. No complaining (Philippians 2:14); no expectation of reward.
- Colossians 3:23-24—Serve with all your heart! Realize that you are serving the Lord Christ, not men.
- Suggested: Psalm 100:2, Proverbs 3:27-28, John 13:1-17, Galatians 6:2, 10, Ephesians 6:7-8, Philippians 4:4-5.

Practicals
- Learn to serve without being asked. Look for needs.
- When asked to help in a particular way, *be responsible!* for example, duties such as children's ministry, ushering, communion, teaching, clean-up, office duty, and food preparation.

IV. OTHER NEEDS: Following God's Way

11—Academics: Obstacle or Opportunity?

God certainly expects excellence of Christian students: if not excellent results, at least excellent effort. Too often (undisciplined) students become Christians and then use evangelism or "church" as an excuse for mediocre performance. We must help students to see academics as a God-given responsibility. There is nothing "unspiritual" about studies. The unspiritual course to take is to neglect academics. Without perseverance the student suffers loss in character, discipline, confidence, and credibility—not to mention future prospects.

Clear commission
- 1 Corinthians 7:25—God called us to be Christians as students for a reason! We have a responsibility to glorify God in academics and evangelism.
- Colossians 3:22-23—*Attitude* is more important than *aptitude*. Academics are a vital part of your "spiritual" life. To have consistent motivation, work for God, not for self.

Evangelistic example
- 1 Thessalonians 4:11—A consistent example has an impact! Classmates will be drawn to those who can help others.
- Mark 7:37—People were amazed by Jesus' all-around excellence. You will amaze family and friends if you excel in all areas. "Ministry *through* academics, not *in spite of* academics."

Powerful preparation
- James 1:2-4—Persevering with academics leads to spiritual maturity: discipline, focus, faith
- Suggested: Proverbs 6:6, 18:9, Philippians 2:14-16, 1 Timothy 3: 7, 4:15-16.

Practicals
- Seek input in the area of academics.
- Get input from professors, lecturers, classmates.
- Attend every lecture. This is important for your example.
- Take good notes, and catch up on missed lectures.
- Go through homework within a day of receiving it and plan how you will get it done.
- Keep current at all times! For conscience's sake, as well as for practical reasons.
- Aim to sleep reasonably, especially during exams.
- Read "Effective Study Habits for University Students" at www. DouglasJacoby.com.

12—Christian Marriage: A Cord of Three Strands

God's Word and power provide us with everything we need for happy, godly, fulfilling lives in every area (2 Tim 3:17, 2 Peter 1:3, John 10:10). The area of marriage is crucial, and if marriage is not going well, serious spiritual problems will also be present. Indeed, Christian marriage is one arena in which disciples of Christ will dramatically outshine the many worldly examples surrounding them. A great marriage draws others to Jesus!

God's plan
- Marriage meets many of our deepest needs (Genesis 2:24, Proverbs 18:22). Your husband or wife should be your closest friend!
- Marry a Christian! (1 Corinthians 7:39).
- Marriage is for life (Matthew 19:9).
- Take advice! (Proverbs 15:22)

Worldly v. spiritual marriages
- Communication
  1. Time together (meals, spiritual talks, unscheduled time)
  2. Listening (especially needful for husbands)
  3. Express, don't suppress feelings
  4. No festering resentments (Colossians 3:13)
  5. Co-ordinate schedules; don't leave each other in the dark about the other's plans!
  6. Communication may increase conflict; expect it, don't avoid it!
- Selfishness
  1. Harsh husbands? (Colossians 3:19) Husbands must serve their wives, being considerate (1 Peter 3:7). Husbands should do their share of the housework, cleaning, taking care of children...
  2. Bossy/nagging wives (Proverbs 21:19, 25:24, 27:15). Wives must learn submission (Colossians 3:18, 1 Peter 3:5-6).
  3. Weak husbands? (henpecked) The man must be spiritual leader in the relationship (Eph 5:22-33).
- Hospitality
  1. Is home life centered only around each other, life in a cozy, selfish, private world?
  2. Hospitality is God's will! (1 Peter 4:9) open your home.
  3. Use hospitality in evangelism.
  4. This is the husband's responsibility even more than the wife's (1 Timothy 3:4)!
  5. An untidy home isn't inviting! (Proverbs 24:30-34)
- Spirituality
  1. Talk about spiritual things when together.
  2. Pray with spouse daily.
  3. Don't "protect" each other when there is lukewarmness or compromise (Acts 5:1-11); speak the truth in love! (Ephesians 4:15).
- Romance
  1. Don't deprive one another (1 Corinthians 7:5).
  2. Remember the special touches! (cards, flowers, presents, surprises...)
- Input
  1. Are you (two) closed to input? festering problems?
  2. Every marriage needs counseling! no one is above it!
  3. All marriages need counseling.

Practicals
- Pray together every day!
- Share your faith together.
- Share Quiet Times from time to time.
- Work on the church classes together. Expect the best of each other!
- Spend an evening a week alone together, showing your love for each other and really communicating.
- Read and discuss 1 Corinthians 13.
- Read Song of Songs to one another! (*Lover* and *Beloved* parts)
- Pray daily that you will be able to study with one couple together.
- "Double dates."
- Discuss your schedules together.
- Plan an overnight trip together (without the children).
- Read a great book on marriage and discuss it.[1]

13—The Christian Family: Parents and Children

The family is the basic social unit, and to understand the desperate plight our society is in, you need only to look at the desperate straits the average family is in! In stark contrast to families in the world, with their narrow outlook, poor communication, brewing resentments, undisciplined children, and decaying marriages, the Christ-centered family is a breath of fresh air and a ray of hope.

The family following God's Word is a happy, communicative, warm, loving, committed and fruitful family. Just as Christian marriage is God's wise plan for men and women to love and live together, so the Christian family is both God's answer to the ungodliness and selfishness of society and his plan for character development in his most precious gift to parents: their children.

Spiritual focus
- Chain of command (Christ—husband—wife—children)
- If you want a great family life, you need input!
- Aim to have an evangelistically fruitful family!

Bringing up children
- Basic need for security and happiness:
    1. Time—you'll need to re-order your priorities!
    2. Affection—without it, they will become insecure, cold, introverted, awkward around strangers.
    3. Spiritual examples (parents)—Ephesians 6:4, Deut 6:7.
- Discipline—it's unloving not to give it (Proverbs 23:13-14). Discipline is training.
    1. Encouragement is necessary (Colossians 3:21)
    2. Discipline is essential
        a. God commands it (Proverbs 22:15, 29:15, 17, 19, 21)
        b. The husband is the chief discipler.

    c.   Wife and husband should agree on the "rules," lest the children pick and choose whom to obey!
    d.   Areas of training (Proverbs 22:6)
- Respect toward authority
- Speech and openness
- Affection
- Manners
- Tidiness
- Moodiness

    e. Regular spiritual times with each child!

Other Important Matters
- Regular, consistent family devotionals.
- Be on time to church. Allow extra time, particularly considering the children. Plan to come early!
- Pray with the children before they go to bed.
- Have a weekly family time.
- If you have Christian children, work with the pre-teen or teen ministry. Embrace feedback. Don't be defensive.

Practicals
- Create a simple system of allowances and incentives for the children.
- Take the whole family out evangelizing. Reach out to other families as a family.
- Ask Christians you respect to recommend helpful books.[2]

Follow-up Studies: Closing Considerations
Follow-up studies can be covered at the rate of about one to two per week over the period of a few months. Depending on the needs, they may be used in any order. In addition to the studies presented in this chapter, it may be helpful to use some of the Guard the Gospel studies not covered in your personal study with the young Christian. And, by all means, do not consider that your work with a young Christian ends after the follow-up studies have been completed! No, for you are still only in the *middle*.

Notes
[1] For example, Sam and Geri Laing's *Friends and Lovers: Marriage as God Designed It* (Woburn, Mass.: DPI, 1996).
   [2] For example, Sam and Geri Laing, *Raising Awesome Kids in Troubled Times* (DPI, 1994) and Douglas & Victoria Jacoby, *The Quiver: Christian Parenting in a non-Christian World* (IPI, 2005).

17

In the Hall of Tyrannus

Effective Group Bible Discussions

An invaluable part of shining ever brighter is learning to share the faith not just with individuals, but also with groups. If you are like me, you will benefit greatly from the practicals offered in this chapter.

Luke records, "But some of them became obstinate; they refused to believe and publicly maligned the Way. So Paul left them. He took the disciples with him and had discussions daily in the lecture hall of Tyrannus" (Acts 19:9). Two thousand years ago, Paul saw how informal discussions were a great way to get the word out. His flexibility creativity allowed him to try new things and go with what worked. And so preaching in the synagogue gave way to the discussion group in the rented facility.

Discussion is fundamentally different to preaching. Preaching confronts forcefully; discussion confronts gently. Preaching is primarily one man interacting with the group, while discussion is every member in the group interacting. Many people not so eager to come to a "big" church service are actually enthusiastic when invited to a discussion. Another positive aspect is that the discussions give women opportunities to teach and to lead other women.

And so "the hall of Tyrannus" becomes a forum more attractive for many than the "synagogues." Ten suggestions on how to lead effective group discussions follow.[1]

1. Preparation

The first principle of effective discussions is preparation! Put in as much time as you need to produce an excellent study. (You want people to come back!) I can never forget my first study—though I would like to! My friend Gary asked me several times if I had practiced it, if I had thought it through. Even though my thinking was very muddled, I did not realize how ill prepared I really was. When my embarrassing, rambling stab at a unified discussion was finally over, one of my visitors patted me on the back, and said, "Nice try." More comments like that eventually sold me on the importance of preparation.

From that initial attempt as a bumbling teenager, within a few short years I would be leading effective group discussions brimming with visitors and interactive dialog – keeping the guests in my dormitory room long after the study had officially concluded. A few years later and

I was leading two studies that saw twenty people become Christians in the span of six weeks.

Preparation does take time, though. Don't short-change the "workers" who are inviting their friends to your study. Be prepared; your people will appreciate it!

2. Atmosphere

The physical atmosphere of the room is important. Is the room a bit warm—we don't want our guests getting *too* "comfortable"! Are there enough chairs? Are there refreshments – especially things to drink? (Refreshments also discourage people from running off as soon as the Bible is closed—singles especially!) Good lighting is helpful. I also suggest music as a cue for discussion. The music plays as people are coming in and socializing. You turn it off when it's time to start—and back on again once the study is over. This creates a relaxing "wind-down" effect, as well as making it easy to control the over-talkative guest! Be alert and consider how you can improve the physical atmosphere of the discussion setting.

3. Opening question

An opening question breaks the ice for visitors who may be wondering, "Why am I here?" Just getting people talking builds their confidence and imparts strength to the group. Obviously, when you are choosing an opening question, strike a balance between the overwhelming "Can you explain the meaning of the universe?" and the less taxing "What part of town do you live in?" Ideally, pose a question related to the topic of the discussion. (Do be wise who you start with – maybe best to begin with a friend you can rely on to share smoothly and relatably.)

Ask questions throughout the discussion. Draw people out and prompt them to agree, disagree, or simply add a different thought. Well presented and well thought out questions mean the difference between a dull, dry study and a stimulating, interesting discussion.

4. Illustrations, Analogies, and Humor

Without these elements, though you may preach the truth well enough, it is unlikely your audience will really grasp what you are trying to get across.

As for illustrations, never "preach" them. Always let your illustrations illuminate your scriptures. If you are telling a story, never drag the story out. Once you say "to make a long story short," it's already too late. And don't try to construct discussions around a single illustration. Analogies should be simple enough to require no further explanation. (Woe to the analogy which requires a second analogy to illumine it!)

As for humor, the best kind is that which arises spontaneously from your situation, whether originating in comments of the group or in creative lateral thinking. If you are planning humor into your "script," be careful that you do not belittle others, laugh at another's pain, or joke about sensitive areas – mental health, death, surgery, etc. Also, in these days of easily available and often recycled internet humor, watch out for the "new" joke that others may have already read six months ago!

5. Personal sharing

It's worth noting that humor is best used and easiest done through personal sharing. People enjoy laughing with people at their foibles, and humor used in this way will draw the people to the speaker. And remember, the main reason for being humorous in group Bible discussions is to make people relax, so that their hearts will open more easily to the Word.

Personal sharing should not shift the focus from Christ to you. Paul said, "We do not preach ourselves, but Christ Jesus as Lord, and ourselves as your servants for Jesus' sake" (2 Corinthians 4:5). Sharing is not entertainment, though it may be entertaining. It is to illumine the scriptures and to give people hope that they will be able to obey them.

6. Use of scripture

A Bible discussion is focused above all on *the Bible*. It is not an encounter group, therapy session, or ventilation forum. A few tips for bringing the Word of God to life:

- Use a contemporary version. In English there are over a hundred versions, of which the NIV (New International Version) is currently the most popular. Compare, for instance, the NIV rendering of 1 Peter 3:21 against the traditional KJV ("The like figure whereunto even baptism doth now save ye also..."!) The NLT (New Living Translation) is also very readable, as is the HCSB (Holman Christian Standard Bible), which has the additional advantage of being one of the most accurate versions out.
- Don't use too many passages in the study. Sometimes it is best to stick with just one passage. For example, you could base a whole study around Philippians 1:21 ("For to me to live is Christ, and to die is gain").
- Passages should be presented in context. It is poor training for the group, even if your point is correct, if the passages on which you are basing it do not support the point.
- Make it clear at the outset that the assumption of the study group is that the Bible is God's Word – that it will serve as the standard and authority for the discussion.

7. Overall length

My personal policy is to start the discussion a little "late" and finish a little early. Thirty to forty-five minutes is normally plenty of time! For example, with a 7:30-8:30 slot, guests begin arriving around 7:15 or 7:20 for an informal time of getting to know each other. Begin the discussion proper (turn off the music) at 7:40 and aim to finish around 8:20. With the music, refreshments, and more individual discussion following, most people will probably not begin leaving until after 8:45 or 9:00. As one sage said, "The mind can only take in as much as the seat can endure." (And remember, you said "discussion," not sermon!)

7. Rapport and captivation

It is interesting how some Bible discussion leaders just seem to "have a way" with visitors, and how others often seem to have conflicts. This comes down to rapport. Rapport with visitors starts before the discussion begins. Befriending potential troublemakers at this point can eliminate unnecessary embarrassment later. As the visitors are giving their names during the opening question, make a mental note of them—it will make a tremendous impression on them when they are called by name later. Ask visitors to read a chosen scripture. It is an easy task, and yet it helps them to feel involved and part of the discussion. Always thank whoever reads, whether a Christian or a non-Christian, but don't flatter. ("Wow, thanks, that was really great! I've never heard anyone read so eloquently before!") It's also vital not to belittle visitors' comments, no matter how much they disagree with you or how odd or silly they may sound. Try to correct them respectfully, but don't make fun of anybody. After the study, personally thank the visitors for coming and also thank them for their comments and/or questions and feedback. Make sure the evening ends on a positive note, so that the visitors are encouraged and want to come back again.

Contrary to how the word sounds, "captivation" is the ability to make the discussion and the evening so gripping that no one wants to leave. (Not making them feel captive against their will!) There will be the unspoken feeling, "What—the study is already over? I was enjoying myself so much I lost track of the time. Captivation requires that you as leader speak with dynamism, animation, depth, conviction, and personal warmth. Your enemies: monotone presentation, lack of gestures, shallowness, absence of heartfelt sharing and challenge, and clinical presentation of truth. Overall captivation will be a result of all ten points in this lesson. Like rapport, captivation for most of us is more of an art than a given. You can tell in your heart (after the study and even during it) whether the group was captivated.

9. Conclusion

Imagine you are on an airplane. The flight (running on time) is nearly over, and the captain announces that you are beginning the descent. The landing gear is down. You've put your seat into the upright position, stowed your tray table, and are enjoying the view out the window as the plane approaches the runway. Suddenly, about to land, it touches down – only to lift off awkwardly back into the air!

So it is with some Bible discussions. They should have ended seven minutes earlier. The "captain" falsely led the group to prepare for "landing," yet he hadn't adequately prepared for the conclusion. The troops are getting restless and the returns diminishing.

To avoid this situation, plan your wrap-up. Ensure that when it is time end, there is no false sense of conclusion. Recap the major points— not re-teaching, just summarizing them. This ensures that visitors will leave with a clear idea of what they have just learned. Plan a firm and definite conclusion. Do not assume you will "just know" when to stop!

10. Bringing visitors

What can be said after point 9, "Conclusion"? Only one thing. It goes without saying that a discussion without guests is a superfluous evangelistic event. The best way to guard against this is for you, as the leader, to set the pace in bringing non-Christians to the meeting. Leaders, you need to bring your own visitors!

How about you? Are you working that hard to spread the Word? I learned to lead discussions in my university years. Throughout most of this period (it was not short!), I averaged three or four guests a week to my group Bible study. (There were a good few times when ten or fifteen men and women I invited showed up!) Yet in the years following, I did not bring visitors as frequently.

I was an evangelist, and I remember clearly a challenge in 1990 from a fellow evangelist. He said, "It seems to me that *evangelists* should *evangelize*. What do you think about that, Doug? I don't see you bringing many guests." Instead of acknowledging my sin, I was defensive. "That isn't really my role. Others can bring them, I can give direction." (The problem was, I *was* "giving direction" – wrong direction!) Several years later (yes, years!) I repented of this lazy attitude. The visitors came, my personal ministry flourished, God gave (and still gives) the increase.   At this very moment, are you (evangelist or not) deftly deflecting challenges to share your faith? Are you "hard to pin down"? Don't be like I was. Isn't this why you bought this book, anyway? I guarantee you that if you as leader set the pace, you will rarely have to "challenge" the group very hard to follow. They will appreciate your genuineness, imitate your faith, and arrive at the discussion with a sense of anticipation and enthusiasm.

Conclusion

Brothers and sisters, that's how to lead stellar discussions! Nothing further needs to be said, does it?

Notes

[1] If you want even more ideas, consider the following *dos* and *don'ts,* which are good suggestions for everyone taking part in the discussion.

- Do share from your life—people are always interested in personal stories, provided they are of reasonable length. It makes them see you as a normal person with a normal life and helps them relate to you. Involve names of other people in the group Bible study in stories, as well as other comments.

- Do introduce your guests to others and vice versa—it makes them feel special and part of the group. They become more comfortable once they know people's names. Also, the more relationships that they develop in the church, the easier it is for them to make the transition to being Christians.

- Do share Bibles—make sure every visitor is looking at a Bible. Have Christians near all the visitors, to help them find the passages. Be relaxed and natural when helping them find a book in the Bible, lest they feel stupid. Be patient.

- Do be positive about your friends—avoid sarcasm and try to be as encouraging as possible without being false. It is very unusual in the world for people to express appreciation for qualities in anybody else's life. We should take the time to say things like "Joy is an important quality in anyone's life, and that's why I like spending time with Linda—she's a lot of fun."

- Don't use religious jargon—"quiet time," "prayer partner," and "when I was a [name of denomination], before I was a Christian" will be confusing at best and offensive at worst. People do not understand, and the jargon is perceived as bizarre. It makes it difficult for them to relate to you, and they may view you as part of a strange religious group.

- Don't come in late—lateness is selfishness! Group Bible discussions are designed to meet the needs of non-Christians. As a Christian, you are there to serve and help to fulfill those needs. By coming in late you can easily destroy the atmosphere that has developed.

- Don't answer every question—wait a few seconds. Give the more timid people a chance. However, don't let silence go too long. Visitors can answer some of the questions, and it makes them feel more at ease and part of the group when they get a chance to contribute.

- Don't be silent or appear bored—the visitors will reproduce your behavior. You are there to set an example, and if you look interested and excited, they are more likely to feel that way themselves. Avoid thumbing through the Bible or fiddling with your nails, glasses, shoelaces, etc.

- Don't disagree with the leader in public—if you have a crucial question to raise, do it later, after the study. You do not want to get the study off track. It distracts everyone and reduces the impact. If you are seen as conflicting with the leader, it can undermine the people's confidence that a right answer can be found. They may well reason, "If these two Christians can't even agree, you must not be able to know what is right—so why bother trying?" Of course this does not mean the leader is always right, or that it is always wrong to take a stand (Galatians 2:11). But the group discussion is probably not the best setting for this.

- Don't be too intense after the study—the group discussion was probably intense enough for them, so make them feel relaxed and at ease in the fellowship time afterward. People can take challenge for only so long, and then the law of diminishing returns takes over. Allow people to "digest" their spiritual food—don't force-feed another meal.

If each member will follow these simple *dos* and *don'ts,* the study will go smoothly. In short, each member must do his part—no more, no less.

18

A Fountain of Life
Fourteen Studies and How to Lead Them

Proverbs 13:14 states, "The teaching of the wise is a fountain of life, turning a man from the snares of death." To enable you to become the "wise teacher" whose evangelistic discussion group leads many to Christ, this chapter contains fourteen Group Bible Studies.

Each discussion is thoroughly presented, including passages, questions, and points. For group Bible discussion leaders, it's always a joy to come across new material. Hopefully these studies will whet the reader's appetite to design other new studies. The standard format studies in this chapter are:

I.	Jonah
II.	The Demon-Possessed Man
III.	Matthew 7
IV.	Naaman
V.	The Blind Man
VI.	Jesus, a Man of Power!
VII.	The Woman at the Well
VIII.	The Great "I am"

Variety is the spice of life, and innovation is the spice of group Bible studies. There are many times, in fact most times, when a "standard" study is the best choice. But if you are like most discussion leaders, you can slide into the rut of using those old, familiar studies time and time again. Non-Christian visitors—and especially the regulars!—will appreciate a change of pace or a variation in format. The following are six such studies.

IX.	Jehoiakim
X.	The Seven Churches
XI.	Herod's Dilemma
XII.	Convert the Heathen
XIII.	The Book of James
XIV.	The Man at the Pool

These last six studies "break the monotony" of the "one-more-night-on-the-Parable-of-the-Sower" syndrome. Relief is on the way!

Since one of the easiest ways to "melt the ice" is to ask a good (interesting or thought-provoking) opening question, most studies begin with a question ("Q") to "get things rolling.

I. Jonah (8ᵗʰ century BC)

This study moves through the four sections of the book of Jonah, allowing each person in the discussion group to identify which phase of Jonah's life best relates to his or her life.

Opening
- Q: If you had $50,000 to spend on a trip, what part of the world would you visit? Another good opening question is, What is the farthest away from (your current) home you have ever been?

1. Running away from God
   - Reading: Take turns reading first eleven verses. Assign different parts: Jonah, God, narrator, captain, sailors (in unison).
   - Q: What is Jonah doing and why?
   - A: We don't run from God—but from his will. (May read Psalm 139:7-9.)
   - Q: How do we do the same?
   - A: For non-Christians—avoiding becoming Christians... For Christians—not living Christian life—being caught up in materialism, sin, etc.
   - Personal illustration
   - Jonah slept—slept during storm, like Jesus (Mark 4:38), but Jesus slept because he knew he was in the hand of God. Do we have the humility to admit we're running from God, or do we blame God? Jonah had the humility to admit that he was the problem.
   - Q: What does Jonah do in verse 12?

2. Turning back towards God (repentance)
   - Reading: 1:12-2:1
   - Jonah's prayer—turning to God (repentance). God wanted Nineveh saved whether Jonah saved it or not. They too had to make a firm decision—repent.
   - Illustration: Share about one or two people you have studied the Bible with who illustrate the point.
   - Q: How do you define repentance?
   - A: Repentance means more than just saying "sorry." (May read 2 Corinthians 7:10-11—actions must back up our sorrow.)

3. Walking with God (obedience)
   - Reading: 3:1-5, 10.
   - Jonah could have made excuses: the city was too large, people too hard-hearted...
   - Q: What kinds of excuses do you make for not obeying God?

- Jonah obeyed—and the city repented in one day. This made Jonah so mad that he wanted to die—but he still obeyed God. (Jonah, representing the Jews of his day, was prejudiced against the Gentiles.)
- With us—obedience means going against our feelings and doing things not convenient at the time—resisting temptations to sin, giving up immoral relationships, evangelizing—even when not inspired to do so, going to church even when tired.
- Q: Have you denied yourself—are you going against feelings in your obedience to God or does your obedience entail only going with your feelings?

4. Running Ahead of God (If time is running short, omit this point.)
    - Leader summarizes Jonah 4
    - Jonah doesn't have a good ending—Jonah wasn't happy that everyone repented. This is like us today—prejudice against _____ (ethnic or national group). We think _____ are hard-hearted and have no chance of being right with God. Other prejudices—poor against rich, rich against poor, e.g.
    - Q: Jonah "obeyed God"—but why was he still wrong?
    - A: The problem was that Jonah did not deal with his heart. We can sometimes obey God on the outside but our hearts may not be right.
    - Q: In what areas might we obey outwardly but not with our hearts?
    - A: Going to church, reading Bible, praying without one's heart being in it.

Conclusion
- Get the visitors to summarize the points of this study.
- Challenge: Make sure you're running with God, and when you do, run with God from the heart.

II. The Demon-Possessed Man

Opening
- Q: What is one of the most frightening things you've ever seen?
- Reading: Mark 5:1-20 (assign to a series of volunteers, or go around the room).
- Note: The study is not centered on demon-possession or exorcism, but on how life is changed after an encounter with Christ.
- We will take a look at three aspects of his conversion: his (1) condition, (2) change, and (3) commission.

1. His condition
    - Paint picture of strange man. Believe it or not, you can learn from how this insane man, who lived naked in a graveyard and cut himself with stones, changed when he met Jesus.

- Q: As for us today—what are we living for? What is our purpose?
- Q: What difference does our life make?
- Q: Are we restless—always looking for more?
- Q: "Cut with stones"—How do we hurt ourselves today?
- A: Self-destructive habits
- Q: He was controlled by an evil spirit—what are some things we are controlled by?
- Personal illustration of a controlling sin.
- Q: He was scared of Jesus. Why do you think people today are scared of facing the truth?
- We must admit the condition we are in. Don't be proud. Face up to Jesus and find the truth in the scriptures.

2. His Change
   - Reading: Mark 5:6-7
   - Q: What does this tell us about him?
   - A: He has a desire to change, yet there is resistance. If you are undecided, come to church, come to a group Bible discussion, study privately...
   - If you are afraid of this challenge—you are more like this man than you thought. When you come to Jesus, there will be change.
   - Note: the pig farmers were doing nothing illegal. They were Gentiles raising pigs in Gentile territory (on the east side of the Sea of Galilee) for Gentile consumption.
   - Reading: Mark 5:16
   - Q: If you were one of the crowd, what changes would you notice?
   - A: The man is sitting there—at Jesus' feet! Fully clothed, in right mind, no longer the wild look—but peace, no longer hatred in heart—instead love, no longer confinement and frustration—now, right mind, purpose, etc. He met Jesus, and was changed drastically.
   - Reading: 2 Corinthians 5:17
   - Q: What does it mean to be a new creation?
   - A: Not just read Bible, not just go to church, not just have Christian friends. Concerns thoughts, motives, desires, purpose.
   - Q: Have there been such changes in your life?
   - Excellent time for leaders to share personally.
   - Q: Why did they plead for Jesus to leave?
   - A: He challenged them (verses 14-17)—he highlighted their own need.
   - Q: What are some things you need to give up to become a Christian?

3. His Commission
   - Q: What motivated him to spread the good news?
   - A: The mercy of the Lord (verse 19).
   - Note: the Decapolis, where "Legion" shared his faith, is the name of the Gentile *region* in which the demoniac had been living. (Speaking in the Decapolis does *not* mean that Legion evangelized ten cities.)

- Q: Did he have to be coerced into sharing his faith?
- Q: Is being evangelistic an option?
- Q: Why do people/Christians today not share their faith?

Conclusion
- We must realize our condition—lost. We must find truth in scriptures.
- We need to make a firm decision to change.
- As Christians, we have been commissioned to share our faith. It is our mission in life.

III. Matthew 7

Often an entire chapter of the Bible can be made into a study. The advantage of such an approach is that it keeps the study in one place, avoiding too much flipping from page to page. It is easier for the regulars to anticipate where the leader is going. Moreover, passages can be explored with much greater depth than in a study that relies on three or four separated sections of scripture. Finally, if time is getting short or if one passage has received a disproportionate amount of attention, the leader can skip over one or two of his points without losing the effect of covering the chapter thoroughly.

Reading tip: Have only the section you are about to discuss be read. (Read a section, discuss it, read the next, and so on...)

Opening
- Explain that we are going to study just one chapter of Matthew, the third and final chapter of the "Sermon on the Mount."

1. Judging others
   - Reading: Matthew 7:1-5
   - Q: Is it wrong to judge others?
   - Describe dramatically what verse 4 is saying.
   - Jesus is condemning hypocritical judging. Not all judging is not wrong. In the New Testament many types of judging: hypocritical (Matthew 7:1), slandering or grumbling against a brother (James 4:11), superficial judging, before getting all the facts (John 7:24), disciplinary "judging" for members of the church (1 Cor 5:12), and final judgment, reserved for God alone (Hebrews 10:30), to name just a few.
   - Q: Why do people so often accuse well-meaning Christians of "judging" them?
   - A: They are defensive because of their own sin. (Concede that sometimes Christians are less tactful than they ought to be.)

2. Pearls to swine
   - Reading: Matthew 7:6
   - Q: What does Jesus mean? Is he saying that some people are swine?

- Explain that Jesus taught we are to love all men, but because of the need to get the message out we need to focus on those who are willing, or open. Refer to Matthew 10:14 if necessary. By the way, here is a perfect example of the need for using one's judgment, proving that the judging condemned in verse 1 is not referring to all judging.

3. Seek and you will find
   - Reading: Matthew 7:7-11
   - This is a very positive promise! There are many things you could seek in life and yet never find (riches, UFOs, promotions, good grades, etc).
   - Q: Why does God promise this?
   - A: God wants people to seek him. Express appreciation for everyone showing up for the Bible discussion.
   - Humor: Illustrate verses 9-10 graphically, describing a restaurant that serves stones and snakes.
   - Q: Why is it that many seem to be seeking but few are finding?
   - A: Looking in wrong place, not seeking the kingdom of God first (Matthew 6:33), seeking with wrong motives, etc.

4. The Golden Rule
   - Reading: Matthew 7:12
   - Point out that in most religions it is the "negative" golden rule that appears. Christianity turns it all around.
   - Q: Which is more challenging, the negative or the positive version?
   - Challenge: Live just *one* day putting others first in everything. Many claim to be living by the Golden Rule, but what they usually mean is that they try not to hurt other people—the *negative* golden rule.

5. The narrow road
   - Reading: Matthew 7:13-14
   - There are only two roads—no comfortable third option.
   - Comment: If you are comparing yourself to everyone else, and think you're as good as the next person, realize that being in the majority is not necessarily a good thing. It means you're lost!
   - Q: Why is it that only a few are finding? Is it that God does not want a lot of people in heaven?
   - A: No—few finding means few are seeking.

6. False prophets
   - Reading: Matthew 7:15-20
   - Q: How can we tell the false from the true prophets?
   - A: Look at their fruit.
   - Q: What sorts of people do you think could be false prophets?
   - A: Fakes and frauds, people who deny Jesus—even nice people and clergymen.
   - Q: How do false prophets gain a following?

- Q: What is it that makes them *false* prophets?
- A: They don't follow God's word.

7. "Lord, Lord"
   - Reading: Matthew 7:21-23
   - Q: Are these religious people?
   - A: Definitely.
   - Q: Are they committed?
   - It would seem so—verse 22.
   - Q: Are they sincere?
   - A: There is no indication to the contrary.
   - Q: Are they saved?
   - A: No.
   - Q: Why not?
   - They haven't done the will of God (verse 21).
   - They were relying on their own experiences, and they made a dangerous assumption: that they were saved, when in fact they were not following God's word.

8. Wise and foolish builders
   - Reading: Matthew 7:24-27
   - Q: What is the solid foundation we should build on?
   - Q: How do we fail to build on the solid foundation?
   - A: We neglect to put Jesus' words into practice.
   - Q: What does the "great crash" refer to?
   - A: Judgment Day, the storms of life, or both.

Conclusion
   - Reading: Matthew 7:28-29
   - Q: What kind of teacher was Jesus?
   - A: Authoritative.
   - Q: Why are so few people (including preachers) these days confident and authoritative?
   - A: They lack conviction, don't know the Bible, are living double lives, etc.
   - Let's be confident as we live out the words of Jesus and share them with others.

IV. Naaman

2 Kings 5:1
   - Q; Who was Naaman? What kind of person was he?
   - A: Great man, very popular, well respected, valiant, good leader, etc. Name a few modern military chiefs.
   - Q: What was his problem?
   - A: Leprosy (or some similar skin condition).
   - Q: Can anyone describe what leprosy?

- Leader—look up the disease and be prepared to describe it.
- Although Naaman's disease was probably in its early stages, a horrible future was awaiting him if he did not get help.
- Q: Has anyone ever seen the Michael Jackson "Thriller" video?

2 Kings 5:2-6
- Q: What advice is Naaman given?
- Q: What does Naaman do?
- Q: What is the King's response?
- Q: Look at the things Naaman takes with him. Why does he take so much with him?
- A: In order to pay for a cure.
- Q: Is Naaman's health important to him?
- Q: What are the things that we, today, may consider important to us?
- A: Health, money, family, career, academics, food, sports, relationships, etc.
- Q: In eternity, though, what's the only thing that will matter?
- Our relationship with God. Many of the things mentioned are very important. We do need to do well academically, take care of our families, health, etc. But ultimately the thing that is most important is not our physical health but our spiritual health!

2 Kings 5:7-10
- Q: What happens when the King of Israel receives the letter?
- A: He gets very upset, begins to despair. He thinks that the King of Aram is trying to pick a quarrel with him and in his sorrow he tears his clothes.
- Q: Who is Elisha?
- A: He was a prophet, the man of God.
- Q: What does he do when he hears of the king's predicament?
- A: He says to send Naaman to him.
- Q: Why does Elisha say, "He will know that there is a prophet in Israel?" He is expecting God to work through him to cure Naaman. He knows God's power.
- Q: So what does Naaman do?
- A: He goes to Elisha.
- Q: Then what happens?
- A: Elisha sends out his messenger with specific instructions.
- Q: If today we want to find out God's instructions in order to be cured spiritually, where do we go?
- A: The Bible.

2 Kings 5:11-12
- Q: The instructions that Elisha gave, are they difficult to understand?
- Q: What is Naaman's response?
- Q: Why? How do we do this today?

- A: People today may allow pride to prevent them from being cured spiritually—for example, not willing to give up control of their lives to God.
- Preconceived notions—"I thought..." many have preconceived ideas of how to obtain God's spiritual cure, forgiveness of sins (infant baptism, pray Jesus into your heart, born a Christian) rather than obeying God's Word.
- Rationalization—these instructions, when considered, do sound too ridiculous to be true. Some today rationalize God's plan of salvation. For example, "how can just being dipped in water cause your sins to be forgiven?"
- Embarrassment—being a respected commander he might have felt silly obeying these instructions. Some today are embarrassed to be known as Christians, and to live the Christian life.

2 Kings 5:13-14
- Q: Would Naaman have been prepared to do "some great thing," like climb Mount Everest to be cured?
- A: Yes. (verse 13).
- Too often people are prepared to go out and do great things for God, like raising money for charities, helping the poor, sick, etc, but they are not prepared to follow the simple steps necessary to be spiritually cured—repent and be baptized.
- Q: What does Naaman do?
- A: He obeys—he dips seven times, and he is cured.
- Q: Would he have been cured if he had only dipped five times or six times?
- No!
- What if he had been sprinkled as opposed to dipped?
- A: No!
- There was nothing in the water that cured him; it was God's power; but only after he had obeyed completely. Example: when you are prescribed a medicine for an illness, the medicine cures you, but it will do no good if you just sit and look at the bottle. You must obey the instructions and drink the medicine.

2 Kings 5:15-16
- Q: Why does Naaman offer Elisha a gift?
- He is grateful and acknowledges God's power working through Elisha.
- Q: Why doesn't he take the credit for himself—after all, he's the one who dipped himself seven times?
- A: He was cured, but not by his own actions. It was by God's power. Similarly, our salvation is not earned, but comes from God through faith shown by obeying his commands.
- Q: Naaman ended up by saying, "Now I know that there is no God in all the world except in Israel." How did he come to this conclusion?

- A: By obedience. If we are prepared to put God's commands into practice we can be certain whether or not he exists. Spiritual health is so important, there is so much at stake, that it is illogical not to "test" God's instructions (the Bible), and see if it is true.

V. The Blind Man (John 9)

The entire study comes from this single chapter. As things turn out, all characters in the story are blind, except for Jesus. The incredible irony of the situation (spiritual blindness) is heightened as the story progresses and we see that all characters have this spiritual disease in common, though in different ways.

Opening
- Q: "What's one sickness (disease or medical condition) you would dread getting, and why?" Possible answers: cancer, diabetes, leprosy, brain tumor, deafness, amputation... As the leader, you go last, and mention blindness.

Blind Physically
- Explain that the first character on the stage is a man who's been blind from birth. Bring it to life: imagine never having seen nature, buildings, TV, the faces of friends and family... Intense!

Blind Disciples
- Reading: John 9:1-7
- Q: Who's really blind here?
- A: The disciples! They are "blind" because they can't see the man for what he really is: a human being in need. They see him rather as a *theoretical problem*. Discuss their preconception: in this case specifically, that disease is the result of sin—bad karma! It's amazing how religious people throw around terms like "the love of God" and "heaven and hell," and yet are so hardened to the world around them! This discussion is about spiritual, not physical, blindness (verse 5).

Blind Neighbors
- Reading: John 9:8-12
- His neighbors and those who frequently saw him also are "blind."
- Q: Is it surprising they didn't recognize him? How were these neighbors blind? How can we be around the same people day after day without ever really "seeing" them? What are relationships in the world like? Do people care about their neighbors? How should Christians be different? (These are just a few of the questions you could throw out to stimulate discussion.)

Blind Pharisees
- Reading: John 9:13-17
- The Pharisees are "blinded" by their traditions. (Be sure to explain that Jesus did not violate the Old Testament, only the Pharisaic interpretation.)
- Q: What sorts of traditions obscure the truth for us?

Blind Families
- Reading: John 9:18-23
- Peer pressure and fear of rejection are powerful forces in blinding people to the truth. Share about a time *you* gave in to peer pressure.
- Q: Would traditional religion really reject someone today just because he/she was trying to follow Jesus? Why?

The Blindness Continues
- Reading: John 9:24-34 (The leader should read this section. Read dynamically and dramatically! Be animated during this transition section, though spending no more than about three minutes in reading and explanation.)

Spiritual Sight
- Reading: John 9:35-39
- Q: What's 20-20 vision spiritually? What do you notice about the man?
- A: Willing to take a stand on truth, not popular consensus; open to Jesus, despite limited knowledge; respects (worships) God. How can we open ourselves to the truth about Jesus?

Paradox of Blindness
- Reading: John 9:40-41
- The Pharisees are offended by Jesus' comment.
- Q: What did he really mean?
- A: People who claim already to see (who aren't really open) are blind, while those who recognize their blindness (or ignorance) can see.
- Are you an open person? Can you really see? Or are you controlled by your preconceptions, traditions or what others think?

Conclusion
- Q: Which is worse, *physical* or *spiritual* blindness?
- A: Spiritual blindness is much worse—you never learn the truth about life, God or even about yourself. Many think they see, but they're blind.
- Q: If the story continued and *you* were included, what would be said about you?

VI. Jesus, A Man of Power

This study has many possible verses, so choose the ones you can most best teach with conviction. As we will see, Jesus was a man of power! For first-timers, this will be a study full of surprises!

Opening
- Q: What pictures of Jesus are common in our society? Or what concept were you taught growing up?
- Emphasize what Jesus is *not*: (1) Effeminate—he was not "a woman with a beard" who uttered nice things, (2) a weakling—he was a strong ex-carpenter, no fixed address, direct and to the point, (3) insecure or indecisive—he had a clear life objective and a calm demeanor, not from meditation, but from knowing he was doing the right thing. This strength and confidence can be traced back to his childhood.
- Reading: Luke 24:19—After his death, people remembered Jesus Christ as a powerful man, not a sissy.

Pictures of Jesus:
- Luke 4:1-4—Power to resist temptation! Discuss several activities associated with "being a man." Real men don't follow the crowd at parties to show he can "hold his liquor"; real men go against the stream when it's flowing in the wrong direction.
- Luke 4:28-30—Authority! Taking a stand against prejudice, first message to hometown! They try to throw him off a cliff. If twenty or thirty men tried to throw you out the window, could you stop them? Clearly Jesus was no pushover! His authority was felt.
- Luke 4:33-37—Speaks sternly to demon. I would have fled in terror!
- Luke 4:42—Up early after busy night. *Packed*, not *wimpy* schedule!
- Luke 7:14—Against social convention when necessary. Imagine the guts needed to stop a funeral procession!
- Luke 11:37-39, 44-46—Strong talk to religious leaders—as guest at a dinner party! Have you ever talked to anyone that way?
- Luke 12:49-51—What drive he had! What a radical message!
- Luke 13:24—"Make every effort": Greek *agonidzesthai*, contend for the prize = agonize. To follow Jesus you have to really "go for it"!
- Luke 23:34—It takes strength to forgive. Any fool can harbor a grudge or take revenge, but it takes a real man to love and to forgive!

Conclusion
- Reading: Luke 2:34-35
- People reacted strongly to Jesus, because he was such a strong character. Is this the Jesus you want to follow? If so, you are destined to become more and more like him. Watch out!

VII. The Woman at the Well (John 4)

Have you ever had a study with only a few visitors? Don't get frustrated – get creative! This study meets needs of both Christians (we need to share our faith) and non-Christians. It's rewarding to study an entire chapter of the Bible, and avoids unnecessary turning of pages in an extended trek across the testaments.

Opening
- This simple story has two main characters: a woman of Samaria and Jesus. The Samaritans were half-caste racially and half-Jewish in their religion, hated by the Jews as compromisers. But Jesus never gave in to prejudice. In fact, he makes Samaritans the heroes of his stories. (Remember the Parable of the Good Samaritan and the Healing of the Ten Lepers, Luke 10 and 17?) Background: the Samaritans, who came into existence in the 8th century BC (2 Kings 17), eventually built their own temple atop Mt. Gerizim. It was destroyed in 129 BC, but the Samaritans still claimed that this was the place where people were to worship the Lord, not Mt. Zion (in Jerusalem).

Jesus at the well
- Reading: John 4:4-6.
- Q: How many of you have had a long day?
- Q: What are you like when you're tired?
- Describe what you are like when you first wake up, or how you feel when you come home from work.
- Jesus is taking a break. He didn't just cruise through life without any effort. He was human. He felt fatigue, understood all the pain, sweat, hunger, and thirst that we experience.
- Q: What do you like to drink when you're really thirsty? Jesus offers something far better.

Jesus initiates a conversation
- Reading: John 4:7-9.
- Jesus goes against social conventions. In his day, it was not the custom for Jews to talk to Samaritans.
- Q: What is your experience of prejudice? (Good opportunity for personal sharing.)
- Also, this is a *man* starting a conversation with a *woman*.
- Q: What do you think she might have been thinking when he first started speaking to her? What would you feel if you were the woman?
- Following Jesus means we need to see social conventions in perspective. It *can* be okay to talk to strangers. And men can talk to women out of pure motives.

Jesus shares his faith
- Reading: John 4:10-26.

- He is willing to speak personally to her, even though she's a stranger (verse 18).
- Q: How readily do you talk to strangers?
- He turns the conversation in a spiritual direction, and arouses her curiosity (verse 10). Jesus knows he has something to offer! People pay money for books and courses on becoming confident people. When we know the truth and what life is all about, we don't have to psyche ourselves up to feel important or act big. It's natural.
- Q: What is "living water"?
- What a contrast to her daily routine: making the journey on foot to the well and back a couple of times a day, carrying the heavy water jar, running out of water and having to return again. Outside of Christ our limited resources are fast depleted. In Christ, they never need to run dry.
- The woman at the well progresses in her realization of who Jesus is: from Jewish man (verse 9) to "sir" (verses 11, 15) to "prophet" (verse 19), and finally Messiah (verse 25). Your appreciation of Jesus will deepen the longer you know him.
- If you're meeting him for the first time, you'll very soon realize he's far more than a wise teacher, or even a prophet. You're meeting God!

Disciples challenged by Jesus' example
- Reading: John 4:27-35.
- Q: What does he mean by the fields being "ripe"? What happens when a crop is left too long in the field?
- A: People are ready and waiting; we must act fast!
- Q: How do you refresh yourself when you are tired?
- Jesus' food is evangelism (verse 34)—it keeps us going when we're tired, too. Some say, "I feel too tired to give." Give, and your energy will come back!

The result of one conversation
- Reading: John 4:39-42.
- The Samaritan woman affects her whole community.
- Q: Are you having any noticeable impact on your community? What difference does your life make in the world?
- Anyone can share his faith! This woman was a "beginner." Share about yourself as a young Christian—how little you knew but how a simple faith moved you to action.

Concluding challenges
- Now, having studied John 4, we all know as much about Jesus as she did—even more! Doesn't God expect us to respond in the same way?"
- Take time after the study to read the rest of the gospel of John.
- Disciples—share your faith and have the perspective of Jesus.

- Others—begin a relationship with Jesus as soon as possible. Jesus offers all of us "living water." Why wait? Go for it today.

VIII. "I Am" Statements of Jesus

This study follows the "I am" statements of John, and is excellent for beginners, members of other world religions, and "enlightened" or liberal thinkers who are offended by the idea that one single religion might have the truth. Expect lots of discussion—the points are simple.

Opening
- Q: If you were *extremely* hungry, where would you go to eat?

Jesus the bread of life
- Reading: John 6:35
- Q: What keeps you going when you are tired or inwardly hungry (lack of motivation, focus, perspective, joy, good relationships…)?
- Q: What does it mean to be *spiritually* hungry or tired?
- The O.T. says (Ecclesiastes 3:11) God has set eternity in our hearts. We are *all* religious, or spiritual, whether we realize it or not. But until a relationship with God fills the empty place in our lives, we will never be truly satisfied.
- This statement is either true or false. If it's false, don't worry; but if it's true, the implications are incredible!

Jesus the light of the world
- Reading: John 8:12
- Q: As a child, were you afraid of the dark? Why were we afraid? What's the darkest place you've ever been in? What does it mean to be in "darkness"? (Not sure where you are going in your life, confused, fearful, accidentally injuring yourself…)
- Do you know where you're going in your life? (Or are you always guessing, hoping…?)
- What a bold claim: "I am *the* light of the world"! Jesus does not point to the light and say, "*There* is the light of the world," but *I am* the light…
- There's no in-between! Darkness *or* light, no "gray area." Again, this statement cannot be true *and* false; it's *either* true *or* false!"

Jesus the Good Shepherd
- Reading: John 10:14
- What's the difference between a good boss and a bad boss?
- A: Honesty, personal concern, being a good listener…
- In the same way, Jesus is a *good* shepherd. We are the sheep.
- Q: Why do you think the Bible describes us all as "sheep"?
- God cares about our happiness, about our feelings. He wants us to have the best life possible (John 10:10). But it's not just a good feeling God is offering us; God desires a personal relationship with us. He's even willing to go after us when we stray away. Maybe he's going after you now!

- Jesus is the bread of life and the light of the world, yet the concept of the shepherd is more personal.

Jesus the resurrection
- Reading: John 11:25
- Q: Do you believe in eternal life? What does that mean?
- It's not reincarnation Jesus is offering (Hebrews 9:27), nor is it an "afterlife" Jesus promises (everyone will have that), but eternal life with God! We all will die one day. For worldly people, that is the end. It's awful, irreversible. But for people who know Jesus, it's just the beginning. It's terrific, and no one would want to reverse it!

Jesus the only way
- Reading: John 14:6
- This is an incredibly exclusive claim! People don't "accidentally" believe in Jesus (without knowing it)! It's a conscious decision. (Possibly refer to John 3:18.) In the same way, you don't get married by accident. It's by mutual agreement and happens at a specific point in time. Thus if Jesus is right, no other religion is valid. (We can see why Jesus received such opposition!)
- Like all the other claims of Jesus, it's either true or false; don't monkey around with Jesus' claim! Accept it or reject it.
- Q: How would someone's life change if they really believed this?
- A: In his or her attitude to the Bible, praying to God, eagerness to be at church, evangelism...

Conclusion
- There are other possible "I am" verses we could have looked at (8:58, 10:7, 15:1, etc). But this assortment of just five of the amazing statements of Jesus is enough to give us a good picture of how radical a character he was.
- Q: Is this the Jesus you were shown before? Or is a lot of this brand new?
- Q: Why do you think people misunderstand Jesus today? Why do they fail to realize the seriousness and uniqueness of his claims?
- A: People are unwilling to face opposition, make the time for study and activities, come clean... We need to think through the implications of what Jesus said about himself and make changes accordingly.
- Read one of the gospels and get an accurate picture of Jesus.
- Begin studying the Bible with someone who has a relationship with Jesus already.
- Start taking a stand on the teachings of Jesus. You will notice how well they work, how few practice them, and how your own life is changing for the good.

IX. Jehoiakim

This study is a highly creative way to approach the subject of the Word of God. It falls into two parts. The beauty of the discussion is that the participants create the study.

Opening
- Begin by turning to Jeremiah 36. Assign readings: verses 1-3, 4-6; then the leader summarizes verses 7-19; then have verses 20-26 read.
- Explain that everyone present in the room will be creating the study. The object is to play "Jehoakim"—to identify undesirable elements in the Bible and then "cut them out." The leader explains the aspects of the Bible to be deleted may be things which people have a hard time accepting, or which the individual offering the suggestion has a hard time obeying. Each alteration must be identified by an "undesirable" scripture.

Break
- It is during the break that the difficult parts and accompanying scriptures are to be located. Make sure that all the non-Christians come up with something—after all, the study is for them! Christians need to be alert and help them voice what they are thinking during the intermission.
- Let the break run for ten minutes (serve refreshments).

Second part
- The group re-assembles.
- The leader has each participant read the passage he has chosen for deletion. (No need for everyone to turn there.) The reason for deleting the passage from the Bible is explained.
- This is not a time for discussion; the leader just takes down the verses and objections on paper. (Common deletions include verses against lust, church attendance, the existence of hell, etc. It is fun to see what the group comes up with!)
- Next the leader brings to life the new "version" of Christianity. Going through the list of corrections he got from the group, he paints an enticing picture of the "easy" version of Christianity now that the Bible has been edited. "Wouldn't that be great?" the leader says.
- It also be a time to suggest a name for this new, improved Bible.

Then return to Jeremiah 36:27-28, 31-32. Ask the group what the lessons to be learnt are.

Conclusion
- Ignoring the Bible, or parts of it, no more changes the truth than ignoring a problem or a disease makes it go away (Jeremiah 6:13-14). Something must be done. We have no right to play games with God's word.
- Telling the truth may make you unpopular, but God is the only one whose opinion really counts.

X. The Seven Churches

Revelation 2 and 3 provide a very clear outline for a seven-part study that can be delegated to various members of the discussion. The leader introduces the topic, and then assigns each church to one or more individuals to study and briefly summarize. After allowing ten to fifteen minutes for preparation, people report on the messages to each of the churches.

The leader follows each report by making practical applications.

Tips

- This is an especially good study for larger groups, especially where there are at least seven guests and seven believers.
- Be sure to place at least one fairly knowledgeable person in each group.
- The leader usually takes the seventh church because it is the most challenging.

XI. Herod's Dilemma

Get ready for a lively time! (Not a study for leaders afraid of the theatric!)

Opening

- Q: What is one difficult decision you have had to make?
- Reading: Mark 6:14-25
- Q: Why did Herodias have a grudge against John?
- A: Because he said it was morally wrong for Herod to marry her.
- Q: What decision must Herod now make?
- A: To kill or not to kill John.
- At this point, split the group into two teams. Assign a leader to each team. Be sure you split the teams in a balanced way, with a dynamic leader for each team.
- You take the role of King Herod. One of the teams is to advise you to kill John the Baptist. The other is to advise against it. Give the teams ten minutes while you go out and make the coffee.

Argumentation

- When the ten minutes are up, have the teams take turns advising you for and against killing John.
- (Be sure to speak to the more mature Christians in the discussion beforehand to ensure a great spirit of involvement and enthusiasm.)
- Following are some possible arguments that may be made. This is not the structure of the discussion, just a peak at how it might go. (As "Herod," your job is not to advise them how to advise you, though your helpers may influence the groups through some of these suggestions.)

Arguments for Killing John	*Arguments against Killing John*
1) "Think of your guests!"	1) "Think of John's supporters; there are many."
2) "He is causing trouble all over the place, telling us to repent, sell our possessions, etc. He's upsetting the system.	2) "It would be murder."
3) "You swore it to your wife's daughter!"	3) "You know he's righteous!" (See verse 20.)
4) "It'll please Herodias."	4) "Your conscience will always bother you."
5) "He'll stop bothering you about Herodias.	5) "If you give in to Herodias, she'll always be one up on you!"
6) "You'll make an example of him for other people who make Trouble. People will fear and respect you.	6) "The Bible says it is okay to free yourself from an unwise commitment" (Proverbs 6:1-5).

Closing
- When the teams have exhausted their arguments, call the debate to a close, and say, "Let's find out what Herod in fact does."
- Reading: Mark 6:26-29
- Q: Why did Herod kill John the Baptist?
- A: Herod gave in to peer pressure (verse 26). Today, we must not give in to the world's view of Christianity, even if our friends and family oppose us.
- Q: By killing John, what did Herod do to his chances of getting right with God?
- A: He may have "killed" his last chance. This can happen to us today when we refuse to change things in our lives and become Christians.
- Q: By killing John, Herod silenced the voice that was convicting him (verse 17). How can we do that today?
- A: Don't study the Bible, don't come to church, don't have Christian friends...
- Challenge: Don't be like Herod. Make the right decision about Christianity.

XII. Convert the Heathen

In this study the leader plays the role of a heathen—usually a drunk who has come into the study after being told that he has one week to live (cirrhosis of the liver, or something to that effect). The alcoholic appeals to the group to teach him—using the Bible—step by step what he must do to be saved.

Tips

- Plan ahead for the kinds of issues you want to focus on. It may be the definition of faith, the need for total repentance, or the terms of discipleship. The discussion of baptism can be extended and explicit or fairly superficial.
- As the leader, you will need to explain the ground rules *before* you start your role playing. Do not break out of character until the very end of the session.
- In your acting, invent excuses, throw questions back to the group, ask whether a particularly good point might not just be someone's own "interpretation."
- Be animated!

The study works best when the visitors are either irreligious or already aware of the plan of salvation.

XIII. The Book of James

Like the study on the Seven Churches in this chapter, this is a particularly ripe portion of scripture to allow members of the discussion to study and present. (It may also be presented by the leader in a more conventional way.)

James divides neatly into five chapters, and the abundance of sharp, penetrating statements gives even the novice confidence in understanding the book. (In fact, there are so many good points that it is possible to extend the discussion into a two or three part series.)

For a period of ten minutes or so, five small groups discuss their chapter and the points they would like to share when the whole group reassembles. Proceed chapter by chapter.

Tips

- The leader should do his best to ensure there is at least one Christian in each group.
- He should also know the book (and its background) thoroughly and to have a list of points from each chapter.

Here is a outline of some of the points that may emerge from each chapter.

Chapter 1

- 2-4: Joyful in trials because trials bring maturity (also 1:12).
- 13-15: Truth about temptation and sin. We do not "fall" into sin; we walk into it. Eventually the feeling of guilt subsides, leaving us spiritually dead.

- 19: "Quick to listen…"—a lesson in itself.
- 22-25: Listening is deceiving if not accompanied by action. (I.e. those who attend church or Bible discussion without really changing.)
- 26: "Worthless religion"—very convicting for many foul-mouthed nominal Christians.
- 27: "Pure religion" means social concern.

Chapter 2
- 1-12: Condemnation of prejudice
- 14-19: Faith plus good deeds: good illustration is husband who says "I love you" to his wife but never shows it.
- 24, 26: Faith without deeds is dead.

Chapter 3
- 1: Strict judgment for teachers—discuss why.
- 3-12: Hazards of the tongue. It is useful to discuss various verbal sins.
- 13-17: Wisdom of the world versus wisdom of God.

Chapter 4
- 4: You can't love both God and sin; love of world equals hatred toward God. E.g. "It's not that I don't love God, it's just that I like getting drunk" etc. Parallel: your wife and another man: "It's not that I don't love you, John. It's just that I love Peter, too." (Create hypothetical examples using people in the discussion for husband, wife, lover.) God is saying you cannot have it both ways; when you choose the world, you sever your relationship with him.
- 13-16: Put God in your plans; decisions about course, career, where to love, etc.
- 17: One of the most convicting verses in the Bible. Sins of *omission* as well as sins of commission.

Chapter 5
- 12: Let your "yes" be yes. Practical areas: punctuality, reliability, openness.
- 16: Confess sins to one another. Why? An opportunity to receive advice on how to overcome sin, grow in your humility, show your seriousness about change.
- 19-20: Bring the wanderers back home (the lost and those who have strayed).

Conclude by summarizing the major points, thanking all present for their participation, and urging them always to read the Bible with a view to letting their hearts be challenged by the Word.

XIV. The Man at the Pool (John 5)
This may be the liveliest discussion you'll ever lead! It's a debate on whether the man at the pool had a good heart or a bad heart.

Opening
- Begin by reading John 5:1-16. Different people take turns reading the story.
- Describe the scene: All those sick people, moaning and complaining!
- Q: How long had he been disabled?
- A: Thirty-eight years! That's longer than many of us have lived! Draw attention to Jesus' question, "Do you want to get well?" (But don't offer any interpretation.)
- Explain that we are going to discuss whether this man had a pure, sincere heart or whether is heart was bad and his motives wrong.
- Make sure you don't "prejudice" the group by sharing your own view.
- Now divide the group in two. The left side argues that the man's heart was good, the right that his heart was bad. It's important that you, as the leader, choose the sides; the participants have no say.

Debate
- Allow each group three to four minutes to confer before beginning the debate.
- The debate begins (twenty to thirty minutes). You're merely the moderator, ensuring the discussion flows. Don't let the crowd address you; rather make sure they debate each other. Many points will come out. (Remember, it's not your job to suggest the points, though the occasional provocative comment can help keep things rolling.)

Possible points—Good heart
- He obeyed Jesus (picked up his mat).
- He shared his faith with Jews, telling them it was Jesus who healed him.
- Weak character doesn't mean impure motives.
- Nothing in the passage says he had a bad heart.
- He'd made efforts to get into the water, but was unable.

Possible points—Bad heart
- He made excuses when asked if he wanted to get well.
- He was wavering on whether to give up his soft lifestyle.
- He got Jesus into trouble.
- Jesus told him to "Stop sinning."

A good case can be made on both sides!

Midpoint
- Halfway through, stand up and stop the discussion. Inform the group that anyone persuaded by the opposite view may switch positions. They should actually *change seats*, so that each (reorganized) group still sits together. Then the debate continues. (Don't let it go too long.)

Close
- End the debate. (There is no "winner.") They'll want to know which side you hold with, but if you're wise, you *won't* share your opinion. (I won't tell you mine, either!) *Do* make the following points:
- Jesus changes us. We all need healing.
- Q: How long have *you* been spiritually sick?
- You must make your own decision and be personally motivated (verse 6). God doesn't force anyone to follow Jesus.
- Whatever his real motives, God knows. And God knows your heart, too. Is it good? Why are you interested in Jesus Christ? For friendship? Attention? Because you want to get something out of it, or because it is right and you want to give your life for others?

Conclusion

Scores of further discussions are "out there"[1]—we suggest you "scrounge" and "scavenge" till your personal repertoire is ample. We hope you enjoyed this "fountain" of fourteen user-friendly discussions. And may God bless your ministry!

Notes

[1] Just a few other possibilities include "Being exposed," on the character of Peter—Luke 5:1-11, John 3:19, Hebrews 4:12-13, "Whose Fool Are You?"—Intellectual fool, Nearsighted fool, Mocking fool, Self-sufficient fool, God's fool, and "Running to win"—1 Corinthians 9:24, 2 Timothy 4:7-8, Hebrews 12: 1; "Vision problems"—Farsighted, Nearsighted, Astigmatic, Cross-eyed; and "Aladdin's Lamp"—1 Kings 3, Ecclesiastes 2. To amply expand your horizons, see David J. Schmeling's *52 Bible Talks for Fun and Fruitfulness* (Woburn, Mass.: Discipleship Publications International, 1999).

PART V

Burning Hearts!

"They asked each other, 'Were not our hearts burning wthin us while he talked with us on the road and opened the Scriptures to us?'" (Proverbs 4:18).

Are our hearts touched by the words of the Master? If so, they burn with conviction, and hence passion to share the light with others. Now it is time to put the challenge into action. The concluding chapter calls us to a common decision of faith and commitment. Truly, the will of God for all of our lives is that we "shine like stars," always, wherever we are, whatever we are doing, whomever we are with.

19
Burning Hearts!
Translating the Challenge into Actions

So far the book has been fairly challenging. Yet the greatest challenge of all is the subject of this final chapter: putting into practice the principles from God's Word brought to light in these pages. This is the acid test.

For most of you reading *Shining Like Stars*, your hearts are pure and you genuinely want to change. You are keen to develop a powerful evangelistic lifestyle or, if you already have one, to increase your effectiveness. But how easy it is to be caught in the trap into which Ezekiel's hearers fell: approving of the truth without acting on it personally!

> "As for you, son of man, your countrymen are talking together about you by the walls and at the doors of the houses, saying to each other, 'Come and hear the message that has come from the Lord.' My people come to you, as they usually do, and sit before you to listen to your words, but they do not put them into practice. With their mouths they express devotion, but their hearts are greedy for unjust gain. Indeed, to them you are nothing more than one who sings love songs with a beautiful voice and plays an instrument well, for they hear your words but do not put them into practice" (Ezekiel 33:30-32).

These people were not overtly negative. In fact, they were enthusiastic about the things God was trying to show them. (Perhaps some of the most obstinate of them shouted the loudest amens.) No, God does not fault them for a lack of zeal. They lacked obedience; that was their downfall. Yes, with their mouths they expressed devotion, talked about total commitment, fancied themselves to be growing spiritually—but their hearts were greedy for unjust gain.

Could it be that, just like the people of God 2600 years ago, churches have grown "greedy for unjust gain"? Brothers and sisters, the world is lost. Therefore any lifestyle which does not seek at all costs to improve the situation is fundamentally "unjust." Any congregation of the Lord's people which has forgotten the mission – love for the lost and concern for the needy – is *de facto* unjust. We have no right to focus inward, to surrender our distinctiveness and blend into the world around us, to hoard our salvation, while the vast majority of mankind has never heard the truth about Jesus.

Many of us, instead of shining like stars, are as silent (and unnoticeable) as a cold and lifeless asteroid. That is unjust! Every Christian, every congregation, must strive to be on fire, incandescent with the light of the gospel of Christ.

In prophesying the ministry of Jesus, the great prophet Isaiah said, "The people who walked in darkness have seen a great light; those who lived in a land of deep darkness – on them light has shined" (Isaiah 9:2, NRS). How thrilling it is to witness the spread of this very light across the globe! And yet it is possible to *applaud* this perspective without truly *applying* it. If this is the case, we are being *entertained* by the truth, but not *entering into it* and incorporating it into our deepest being.

In my ministry I have struggled to understand these principles, and realize that my understanding of evangelism is at this point "under construction." I for one have far to go in the area of relational evangelism, and far to go in the fight against "the pattern of this world" (Romans 12:2), which vies for our very souls. Certainly there is much the Lord will continue to teach us, and much ground to cover before we will have evangelized this planet.

Hopefully you have been not only stimulated by these exciting principles, but also sensitized to the will of God. As God promised Israel in Ezekiel 36:26-27,

> "I will give you a new heart and put a new spirit in you; I will remove from you your heart of stone and give you a heart of flesh. And I will put my Spirit in you and move you to follow my decrees and be careful to keep my laws."

Has your heart been changing? It is sad that the people of Israel frequently lost their capacity to respond to the voice of the Lord; their hearts were like stone. All of us know what it is to lose our spiritual edge, to be dull to the living and active word of God. Yet God yearns for all his children to have "hearts of flesh." That is why it is so important not to forget what you have heard.

The key is obedience. In the words of James (1:22), "Do not merely listen to the word, and so deceive yourselves. Do what it says!"

An action plan is needed. I would urge you to (1) pray through the ideas that struck you, (2) talk about them with a Christian brother or sister, seeking advice, and (3) set some goals. The conviction you feel at this very moment—capture it, fan it into flame. Let that burning heart never be extinguished!

Appendix A
Bringing Back the Stray

"My brothers, if one of you should wander from the truth and someone should bring him back, remember this: Whoever turns a sinner from the error of his way will save him from death and cover over a multitude of sins" (James 5:19-20).

"Brothers, if someone is caught in a sin, you who are spiritual should restore him gently. But watch yourself, or you also may be tempted. Carry each other's burdens, and in this way you will fulfill the law of Christ" (Galatians 6:1-2).

Whereas the Lord *restores* our souls (Psalm 23), and those who are spiritual ought to restore the one caught in sin (Galatians 6:2), this appendix is talking about *bringing back the stray*. Properly speaking, this is not "restoration," since restoration, though in some ways a similar process, is not limited to those who have wandered away from the flock. In many cases they have wandered far from the Lord. What exactly is bringing back the stray?

- It is a process of freeing a drifting brother or sister (Hebrews 2:1) from the allure of the world and bringing him or her back to the fold. This process takes time. It is much more than simply adding someone's name back to the membership list.[1]
- It is carried out gently (Galatians 6:2). This means caring for the individual, hearing him or her out, not rushing but carefully retracing steps back to the place he or she got off the narrow road. More often than not, those wishing to return to the fold already have plenty of guilt and shame. They need assurance, not just an "I-told-you-so" telling off (2 Corinthians 2:6-8).
- Not all Christians are able to bring back the stray. Maturity, experience, and spirituality are essential. This is a pastoral duty, though not necessarily limited to church leaders. All Christians are "shepherds" of the flock in some sense. Many congregations contain plenty of mature Christians,

and these are the ones who will be most qualified to bring the wanderers home.

- The process itself is somewhat precarious by its very nature. The temptation to over-identify with the lapsed disciple, taking on his attitudes or championing his grievances, is more than some disciples can handle. In some cases, the sin in which the person to be restored must relinquish is still ongoing.
- To bring back the stray is Christ-like. At times all of us need help in carrying our burdens, don't we?

Practicals

Here is some distilled wisdom concerning working with those who drifted back into the world.[2]

- Always ask, What are the causes of the person's leaving the church? We must make sure that we are dealing with true causes, not *symptoms*. Otherwise, after being welcomed back, they may slip back into the same well-worn ruts.
- Remember that God holds the individual responsible for quitting—no matter what (Romans 2:5ff).
- Sometimes it is largely a leader's fault. Shepherds, through harsh leadership, can scatter the sheep (Ezekiel 34). In addition, sometimes people fall through the sin or lack of forgiveness of another (Luke 17).
- False teaching also has a role in dragging many back to the world (2 Peter 2:1-3).
- Spiritual "starvation" (1 Corinthians 3:2) may also be an issue. Lack of proper appetite may be a factor, but so may lack of proper diet. Milk and meat are both needed. Shallow preaching and or humanistic leadership inhibit our potential to grow. (Still, the onus is on the individual.)
- Always speak to those who were involved in the person's life before he lapsed. Realize, in addition, that in some cases there are "two sides" to the story (Proverbs 18:17). Make sure you are properly informed.
- Call for additional help as required.
- Is someone is not open to returning at the moment, "leave the light on and the door open"! (The Parable of the Lost Son shows the example.) Don't be resentful or take sinful decisions personally. This only causes us to turn a cold shoulder to them, and it prohibits them from coming back.
- Be urgent to see the person progress, but don't rush him. Beware of flash-in-the-pan decisions. Give them time to once again implement spiritual disciplines (personal devotional times, to begin with) and to re-integrate the church schedule into their own routine.

- Study the Bible together. Pray together.
- Expect them to so the same on their own.
- When they have true conviction, they will probably start sharing their faith with their friends again.
- If the lapsed Christian is married, ask the spouse what he or she thinks about the change. The spouse probably has a better vantage point from which to evaluate what is going on than anyone else.
- While not withholding gentle assistance, expect the individual to exhibit initiative. Ultimately, it is not hand-holding that will set them back on the path to the Lord's heavenly kingdom (2 Timothy 4:18).

Probably the best wisdom is to "shepherd" others as Christ would (John 10). The biblical formula for salvation is *not* faith—repentance—baptism. It is faith—repentance—baptism—perseverance (Hebrews 11:6, Acts 2:38, Hebrews 3:14). We all need ongoing input, mentoring, discipling, guidance—call it what you will! Far too many are baptized and then quit. When we love people more—concretely, spiritually, sincerely—they will not want to leave the Lord or their brothers and sisters. An ounce of prevention is worth a pound of cure.

Conclusion

In most cities around the world there are not only active Christians, but also a number of men and women who have turned back from following the Lord. We must reach these individuals to "save their souls from death and cover over a multitude of sins."[3]

Be proactive and preemptive in your ministry. Build solidly and carefully. There will always be some who are lured back to the world (Luke 8:13-14, John 6:60-67), but the number will be reduced when we shepherd the right way. "Restore" *before* they wander off, not just when things have reached a critical point.

Notes

[1] I am avoiding the common term "fallaway" for a lapsed disciple, since the term does not appear in the Bible, and implies, in its simplest understanding (Hebrews 6:4-6), that there is no chance the individual will return to the Lord. The New Testament speaks of those who "wander away" (James 5:19-20) as those we need to seek and bring back into the fold. It is beyond the scope of this appendix to explore the theological implications of the terminology.

[2] For much of this appendix I owe thanks to Wyndham Shaw, a wise elder whom I admire deeply. He has helped to turn many back to the Lord. Adapted from his contribution in the DPI *Leader's Resource Handbook* (Woburn, Mass.: Discipleship Publications International), 1997.

[3] Theirs, not ours.

Appendix B
Index to Study Materials

This index includes thirty-four personal Bible studies and thirteen follow-up studies. (It does not include the 14 group Bible discussions of chapter 18.)

Alphabetical Listing (with series indicated: A = Guard the Gospel A, B = Guard the Gospel B, C = Guard the Gospel C, F = Follow-up Studies))

Bibliography

Barna, George, *Evangelism that Works: How to Reach Changing Generations with the Unchanging Gospel*. Ventura, Cal.: Regal Books, 1995.

Cahill, Mark, *One Thing You Can't Do In Heaven*. Bartlesville, Okla.: BDP, 2005.

Ferguson, Gordon, *Discipling: God's Plan to Train and Transform His People*. Woburn, Mass.: Discipleship Publications International, 1997.

_____, *Revolution: The World-Changing Church in the Book of Acts*. Woburn, Mass.: Discipleship Publications International, 1998.

Girzone, Joseph F., *Joshua*. New York: Simon & Schuster, 1995.

Green, Michael, *Evangelism in the Early Church*. Grand Rapids: Eerdmans, 1970.

Hedman, Tom, *A Life of Impact: Leadership Principles of Jesus*. Toronto: New Life Publications, 1992.

Douglas Jacoby, *The Spirit*. Newton, Mass.: Illumination Publishers International, 2005.

Jennings, Alvin, *How Christianity Grows in the City*. Fort Worth: Star Bible Publications, 1985.

Jones, Thomas (Ed.), *The DPI Leader's Resource Handbook*. Woburn, Mass.: Discipleship Publications International, 1997.

Kim, Frank and Erica, *How to Share Your Faith*. Woburn, Mass.: Discipleship Publications International, 1998.

Little, Paul, *How to Give Away Your Faith by Paul Little*. Downers Grove: Intervarsity Press, 1988.

McKean, Randy and Kay, Ed., *The Mission.* Woburn, Mass.: Discipleship Publications International, 1994.

Pippert, Rebecca Manley, *Out of the Saltshaker: Evangelism as a Way of Life.* Downers Grove: Intervarsity Press, 1979.

Schmeling, David J., *52 Bible Talks for Fun and Fruitfulness.* Woburn, Mass.: Discipleship Publications International, 1999.

Sheldon, Charles M., *In His Steps.* Uhrichsville, Ohio: Barbour, 1993.

About Illumination Publishers International

Toney Mulhollan has been in Christian publishing for over 30 years. He has served as the Production Manager for Crossroads Publications, Discipleship Magazine/UpsideDown Magazine, Discipleship Publications International (DPI) and on the production teams of Campus Journal, Biblical Discipleship Quarterly, Bible Illustrator and others. He has served as production manager for several printing companies. Toney serves as the Managing Editor of Illumination Publishers International, and is the writer and publisher of the weekly "Behind the Music" stories and edits other weekly newsletters. Toney is happily married to the love of his life, Denise Leonard Mulhollan, M.D.

For the best in Christian writing and audio instruction, go to the Illumination Publishers website. Shipping is always free in the United States. We're commited to producing in-depth teaching that will inform, inspire and encourage Christians to a deeper and more committed walk with God.

www.ipibooks.com

Illuminations Publishers International

www.ipibooks.com

ipi

www.douglasjacoby.com

Stayed informed about the International Teaching Ministry of Douglas Jacoby

The site provides daily interactive instruction to help you grow and mature in your Christian walk. Through the website you will be able to:

- Access thousands of pages of teaching archives.
- Follow the latest discoveries in apologetics and archaeology.
- Learn insights to Biblical languages that help interpret the Bible.
- Read helpful suggestions for building strong marriages & families.
- Test your Bible knowledge through the Monday morning quizzes.
- SUBMIT NEW QUESTIONS (please check archived questions first).
- Gain biblical insights into the hot issues confronting disciples.
- Purchase books and audio by Dr. Douglas Jacoby.
- Read field reports from Douglas's teaching trips abroad.
- Financially support the teaching ministry in mission fields around the world.

This will afford all Christians access to reliable teaching and the ability to apply them to daily life!

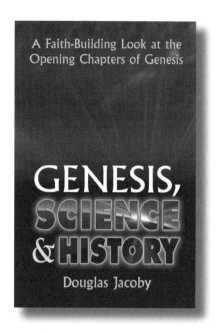

Genesis, Science & History
by Douglas Jacoby

Genesis, Science & History is a faith-building and eye-opening exploration of the scientific and literary themes in the opening chapters of the Bible. With attention to everything from theories about the age of the earth to the extent of Noah's flood, there is something for everyone in this readable, informative look at Genesis 1-11. As the author attempts to show, science and the Bible need not be pitted against one another in the minds of sincere, informed believers. This book will not answer every question that a Bible student may have about Genesis, creation, history and science; but it will point readers in a helpful direction and leave them grateful for the God of the Bible, the God of Genesis, science and history. The author discusses the thorny issues of "theistic evolution" and believes science helps us understand "how" God might have chosen to create. He offers in this book an approach to understanding creation that allows the reader to harmonize differences between the Bible and science while staying true to the text of Genesis.

Published by DPI., paperback, 255 pages, **Price: $15.00**

Available at: www.ipibooks.com

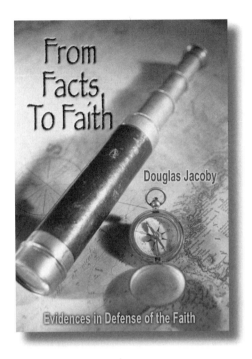

From Facts To Faith

by Douglas Jacoby

This four CD set of messages on evidences will be especially useful for non-believers, Christians with questions of a scientific or academic nature, students with questions about the Bible, and anyone who wants to be better equipped to share the faith with others.

In 1 Peter 3:15, the apostle Peter reminds us not only to make sure Christ is Lord in our hearts, but also to be ready to give an answer to anyone who asks for the reasons for the hope we have. These lessons by Dr. Douglas Jacoby will help further that aim. Over four hours of instruction that will help you answer some of the most challenging questions related to the Christian faith.

The four lessons are:

Why I Trust the Bible
Big Bang, Dinosaurs, Caveman and Evolution
The Problem of Human Suffering
Atheists and Atheism

Published by IPI, 4-CDs, Price: $20.00

Available at: www.ipibooks.com

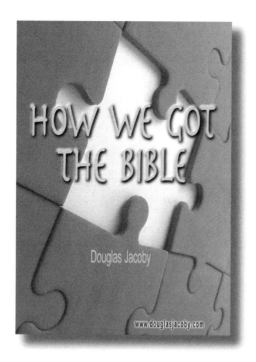

How We Got the Bible

by Douglas Jacoby

Listen to Dr. Jacoby as he tackles the central questions surrounding the formation of the Bible. How We Got the Bible is a four-part audio series explaining why we can have full confidence that the Scriptures have been accurately transmitted through the centuries.

The first two lessons lay out the manuscript evidence for the faithful copying of the Old and New Testaments, including an exploration of the Dead Sea Scrolls—the archaeological find of the 20th century. The third class focuses on canonization—how the individual books of the scripture came together, under the guidance of the Holy Spirit, to form the Bible we have today. The final lesson refutes the erroneous claim of the "missing books," with discussion centering on the Apocrypha, Pseudepigrapha and The Da Vinci Code.

You will appreciate the frankness, clarity, and conviction of these important messages. In addition, helpful notes and articles are provided on each CD.

Published by IPI, 4-CDs, Price: $20.00

Available at: www.ipibooks.com

Reading, Praying & Living THE PSALMS

by Douglas Jacoby

The Psalms: How to read them, understand them, and pray them. This audio set is a practical workshop in improving our relationship with God through studying the longest and most quoted book in all of Scripture. Recorded before a live audience in Orlando, Florida, 3-4 July 2005.

Classes:

CD#1 –Introduction to Hebrew Poetry: How to Read the Psalms
(Includes downloadable outlines)

CD#2–Psalms of Revenge: How to Pray the Psalms

CD#3–Doctrines True and False: How to Study the Psalms

CD#4–Psalms Pointing to Jesus: The Place of Psalms in the Canon

Published by IPI, 4-CDs, Price: $20.00

Available at: www.ipibooks.com

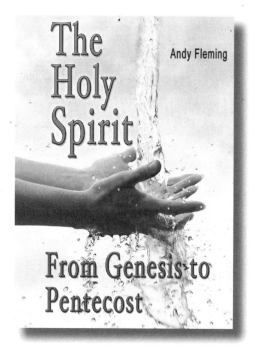

The Holy Spirit: From Genesis to Pentecost
by Andy Fleming

The Holy Spirit is one of the most misunderstood topics in the Bible and at times one of the most divisive. Andy Fleming says that's because people have failed to study the foundational concepts revealed in the Old Testament about the Holy Spirit. Beginning with Genesis, Andy explores what the Old Testament teaches about the Holy Spirit and culminates with its gift to the church on the Day of Pentecost. This series was initially prepared for the Moscow Bible School.

CD#1 Old Testament: The Spirit of God
(Also contains a 21 page outline for downloading)

CD#2 Old Testament: Spiritual Gifts

CD#3 Old Testament: Signs, Wonders and Miracles

CD#4 Old Testament: Prophecies of the future work of the Holy Spirit

CD#4 New Testament: Day of Pentecost

Published by IPI, 4-CDs, Price: $20.00

Available at: www.ipibooks.com